SPLENDOR
OF THE FAITH

**Meditations on the Credo of the
People of God**

Rev. Anton Morgenroth, C.Ss.P.

CHRISTENDOM PUBLICATIONS
Christendom College Press
Route 3, Box 87
Front Royal, VA 22630

L. C. Classification No.: BX 1968.M67

ISBN: 0-931888-14-X

IMPRIMATUR:
   †Most Rev. Glennon P. Flavin
   Bishop of Lincoln
   September 16, 1983

CONTENTS

Introduction   5

Meditations   7

1. The Coming to Life of Faith / 7
2. The Existence of a Creator Who Is Savior / 8
3. The Sacred Power of Procreation / 9
4. God's Oneness . . . and Ours / 11
5. Divine Providence Comes through a Human Heart / 13
6. God's Names: Being and Love / 15
7. Christ Reveals a Triune God / 17
8. The New Creation: Here and Hereafter / 19
9. Redeemed Unity / 21
10. The Responsibility of Christians / 23
11. The Self-Giving of the Son / 25
12. The Son's Priestly Prayer / 27
13. The Son's Eternal Gifts to Us / 29
14. The Incarnation / 31
15. The Blessed Virgin Mary / 33
16. Christ's Human Freedom / 34
17. Our Vocation as Ambassadors for Christ / 36
18. The Kingdom of God: Praying for It Unconditionally / 38
19. Christ Revealed the Father / 40
20. The New Commandment: Extending Christ's Love / 42
21. The Beatitudes: the Heart of Christ / 43
22. The Target and Victim of Sin / 45
23. The Mystery of the Cross / 47
24. The Resurrection and the Sacred Heart / 49
25. The Second Coming / 51
26. Our Response to the Promise of Joy / 52
27. Hell: the Rejection of Love / 54
28. The Holy Spirit: the Spirit of Love and Unity / 56
29. The Holy Spirit and the Church / 58
30. Our Search for God: the Holy Spirit's Role / 60
31. Mary the Mother of God / 62
32. Mary's Untainted Faith / 64
33. Mary's Assumption into Heaven / 66
34. The Queen of Heaven / 68
35. Original Sin and Hope / 70
36. Hints of Joy to Come / 72
37. The Human Struggle / 74
38. Solidarity in Sin and Salvation / 76
39. The Redemption / 78
40. God's Power / 80
41. Baptism into Christ / 82
42. Infant Baptism / 84

43. The Four Marks of the Church / 86
44. The Vicar of Christ / 88
45. The Mystical Body of Christ / 90
46. The Visible Church / 92
47. The Responsibility of the Pilgrim Church / 94
48. The Apostolate of Redemption / 96
49. The Splendor of the Faith / 98
50. The Sacraments / 100
51. A Share in the Paschal Mystery / 102
52. The Church: Holy and Always in Need of Purification / 104
53. Removing Ourselves from the Life of the Church / 106
54. Sin and Expiation / 108
55. The Church and the Jewish People / 110
56. The Church: Teaching, Sanctifying, and Ruling / 112
57. The Teaching Church / 114
58. Preparing to Receive the Word of God / 117
59. Papal Infallibility / 119
60. The Indefectability of True Faith / 121
61. The Rich Variety of Unity / 123
62. Divine Gifts Outside the Church / 125
63. Christian Unity / 127
64. Salvation through Christ / 130
65. Salvation Extends to All / 132
67. The Priest: Christ's Representative / 136
68. The Mass: a Reenacted Sacrifice / 138
69. The Eucharist / 140
70. The Power of the Mass / 142
71. The Real Presence / 145
72. Truths Anchored in the Eucharist / 147
73. Coworkers of God / 149
74. Seeking a Living Faith / 151
75. The Living Heart of Our Church / 153
76. The Presence of the Risen Lord / 155
77. The Kingdom of God / 157
78. Material Progress and the Kingdom of God / 159
79. Growth in Holiness / 161
80. The Virtue of Hope / 163
81. Solidarity in Grace / 165
82. Christian Renewal of Society / 167
83. A Christian Attitude toward Suffering / 169
84. Being Fools for Christ / 172
85. Solicitude for Others / 174
86. The Hidden Battle in Our Hearts / 176
87. Longing for Christ / 178
88. The Way to Eternal Life / 180
89. The Mission of the People of God / 181
90. Victory over Sin and Death / 183
91. Eternal Beatitide / 185
92. The Role of the Saints in Heaven / 188
93. The Communion of Saints / 190
94. The Power of Prayer / 191
95. The Power of the Resurrection / 194
96. The Prayer of Adoration / 195

Appendix: Credo of the People of God (Pope Paul VI)   197

Christendom Publishing Group   204

Introduction

These meditations are not a systematic commentary on the Credo of the People of God, but merely an attempt to point to some possible considerations of revealed reality as formulated in this Profession of Faith. They are intended to be used one or two at a time, completing the whole over a considerable span of weeks or even months. At times, seeking the context of scriptural passages in the Bible might be helpful.

It is *what* we believe, the *content* of our faith, which expands our knowledge of unseen reality into the very infinity of God, our Creator and Redeemer, eternally and immutably Father, Son, and Holy Spirit. Penetrating ever more deeply into the inexhaustible mysteries of God, of His power, wisdom and mercy, that is, of Divine Providence, should be our central and life-seeking concern, to seek the light by which we see the light (Ps. 36:9). For

> only the light of faith and meditation on the Word of God can enable us to find everywhere and always the God 'in whom we live and exist' (Acts 17:28); only thus can we seek his will in everything, see Christ in all men, acquaintance or stranger, make sound judgments on the true meaning and value of temporal realities both in themselves and in relation to man's end. *(Decree on the Apostolate of Lay People*, 4)

Cardinal Newman wrote, "The Creeds have a place in the Ritual; they are devotional acts, and of the nature of prayers, addressed to God" (*Grammar of Assent*, p. 132, Longmans).

Certain themes and words of Scripture will be found quite frequently in these meditations. They were thought to be helpful in the consideration of a great variety of truths. An approach to the theology of redemption will also be found here, an approach which assumes that the causes of the Passion and Death of Our Lord are the Original Sin of our first parents and "the vices and crimes which have been perpetrated from the beginning of the world to the present day and those which will be committed to the end of time . . . and . . . that our sins assigned Christ the Lord to the death of the cross" (*Catechism of the Council of Trent*, p. 57). Christ died *through* our sins, is always the target of sin (Matt. 25:45), and became its victim. The Crucifixion was the consummation of the Fall and its continuation that will only end on the last day. This disaster was transformed by the victory of the redeeming and creative love of Jesus Christ, extended to us, His torturers and murderers, while He suffered and died. The fidelity of His love, maintained while He suffered total rejection, seems indicated in His words, "and when I am lifted up from the earth, I shall draw all men to myself," indicating "by these words the kind of death he would die" (John 12:32-33). This love transformed His dying *through* us into a dying *for* us.

Everything we learn of Christ while He was on earth must be seen in the light of His word, "to have seen Me is to have seen the Father" (John 14:9). Everything during His life on earth reveals facets of the love of God, of the God Whose name is Love (1 John 4:8 and 16). Thus Jesus *is* the "Truth" (John 14:6).

St. Paul seems to teach that the Human Heart of Christ (to Whom all power and authority has been given [Matt. 28:18]) allots to each of us his own share of grace (Eph. 4:7), while by His divine power we "receive what we need for life and for true devotion", gifts through which we "will be able to share the divine nature and to escape corruption in a world that is sunk in vice" (2 Peter 1:3 and 4).

As we become aware of our own positivistic and pragmatic patterns of thought, we should prepare ourselves frequently for the approach to the mysteries of our faith by that great hymn of adoration with which St. Paul closes his meditation on the mystery of Israel:

> How rich are the depths of God—how deep his wisdom and knowledge—and how impossible to penetrate his motives or understand his methods! Who could ever know the mind of the Lord? Who could ever be his counsellor? Who could ever give him anything or lend him anything? All that exists comes from him; all is by him and for him. To him be glory for ever! Amen. (Rom. 11:33-36).

1. The Coming to Life of Faith

"We believe in one only God, Father, Son, and Holy Spirit, Creator. . . ."

By the gift of faith, by the God-given power to believe, we come to know Him who is the source and the goal of our being, the living God, Father, Son, and Holy Spirit. "It is the same God that said, 'Let there be light shining out of darkness,' who has shone in our minds to radiate the light of the knowledge of God's glory" (2 Cor 4:6). And this glory—of which St. John the Apostle wrote, "We saw His glory, the glory that is His as the only Son of the Father, full of grace and truth" (John 1:14)—the glory of God, the radiance of His holiness, is seen "on the face of Christ" (2 Cor 4:6). Because the Eternal Son, Jesus Christ, who alone knows the Father, chose to reveal the Father, and thus Himself (Mat 11:27), this revelation comes to life in those to whom the (now Risen) Christ has given the light of faith, the power to believe.

It is by the light of faith that "the existence of the realities that at present remain unseen" (Heb 11:1) is proven. By faith, we touch the hidden God, "whose home is in inaccessible light, whom no man has seen and no man is able to see" (1 Tim 6:16). But God's gift of incipient faith enables us to hear His word and to understand it only if this "seed" of divine life has been received "in rich soil" (Mat 13:23).

The living God, Father, Son, and Holy Spirit, the Creator, becomes an ever more pervasive reality in our lives, if the soil receiving this "word," this revelation, is "rich." It is rich if we are ready to listen, to trust, to accept; willing to suffer injustice rather than commit it, as Socrates said; willing to take up our cross (Mat 10:38). We then become capable of fructifying the gifts of God which enable us to respond to His call, to His Love, and to His glory: the power which enables us to believe, *faith*; the power which enables us to trust and seek, *hope*; and the essentially mysterious and hidden power which enables us to receive and radiate "the healing power of God's love" (Prayer after Communion, 21st Sunday), *charity*.

A living faith in God is expressed and bears fruit in the keeping of His commandments. "You shall have no gods except me" (Deut 5:7); that is, nothing may be allowed to usurp the absolute priority of God's will and kingdom. The faithful must "live by the truth and in love" (Eph 4:15): by the truth that God is, by the truth that God is God. To live by this truth is to desire, to seek, and to come to possess a living faith. The other commandments, the second to the tenth, simply implement the first.

The specific and living faith of a Christian is to suffuse all thought of God and all prayer with the consciousness of God's fatherhood, His eternal begetting of His Eternal Image or Son (Col 1:15), and their eternal mutual Love, the Holy Spirit. With this faith we seek His Kingdom, by seeking to know and do His will. With this faith, we approach the incomprehensible God through the human Heart of the Eternal Word who became flesh, lived among us, and whose glory was seen in the Child; the Boy, the Man, the tortured and crucified Jesus, "the glory that is His as the only Son of the Father" (John 1:14).

And this God is Creator. This "one only God" is the source of all, "sustaining the universe by His powerful command" (Heb 1:3). He is our goal; it is He whom we are to see "face to face" (Rev 22:4). Of His wisdom, Scripture says: "Within her is a spirit intelligent, holy, unique, manifold, subtle, active, incisive, unsullied, lucid, invulnerable, benevolent, sharp, irresistible, beneficent, loving to man, steadfast, dependable, unperturbed, almighty, all-surveying, penetrating all intelligent, pure, and most subtle spirits" (Wisd 7:22-23). It is He whom, in the words of the Mass, we "have the courage to call 'Our Father.' "

2. The Existence of a Creator Who is Savior

"We believe in one only God . . . Creator of things visible such as this world in which our transient life passes, of things invisible such as the pure spirits which are also called angels . . . ."

(Read Ps 104; Rom 1:18-32; Wisd 13:1-9.)

Nothing can exist, nothing can continue to exist, nothing can happen, nothing can function without the creative thought of God. "It is in Him that we live, and move, and exist" (Acts 17:28).

It is true that the existence of evil and unspeakable suffering, not all caused by man, seems to create a dilemma: either there is no creator, or at least no formative will and intelligence; or, if there is such a power, we cannot possibly attribute to this power those personal dispositions we value, such as justice, goodness, benevolence, fairness, and compassion. Thus may well be that without the revealed knowledge of Original Sin and the revealed promise of a blessed eternity, belief in God is morally impossible. The brutal absurdity of human behavior and of human history, the suffering of the relatively innocent and the success of the wicked seem to contradict the existence of infinite wisdom and power as the source of all that has been, is now, and will be. Without Revelation we would in the words of Scripture, still be "immersed in this world, without hope and without God" (Eph 2:12).

But the Credo reaffirms that God *is* the Creator of all that is and the cause of all that happens. Moreover, it assures us of the existence of pure spirits, whom we "join in their unending hymn of praise," when "we proclaim God's glory with all the choirs of angels in Heaven" (end of the Prefaces for Advent, as well as other Prefaces). Now we know by faith that although we lived (and possibly still live) "in wickedness and ill will, hating each other and hateful ourselves" (Titus 3:3), "the kindness and love of God our Savior for mankind were revealed" and continue to be revealed (Titus 3:4-5 used as Second Reading in the Mass at Dawn on Christmas Day).

And this God, the Creator of the universe, whose infinite power and wisdom are in the service of His mercy ("Almighty and merciful God"— opening prayer, Feast of Christ the King), is the living God, who is both Creator of all and the Savior of man. He is the Eternal Word, "God from God, Light from Light, true God from true God" (Nicene Creed), the Eternal Son, through whom "all things came to be" (John 1:2), who "was made flesh" (John 1:14) and lived among us, and whose glory the Apostles saw: "the glory that is His as the only Son of the Father, full of grace and truth" (John 1:14), the glory that is the radiance of God's holiness and love.

3. The Sacred Power of Procreation

"We believe in one only God . . . Creator in each man of his spiritual and immortal soul."

(Read Pastoral Constitution, *Gaudium et spes*, 12, 14, and 47-52; and *Humanae Vitae*.)

"Yahweh God fashioned man of dust from the soil. Then he breathed into his nostrils a breath of life, and this man became a living being" (Gn 2:7). That man cannot be adequately described in physical, chemical, and biological terms is indicated by the range of man's intelligence and the freedom of his will, both of which far transcend these spheres. We can know what is and what has been; we can plan and arrange the future; we have absract concepts in mathematics that allow us to know certain aspects of nature and to predict the exact positions of moons and planets and manmade spaceships. We know of goodness and beauty.

At the moment of conception, God creates and infuses a spiritual and immortal soul. Conception, once it has taken place, compels, as it were, the almighty and all-knowing God to complete the existence of what has begun on the human-biological level. This newly conceived-created human being will exist forever, and is destined to see God "face to face" (1 Cor 13:12) after an earthly life of seeking Him, whom, as Jesus promised, he will be able to find (Mat 7:7).

Man's capacity to procreate is thereby a power over God which causes Him to create and infuse a naturally indestructible spirit, so that through man's responsible action and God's creative act a new human being is brought into existence. Man's responsible share in this process is meant to be fundamentally joined to God's continuing creation of mankind, a task and responsibility with eternal consequences, as all men are created for God, to "share the divine nature" (2 Pet 1:4). Man is to "be fruitful, multiply, and fill the earth" (Gen 1:28). Man's power to procreate is therefore a most sacred thing; it gives man, as it were, power over God, and brings forth new beings destined for eternal life. The sacredness of man's power to procreate must determine our attitudes toward this area of life. The morality of marriage and of everything that pertains to married life, and the morality of the God-given ability to procreate are rooted in the fact, in the reality, that God is the "Creator in each man of his spiritual and immortal soul." It is as spiritual beings that we have become capable of, and are called to, the beatific vision—eternal life. For we exist, we are created, and we are called to know the Father, "the only true God, and Jesus Christ" whom the Father has sent (John 17:3). "To know" is that marvelous union with God—Father, Son, and Holy Spirit—into which we are baptized (Mat 28:19), which is ours even now, and which will ultimately lead us to see God "face to face" (1 Cor 13:12). It is that marvelous union of vision and love that will be ours for all eternity as we share the joy (John 15:11; 17:13) that God *is* in that mutual love of Father and Son, the Holy Spirit.

The procreative power and duty of man are inseparably joined to that spousal love which is expressed and consummated in the marriage act. Through the sacrament of marriage, "authentic married love is caught up into divine love and enriched by the redemptive power of Christ" (*Pastoral Constitution*, 48). Through the sacrament of marriage, the spouses are called to manifest and actualize toward each other "the mystery of God's love for men" (*Pastoral Constitution*, 45), to be Christ to each other. This love is open to life by the God-given procreative power of man and by God's creating "a spiritual and immortal soul" when conception takes place. Here lies the meaning and sanctity of the gift of man's procreative power, which must not be used except responsibly, within marriage, and without its purpose and meaning being artificially excluded. All morality, all the norms of right conduct in this sphere are derived from this power, duty, and vocation of man to "be fruitful, multiply, and fill the earth" (Gen 1:28), and to thereby give to God new children of the Father (Gal 3:26) who will share His likeness (2 Cor 3:18) and His life (John 14:23; 17:23).

4. God's Oneness . . . and Ours

"We believe that this only God is absolutely one in His infinitely holy essence as also in all His perfections. . . ."

(Read *Dogmatic Constitution on Divine Revelation*, 2-6; Ps 36; 103; 127; 130; 139.)

It is impossible for us to think of perfections in a human being except as distinct additions. Knowledge of physics is quite distinct from the virtue of justice; the ability to play a Mozart sonata is something added to a person's being, and though it affects him as a person, giving him an opportunity of giving joy to others, or to find peace, it is distinct from other abilities. In God, however, what we call His names and attributes exist in totally inconceivable oneness and simplicity.

St. Paul wrote that we are to "put on a new self which will progress toward knowledge the more it is *renewed in the image of its Creator*" (Col 3:10, emphasis added). Could one not therefore expect a growing reflection of God's absolute simplicity and unity in a man as he grows into the image of his Creator? In us, a great multiplicity of dispositions, abilities, and characteristics are able to blend into unity and simplicity if these enable a person to serve God more and more exclusively. The spirit of poverty, necessary for entering and becoming part of the Kingdom of Heaven (Mat 5:3), would seem to integrate variety into unity, when we come to realize, and live by, this description of poverty: that "nothing can happen that will outweigh the supreme advantage of knowing Christ Jesus" as one's Lord

(Phil 3:8), if "for Him I have accepted the loss of everything, and I look on everything as so much rubbish if only I can have Christ and be given a place in Him" (Phil 3:8).

There was perfect unity and single-mindedness, continuity and the peace of God in Jesus Christ, whose "food is to do the will of the one who sent" Him and "to complete His work" (John 4:34); and who said: "I can do nothing by myself; I can only judge as I am told to judge, and my judging is just, because my aim is to do not my own will, but the will of Him who sent me" (John 5:30).

In us this unity and simplicity come about as we realize that "the whole Law and the prophets also" (Mat 22:40) hang on the two Great Commandments, to love God and our neighbor. "All the commandments: You shall not commit adultery, you shall not kill, you shall not steal, you shall not covet...are summed up in this single command: You must love your neighbor as yourself" (Rm 13:9). The absolute, mysterious simplicity and unity of God, the unity in Trinity and the unity of names and attributes, is truly reflected and revealed in a single-minded obedience or love of God, obedience to the commandments of love. *One* love is then manifested in varieties of dispositions, for "love is always patient and kind . . . never jealous . . . never boastful or conceited . . . never rude or selfish . . . ready to endure whatever comes" (Cor 13:4-7).

In a life of growing holiness, firmness will be combined with gentleness, love of justice on all levels of the human family will be combined with a deep pity for everyone who fails; such a life will continually grow to be more unified and consistent, and will become more and more an instrument of that charity which contains all. Single-minded seeking of God's will and its implementation without harshness or Pharisaism, without self-righteousness and vanity, brings about a wonderful unity, consistency, and continuity—and inner peace which "the world cannot give" (John 14:27).

In God, the intensive love for one human being in no way diminishes His love for another, or for all. We can share in this aspect of simplicity and unity. A mother's love for husband and children is not weakened if the number of children grows. A priest's love and care for each one in his flock do not become less if the flock grows. In love, neither arithmetic nor the law of conservation of energy holds. Here, to give is to gain.

In God, whose boundless power and knowledge are in the service of His merciful Providence, all-pervasive knowledge is not an intolerable intrusion into man's privacy, but it is one with His creative power "sustaining the universe by His powerful command" (Heb 1:3), and thus enabling us to exist, to function, to love, to become truly free.

In the lives of saintly men and women, we can see that reflection of God's unity and simplicity. In a great pope or bishop, all plans and activities, the life of prayer as well as concerns about administrative and business matters, can be accomplished in single-minded peace. This is because, with the Church, he pursues "but one sole purpose—that the Kingdom of God may come and the salvation of the human race may be accomplished" (Pastoral Constitution, 45). It is divine charity, originating in God (1 John 4:7), that brings about that unity and simplicity which are marks of sanctity, and therefore reflections of God, whose immutability is one with His manifold attributes and infinite variety of ways of dealing with us. He is the God who changes not, yet whom we ask daily to forgive us. It is the mystery of the fullness of Being, because He is the God whose two principal names are "Being" and "Love."

5. Divine Providence Comes Through a Human Heart

"We believe that this only God is absolutely one . . . in His omnipotence, His infinite knowledge, His Providence, His will, and His love."

In a world where crime pays well and honesty leads to the cross, it seems almost mockery to speak of God's loving Providence. It raises the same question, the same dilemma, as does speaking of God's existence and omnipotence in a world full of sin and suffering. The incongruity is beyond resolution without knowledge of the Fall, of the promise of eternal life, and of the fact that God, in the humanity of the Eternal Son, in Jesus Christ, became the target and victim of all sin, and suffered all while faithfully maintaining His redeeming love. To live with a deep faith in God's Providence, we must also hold onto the fact that God "wants everyone to be saved" (1 Tim 2:4) and that He "has imprisoned all men in their own disobedience only to show mercy to all mankind" (Rom 11:32). And here, as in all attempts to seek understanding of the content of the faith, we express our hope and adoration, praying with St. Paul: "How rich are the depths of God— how deep His wisdom and knowledge—and how impossible to penetrate

His motives or understand His methods! Who could ever know the mind of the Lord? Who could ever be His counselor? Who could ever give Him anything or lend Him anything? All that exists comes from Him; all is by Him and for Him. To Him be glory for ever! Amen" (Rom 11:33-36).

Divine Providence is God's redeeming love, His pity, His tenderness for us pathetic, pitiful, rebellious, vain, proud, somewhat ridiculous beings (Ps 2:4; 59:8); it is also His wisdom which orders "all things for good" (Wisd 8:1). If we cannot see this divine order, let us remember that His thoughts are not our thoughts, His ways not our ways (Is 55:8). "Yes, the heavens are as high above earth as my ways are above your ways, my thoughts above your thoughts" (Is 55:9).

But all power, all authority to direct God's infinite power toward our salvation is now intrusted to the human Heart of Jesus Christ (Matt 28:18). He is not only God "whose home is in inaccessible light" (1 Tim 6:16), for "it is not as if we had a high priest who was incapable of feeling our weaknesses with us; but we have one who has been tempted in every way that we are, though He is without sin. Let us be confident, then, in approaching the throne of grace, that we shall have mercy from Him and find grace when we are in need of help" (Heb 4:14-16).

As the Risen Lord, Jesus Christ is the Good Shepherd, who laid down His life for His sheep (John 10:11): as the Lord with all authority in Heaven and on earth (Mat 28:18), He is "the Lamb who is at the throne [who] will be their shepherd and will lead them to springs of living water; and God will wipe away all tears from their eyes" (Rev 7:17).

Divine love fills the human Heart of Jesus. This Heart, the Heart we have already succeeded in breaking, beholds everyone on earth with that love we have already wounded by sin. It was only by that fidelity which "is always faithful," even when "we may be unfaithful" (2 Tim 2:13), that Jesus "had always loved those who were His in the world" and by which, in going forth to His death, "He showed how perfect His love was" (John 13:1). Whatever Jesus in His human Heart wills, He accomplishes by His divine omnipotence, which is at the disposal of His human Heart. This He did when He forgave the paralytic (Luke 5:20), when He commanded Lazarus to "come out" (John 11:43), whenever His human compassion urged Him to do what surpasses human power. Now, as Lord of Heaven and earth, He deals with *all* men, through His human Heart, but with His divine power.

Herein lies the mystery of His Providence, which seeks to "bring everything together under Christ, as head" (Eph 1:10): divine, infinite power is at the disposal of a human Heart that has been crushed by the Sin of the

World. "The Lamb that was sacrificed is worthy to be given power, riches, wisdom, strength, honor, glory, and blessing" (Rev 5:12). He now continues to "draw all men" to Himself (John 12:32), as He began to do when He was "lifted up from the earth" and rendered helpless by the nails (John 12:32).

It remains for us to set our "hearts on His Kingdom first, and on His righteousness" (holiness) (Mat 6:33). Thus we enter into the hidden ways of His Providence and become signs and instruments (sacraments), "at once manifesting and actualizing the mystery of God's love for men" (*Pastoral Constitution*, 45), as His members (1 Cor 6:15), His branches (John 15:5), and His Church, which is the sacrament of Christ (*Dogmatic Constitution*, 1). And thus we become serious about the prayer we so often say, that God's will be done, that His Kingdom come *to* us and *through* us.

Because "God did not spare His own Son, but gave Him up to benefit us all" (Rm 8:32), we can be certain that God in His Providence, in the perfect, though hidden blending of redeeming love and infinite power, will let "neither death nor life, no angel, no prince, nothing that exists, nothing still to come, not any power, or height or depth, nor any created thing . . . ever come between us and the *love of God made visible in Christ Jesus our Lord*" (Rom 8:38-39, emphasis added).

And so we pray:

Almighty and ever-present Father, your watchful care reaches from end to end and orders all things in such power that even the tensions and tragedies of sin cannot frustrate your loving plans. Help us to embrace your will, give us the strength to follow your call, so that your truth may live in our hearts and reflect peace to those who believe in your love. We ask this through Christ our Lord. Amen.

(Alternative Opening Prayer, 2nd Sunday in Ordinary Time)

6. God's Names: Being and Love

"He is He Who Is, *as He revealed to Moses; and He is* Love, *as the Apostle John teaches us: so that these two names, Being and Love, express ineffably the same divine Reality of Him Who has wished to make Himself known to us, and Who 'dwelling in light inaccessible,' is in Himself above every name, above every thing,*

and above every created intellect."

An uncreated Being, "dwelling in light inaccessible" (1 Tim 6:16), the Triune God, eternally begetting, eternally begotten, eternal love, one in substance with each other, life, light, all-pervasive in His creative and sustaining knowledge—He exists "in Himself above every name, above every thing, and above every created intellect" (*Credo*, above). And He is the same God who pleaded with Israel through her prophets, assuring her of His burning love, always faithful (Ps 136; Is 54:7-10), even though He was rejected again and again; He is the same God Creator whom we see when we see Jesus (John 14:9).

As discoveries in the natural sciences continue to show the inventive and coordinating power of God to an inconceivable extent; as the age, the dimensions, and the complexities of creation are discoverd to be nearly without limit, it becomes more and more amazing when we consider that "the universe itself . . . attains its destiny through [man]" (*Dogmatic Constitution*, 48). Man is the center of the universe; the universe exists to be inhabited and discovered by man. For man, though part of the physical universe, is spirit, and therefore capable of taking hold of anything there is through knowledge. As Romano Guardini wrote, "the world is God's word to man" (*The World and the Person*, p. 143).

God's creative mind is actually touched through the knowledge of what He has created, what He has creatively thought. The living God is the formative cause, the creative mind and will to whom all being and all order is due. This one only God spoke to Moses at Horeb and gave him His name, thereby pointing to His very nature: "I Am who Am" (Ex 3:14). God is the One who simply *is*, who transcends all, and yet is in all by sustaining all (Heb 1:3). He is immutable and yet truly revealed and seen and heard in an intensely human being, in the human life and destiny of Jesus Christ (John 12:4; 14:6-11). "Holy, Holy, Holy is the Lord God, the Almighty; He was, He is, and He is to come" (Rev 4.8). "It is by faith that we understand that the world was created by one word from God, so that no apparent cause can account for the things we can see" (Heb 11:3). Of God the Son, or Word, St. John wrote: "Through Him all things came to be, not one thing had its being but through Him" (John 1:2). And therefore we stammer His name: *Being*.

But "the same divine reality of Him who has wished to make Himself known to us" (*Credo*, above) is also expressed by the name *Love* (1 John 4:8), God's eternal, ineffable Love. He Himself is the Love that He extends to us with a fidelity which even we cannot discourage (2 Tim 2:13;

Heb 6:17-18; Rom 8:38-39; 11:28-29); the Love that let God the Son empty Himself to become Man, servant, and finally the target and victim of all sin, "obedient unto death, even death on a cross" (Phil 2:6-8).

Christian love derives its character and its power from divine love. It is for us, as it was for the Son of God, an obedience demanded by divine commandments (John 13:34; Deut 6:4). For us, love is an obedience of and in faith, because the divine gift of love shares in the mystery of God, and like the Giver and Source of love is "above every name, above every thing, and above every created intellect" *Credo*, above).

It is an astonishing truth that God is *Creator, and* in this love for man, thereby also *Savior* (Titus 2:13). It assures us that, although man's history, thoughts, and actions seem to contradict the fact that God could care for man, these many evils "cannot come from his good Creator" (*Pastoral Constitution*, 13).

God's name—Love—becomes credible in the light of three facts, all of them revealed. First, through Original Sin and the continuation of the Fall, man is no longer what he was intended by God to be. Second, we still are called and enabled to enter eternal life, eternal blessedness, where "God lives among men [who] shall be His people, and He will be their God, [a God who] will wipe away all tears from their eyes" (Rev 21:3-4). Third, God the Son, through assuming humanity, was the target and the victim of all of man's sins, and responded with redeeming, transforming love, by which, on Calvary, He drew, and now from Heaven continues to draw, all men to himself (John 12:32).

7. Christ Reveals a Triune God

"God alone can give us right and full knowledge of this Reality by revealing Himself as Father, Son, and Holy Spirit. . . ."

For "no one has ever seen God; it is the only Son, who is nearest to the Father's heart, who has made Him known" (John 1:18). And as Christ Himself assured us, "no one knows the Son except the Father, just as no one knows the Father except the Son and those to whom the Son chooses to reveal Him" (Mat 11:27; see also John 6:46; 7:29).

The Son has completed His revelation of the Father by word, by silence (John 19:9), by tears (John 11:35; Luke 19:41), by His actions, by His Passion, by His Death, and by the example of His own person as He was seen while on earth (John 12:45; 14:7-11). But more is needed than the revelation of the Father, and of Jesus Christ as the Eternal Son and as the visible "Image of the invisible God" (Col 1:15); more even than to have met Jesus in Palestine, which did not bring faith to all those who saw and heard Him. "Do you know why you cannot take in what I say? It is because you are unable to understand my language. The devil is your father, and you prefer to do what your father wants" (John 8:43-44).

Ill will, bad faith, and devouring selfishness absolutely blind us to divine truth. Even where there is good will, ordinary decency, respectability, natural virtue, the word of God can still remain alien to us. "Rich soil" (Mat 13:23) in which the word can take root and yield a rich harvest needs a growing realization on our part that we are blind and weak, entangled in sins of pride and vanity; that we still may be "ignorant, disobedient, " living in "wickedness and ill will, hating each other and hateful ourselves" (Titus 3:3); that we are "neither cold nor hot" (Rev 3:15; read the whole passage, verses 14-22). Then, moved by our conscience, we must *seek*, and if we do, we will *find*, for we have the infallible promise of God (Mat 7:7). We must persevere in our seeking, for God gives in His own time and His own way (Lk 18:1-8). His ways are not our ways (Is 55:8-9). His wisdom is not ours, either (1 Cor 1:25; read 1 Cor 1:17-2:9). We must prepare and cultivate the soil to become that rich soil which alone is capable of making the seed, the word of God, take root and bear fruit.

There must be a readiness to leave everything and follow Him (Luke 5:28), above all, to abandon dispositions of the heart that are simply incompatible with friendship with God (John 15:15; Col 3:5-7), whose name is Love (1 John 4:8; 4:16). We must allow the word of God to prune us (John 15:2), to become a word of redeeming contradiction, to destroy, to build, and to transform. Only then can the word of God bear fruit. Because "the word of God is something alive and active: it cuts like any double-edged sword. . . . It can judge the secret emotions and thoughts" (Heb 4:12).

The realities revealed by the word can then become a living faith and are realized in a far-reaching and ever deeper manner. But for this to happen, we must receive, each one personally from the Lord, the light in which "we see the light" (Ps 36:9), the light that must shine "in our minds to radiate the light of the knowledge of God's glory, the glory on the face of Christ" (2 Cor 4:6). Only then will the general revelation, entrusted to the Church and meant for all men, also become a true light for each one of us. Only then will Jesus, by His personal gift of faith, become for each of us "the Way, the Truth, and the Life" (John 14:6).

He, "whose home is in inaccessible light" (1 Tim 6:16), came in Jesus Christ. "He lived among us, and we saw His glory, the glory that is His as the only Son of the Father, full of grace and truth" (John 1:14). His love or obedience to the Father and His redeeming love for us sinners, which has its origin in the Father (John 15:9), gives us a glimpse of the love of the Father for the Son and of the Son for the Father, that love which floods the human Heart of Jesus, that love which *is* the Holy Spirit. And so in Him, the Eternal Son, "true God from true God" (Nicene Creed), there is revealed the Father, of whom the Son is the Image made visible in Christ Jesus (Col 1:15); and the Holy Spirit, "the spirit of sons," which "makes us cry out, 'Abba, Father!' " (Rom 8:15). And so, by God's grace, we come in faith, to the "right and full knowledge of this reality" when God, through Christ, revealed "Himself as Father, Son, and Holy Spirit" (Credo, above).

8. The New Creation: Here and Hereafter

In God's "Eternal Life we are by grace called to share, here below in the obscurity of faith and after death in eternal light."

He who revealed Himself as Father, Son, and Holy Spirit is the one into whom we are implanted by the sacrament of baptism. We are baptized *into* Christ (Mat 28:19; Gal 3:27; Rom 6:3-4). With, through, and in Christ, the Eternal Son, we received this new life, this new relationship to the Father, this actual sharing of "the divine nature" (2 Pet 1:4): we become that "new creation" (*in* Christ) (2 Cor 5:17) which we were originally meant to be, and which is now restored to us by Christ's Redemption. We are meant to be children of the Father, "sons in the Son" (Pastoral Constitution, 22), *children*, because in a new birth we have received that life which is the very life of God (John 3:5; Rom 6:4). Moreover, as children, we are meant to grow into a likeness to the Father by becoming "true images of His Son" (Rom 8:29), the Son whom to see in His sacred humanity, in Jesus Christ the Man, is to see the Father (John 14:9).

By baptism we are implanted into the life of the Eternal Son. "Lifted up from the earth" (John 12:32), "sitting at the right hand of the Father (Eph 1:20-23) He is continually active in the world in order to lead men to the Church and, through it, join them more closely to Himself; and, by nourishing them with His own Body and Blood, make them partakers of

His glorious life (2 Pet 1:4)'' (Dogmatic Constitution, 48).

In this way we grow more and more into the life of the Eternal Son. As our selfishness begins to diminish by the "healing power of God's love" (*Prayer after Communion*, 21st Sunday in Ordinary Time) we become more capable of giving ourselves, with, and in the Son, to the Father. The Son, eternally begotten of the Father, as the Father's Word, as His eternal utterance, "the radiant light of God's glory and the perfect copy of His nature" (Heb 1:3), draws us through His Spirit into Himself, into His infinite response to the Father. The Son—Eternal Word *of*, and Response *to* the Father—extends Himself into us, and through us into the world, so that we might become "fellow workers with God" (1 Cor 3:9) and "ambassadors for Christ" (2 Cor 5:20).

When this indwelling of the Son (with the Father and the Holy Spirit, see John 14:23; 1 Cor 3:16) becomes deeper and more pervasive and as our diminishing selfishness makes room for Him, gradually St. Paul's description of Christian existence may be applied to us. It is the "new creation," which here on earth still involves the Cross. "I have been crucified with Christ, and I live now not with my own life, but with the life of Christ who lives in me" (Gal 2:19-20). Our own selfish and unredeemed life is to be replaced by our own true life, which comes from Jesus Christ, and is based on coming to possess the mind of Christ. This is described by St. Paul as an emptying of oneself; for God the Son emptied Himself by becoming a Man, a servant, and one who in obedience finally accepted death (Phil 2:5-8). This is the revelation of the mind of Christ, who extended His eternal self-giving to the Father into His earthly destiny and into the total emptying of Himself even unto death on the Cross. This is the pattern and source of true Christian life, a life and death which find meaning in resurrection and eternal life. Suffering and death are to become for us expiation of sin—of our own sin, and of the Sin of the World (Col 1:24).

This "is all God's work" (2 Cor 5:18). It is our part to allow ourselves to be pruned (John 15:2), to struggle with evil in and around us, and to be willing to bear the crosses that following Christ inevitably brings (Mat 16:24-26; 10:17-25). To have Christ living in us—to "put on the new self that has been created in God's way, in the goodness and holiness of the truth" (Eph 4:24)—always brings with it being "crucified with Christ" (Gal 2:19).

All this takes place now "in the obscurity of faith" (Credo, above). Our true life, Christ living in us, and in eternal union with Him the Father and the Holy Spirit, remains hidden while we are on earth. We "have died, and now the life [we] have is hidden with Christ in God" (Col 3:3). By that faith which alone can guarantee "the blessings that we hope for, or prove the existence of the realities that at present remain unseen'' (Heb 11:1—by that faith do ''we know, too, that the Son of God has come, and has given us the power to know the true God. We are *in* the true God, as we are *in* His Son, Jesus Christ. This is the true God, this is eternal life'' (1 John 5:20; emphasis added).

Only when, in death, life has been ''changed, not ended'' (Mass for the Dead, 1st Preface) will we enter eternal light. Of God, in this life ''we are seeing a dim reflection in a mirror.'' Only in the resurrection will we see Him ''face to face'' (1 Cor 13:12), will we enter into the blessed vision of peace, for which we are created and without which human existence would be cruelly absurd. Our prayer therefore is: ''Come, Lord Jesus'' (Rev 22:20).

9. Redeemed Unity

''The mutual bonds [relations] which eternally constitute the Three Persons, who are each one and the same Divine Being, are the blessed inmost life of God Thrice Holy, infinitely beyond all that we can conceive in human measure.''

''The Lord Jesus, praying to the Father 'that they may all be one . . . even as we are one' (John 17:21-22), has opened up new horizons closed to human reason by implying that there is a certain parallel between the union existing among the Divine Persons and the union of the sons of God in truth and love'' *(Pastoral Constitution, 24)*. This means that ''the blessed inmost life of God,'' although it is ''beyond all that we can conceive in human measure,'' is nevertheless reflected in human relations of genuine unity. In other words, when men are united in unselfish union—in true charity and with a readiness to bear one another's burdens (Gal. 6:2—the Law of Christ)—they actually reflect, and thereby reveal, the unity of Trinity which is God. Because our Lord did pray ''that they all may be one *as we* [Jesus and the Father] are one'' (John 17:22, emphasis added), we should be able to discern in human unity and love a real sign of the unity and love which God is: three Persons, one God. At the same time, we must remember that this revelation of divine reality grants us a mere glimpse of Him who is the creative source of all there is. We must remember that all that exists and all that happens could not exist or happen without God's creative thought bringing about both *what* is or happens, and *that* it exists or happens. For

God, in His creative Word, sustains "the universe by His powerful command" (Heb 1:3).

The extent to which something is able to reveal God depends, however, on its degree of nobility. "Ever since God created the world His everlasting power and deity—however invisible—have been there for the mind to see in the things He has made"(Rom 1:20). But the astronomical universe in its immensity and the biological world in its coordinated complexity reveal the Creator much less than the human person with his capacities for thought and action. Human forgiveness, human joy, human "poverty in spirit, meekness, suffering borne with patience, thirst after justice, purity of heart, will for peace"(*Credo*, resume of the Beatitudes) reveal what it is to be Christlike, and therefore to reveal Him whom we see when we see Jesus (John 14:9). They reveal "God's glory, the glory on the face of Christ" (2 Cor 4:6).

Ours is to be the mind of Christ (Phil 2:5). And Christ revealed the disposition of His mind when, in obedience to the Father, He emptied Himself, becoming a Man, a servant, and the crucified victim of the Sin of the World (Phil 2:5-8). And He who emptied Himself by His Incarnation is God, God the Son—"true God from true God" (Nicene Creed). Man, human beings, by being transformed into the likeness of Christ (2 Cor 3:18; Rom 8:29), like Christ Himself, though on a very limited scale, actually reveal God's presence and His Face (*Dogmatic Constitution*, 50). And as Christ's relation to the Father (as in Matt 11:25-27; and John 17), so does the (eternal) relation of the Eternal Son to the Father shine through saintly people in their obedience to God and the fidelity of their love.

Our Lord prayed that we may "all be one" (John 17:21), that we may regain that unity which sin has destroyed and continues to destroy. He showed us how this would come about in His prayer to the Father (John 17:21-23). He showed us that this redeemed unity has its source (John 17:23) and its exemplar (John 17:21) in the uncreated unity of the Trinity. And this redeemed unity can come about because God the Son has emptied Himself by becoming Man, that is, by the created unity of the Incarnation. He could then, as Man, become the victim of the Sin of the World and conquer sin by His redeeming love. He could draw all men to Himself (John 12:32) on the Cross. He now continues to do so at the right hand of the Father "until He has put all His enemies under His feet" (1 Cor 15:25; see also Ps 110:1) and until "God may be all in all" (1 Cor 15:28).

Thus we should meditate on the redeemed unity that is to be restored in us and through us and among us. Having done this, we can then live by that capacity for self-giving and generosity, which makes us in our personal relations to God and our fellow men a sign of that total mutual self-giving, of those "mutual relations which eternally constitute the Three Persons, who . . . are the blessed inmost life of God Thrice Holy"(Credo, above).

10. The Responsibility of Christians

"We give thanks, however, to the Divine Goodness that very many believers can testify with us before men to the Unity of God, even though they know not the Mystery of the Most Holy Trinity."

(Read Rom 9-11; *Dogmatic Constitution*, 16; *Pastoral Constitution*, 19-21; *Declaration on the Relation of the Church to Non-Christian Religions*, 3-4.)

Judaism. Christ's own people, the Jews, today present a wide spectrum of belief, from Orthodox Judaism to atheism. The latter, the conviction that there is no God, also demands a leap of faith. St. Paul wrote of his own people: "If our Gospel does not penetrate the veil, then the veil is on those who are not on the way to salvation . . . whose minds the god of this world has blinded, to stop them seeing the light shed by the Good News of the glory of Christ, who is the Image of God" (2 Cor 4:3-4; see also Col 1:15). But looking back we realize that centuries of vile anti-Semitism have made it difficult for many Jews in recent years to consider the Gospel of Incarnation and the Triune God anything but sheer mockery, if it is by their fruits that we are to know the followers of Christ (Luke 6:43-44). And one wonders what veil prevented so many anti-Semitic Christians from reading the words of St. Paul, inspired by God (read Rom 9:1-5; 11:28-32) when he said of the Jews: "they are still loved by God, loved for the sake of their ancestors. God never takes back His gifts or revokes His choice" (Rom 11:28-29). To hate where God loves is the beginning of damnation. For it is man who damns himself if he should persist in refusing, till the moment of death, the God whose name is Love (1 John 4: 8, 16). It is only what St. Paul wrote at the end of his meditation on the Mystery of Israel (Rom 9-11) that gives us hope for these who have hated God's people, the Jews (read Rom 11:32, 33-6; 1 Tim 2:4).

Islam. The Unity of God—the one living God in His infinite majesty— the center of the faith of Islam. The Muslims maintain strict obedience to the commandment: "You shall not make yourself a carved image or any likeness of anything in heaven above or on earth beneath . . . you shall not bow down to them or serve them. For I, Yahweh your God, am a jealous

God'' (Deut 5:8-9). Is not the lack of a sense of the majesty of God and of the sacredness of God's ways the most frightening symptom of the sickness in the Catholic Church in so many places? Some Christians have rediscovered their faith in observing Muslims in North Africa at prayer; have been moved to a better faith by a similar reverence for the transcendent mysteries of God among Catholics, especially the mysteries of the Death and Resurrection of Jesus Christ at Holy Mass?

Atheism. The only consistent alternatives to belief in the one living God seem to be either suspension of judgment (agnosticism) or atheism.

Some feel compelled to choose atheism, an atheism of deep regret, for they believe that a God who does not possess the moral qualities dear to us—justice, wisdom, mercy, love—could not *be*. And if there is a God of justice, holiness, and love they ask, why is He in His omnipotence not reflected in the world of man? Why does evil prevail (read Ps 73)? Why did the great Cardinal Newman write that he did not see a reflection of the Creator in this busy world of men—that he would be an atheist, or a pantheist, or a polytheist when looking into this world, if he did not have this clear voice of conscience speaking in his heart assuring him of the existence of God (*Apologia pro Vita Sua*, Ch.VII)? But then, this faith is a free gift from God.

Christians may, at times, share the responsibility for this atheism of deep regret "to the extent that they are careless about their instruction in the faith, or represent its teaching falsely, or even fail in their religious, moral, or social life," concealing rather then revealing "the true nature of God and of religion" (*Pastoral Constitution*, 19).

An atheism of deep regret throws man upon his own resources; it leaves man "immersed in this world, without hope and without God" (Eph 2:12). And we see with ever greater clarity what man can, or eventually will do without God: build concentration camps and gulags; find entertainment for rulers, philosophers, poets, and the mass of people in the Roman Circus, watching torture and murder (read Rom 1:18-32); eliminate entire populations systematically (genocide) or force them into mass migrations. And now, even the total extermination of mankind is within our power.

Godlessness or atheism—whether chosen with regret or in rebellion, whether accepted with uncritical conformity or as a result of being scandalized by unacceptable alternatives—is a dreadful condition of silence, of boredom, of hopelessness with alternating presumption and despair, a living as if one were in solitary confinement, a loneliness so common today, and a foretaste of Hell. In this state, human existence is experienced as a curse, with only temporary escapes, which give way to a meaningless waiting for extinction which is viewed almost as a liberation. Is it not the most elementary obedience of charity commanded by Christ (John 13:34) to be the "light of the world" (Mat 5:14), to be a "light in the Lord," to be "like children of light . . . seem in complete goodness and right living and truth" (Eph 5:9)? It is through and in the Church that Christ gives "light to those who live in darkness and the shadow of death" and guides "our feet into the way of peace" (Luke 1:79). And we, you, are the Church. We must not fail.

11. The Self-Giving of the Son

"We believe then in the Father who eternally begets the Son, in the Son, the Word of God, who is eternally begotten, in the Holy Spirit, the uncreated Person who proceeds from the Father and the Son as their eternal Love."

"His state was divine, yet He did not cling to His equality with God but emptied Himself. . . ." (Phil 2:6-7). *Who* emptied Himself? That a man would accept being a servant and in obedience choose death and even the horrors of crucifixion is within the possibilities of human existence. But here it is Someone whose "state was divine" who emptied Himself, to *become* and *be* Man and servant, to suffer death as the victim of hatred, contempt, intrigue, brutality, and sadism. In Him the converging sin of the world found its ultimate target, because He was God-among-us in visible weakness. As Incarnate Love, He provoked all that is evil, selfish, murderous, resentful of truth and goodness, and exasperated by purity. He, the Word made flesh, living among us and revealing "His glory, the glory that is His as the only Son of the Father" (John 1:14), could now, seemingly, be removed once and for all. Apparently, evil would no longer have to suffer the pain of being unmasked and threatened by Him in whom we "see our God made visible" (Christmas Preface I). The prophetic words of the Book of Wisdom describe sin's response to holiness: "Let us lie in wait for the virtuous man, since he annoys us and opposes our way of life, reproaches us for our breaches of the law. . . . He claims to have knowledge of God, and calls himself a son of the Lord. Before us he stands, a reproof to our way of thinking. . . . Let us test him with cruelty and with torture, and thus explore this gentleness of his . . . " (Wisd 2:12-13; 19). Thus was He tested, He who is eternally the "Image of the invisible God" (Col 1:15), who is eternally one with the Father (John 10:30), and who, as Man, became the visible Image of the invisible God (read 1 John 1:1-3). It was the Creator of the universe, who sustains "the universe by His powerful command" (Heb 1:3) who emptied Himself in obedience. The obedience *of* God (the Son), *in* God, to the Father—what can this possibly mean? For this is what St. Paul implied when he described the mind of Christ (Phil 2:5-8) which is also to be ours. How can we speak of the obedience of God-the-Son to God-the-Father without destroying the unity of God? Are the Son and the Father not one? And yet, Christ suffered crucifixion in obedience, and whatever we learn of Christ does reveal the invisible God. Whatever Christ did was ultimately an act of a Divine Person, an act of the Son of the Eternal Father.

The life of the Three Persons who constitute One God is one of eternally mutual relations. The Father eternally begets His likeness or Son; and the Son is what He is because in begetting, the Father gives Himself totally to the Son, who, in turn, gives Himself to the Father. The foundation of this mutual self-giving is Love, and the same Love in turn flows from this mutual indwelling, this perfect community of Father and Son (John 14:10, 11; 10:38). And this Love in its overflowing might and intensity is a distinct Person, the Holy Spirit. Romano Guardini wrote: "God is Himself the speaker, the one spoken, and the loving comprehension of the eternal speech" (*The World and the Person*, p. 135).

The Incarnation is the reentering of God's Word into a world imprisoned in its own disobedience (Rom 11:32) and rampant self-seeking, a world sullied by the Original Sin or first rebellion, and by the continuation of this rebellion ever since. It was inevitable that God as Man would be a sign that would be rejected (Luke 2:34) as He, in His teaching and life, inevitably would become a sign of contradiction to a sin-infested world. His divine self-giving as Son of the Father was now extended into the world. We became able to see it revealed in Christ's obedience, a human obedience. "My aim is not to do my own will, but the will of Him who sent me" (John 5:30).; "My food is to do the will of the One who sent me" (John 4:34). The obedience of Christ became an ever more radical self-effacing or emptying of Himself until He sustained in His redeeming love the utmost humiliation and pain during the seemingly endless hours of torture and crucifixion. And in this way, the eternal self-giving of the Son was extended into the total emptying of Himself, the Almighty, in helplessness on the Cross. God's names are "Being and Love," expressing "ineffably the *same* divine reality" (*Credo*, emphasis added). And now the fullness of Love came to be an emptying even unto death on the Cross (Phil 2:8). This is the Mystery of the Cross—the invisible victory of redeeming Love drawing all men to itself (John 12:32), and thereby transforming the greatest disaster into the very source and center of Redemption. This was a victory of Love, even while being crushed by evil and hate—a Love that would rise and ascend into Heaven, to be in the Heart of Jesus sitting at the right hand of the Father. And from Heaven His Love would continue to go out to all men to draw them, by His divine power, to Himself (John 12:32; 2 Pet 1:3), to restore men to that redeemed unity brought about by Jesus Christ coming to live in men while the Father lives in Him (John 17:23).

Divine wisdom (1 Cor 1:20-31) consists in this: that God the Eternal Son emptied Himself unto death on the Cross: He revealed His boundless love, which is one with His infinite power and majesty, by the total dispossession of Himself. This is the paradox of God's wisdom. "God's foolishness is wiser than human wisdom, and God's weakness is stronger than human strength" (1 Cor 1:25).

12. The Son's Priestly Prayer

"Thus in the Three Divine Persons, coaeternae sibi et coaequales, the life and beatitude of God perfectly One superabound and are consummated in the supreme excellence and glory proper to un-created Being, and always 'there should be venerated Unity in the Trinity and Trinity in the Unity.' "

(Read John 17; Heb 5:1-10.)

Eternally One in their mutual relations and eternally equal in their infinite Godhead (which Father, Son, and Holy Spirit *are* and share), their life and joy are radiance and light, the glory of "God Thrice Holy" (*Credo*). This eternal, boundless, and yet self-contained glory—a love that is total self-giving, total generosity, threefold personified altruism, a total unreserved sharing of divine power—is "made visible in Christ Jesus our Lord" (Rom 8:39). It is "the radiant light of God's glory" (Heb 1:3), "the glory on the face of Christ" (2 Cor 4:6).

"No one has ever seen God; it is the only Son, who is nearest to the Father's heart, who has made Him known" (John 1:18). He, the Son, Jesus Christ, has made God known, as He freely became the target and victim of all human sin, as He freely maintained His redeeming love for us all while we crucified Him by our sins. This is the ultimate revelation of eternal love of the Son for the Father. In Christ, "God's weakness [became] stronger than human strength" (1 Cor 1:25).

His sacrifice reveals Him as "the Resurrection and the Life" (John 11:25). His human words to the Father reveal Jesus the Man as the Truth (John 14:6). The Truth—the fact of His eternal relation to the Father as the Only-Begotten of the Father—shines through His human words spoken to the Father, above all in His priestly prayer (John 17)—His last words before going forth to His death, when He "knew that the hour had come for Him to pass from this world to the Father," when He was to show "how perfect His love was" (John 13:1).

His successful attempt to maintain the flawless harmony of mercy and power, of burning desire to achieve man's salvation in obedience to the Father and knowledge of how it must be achieved increased the tension and suffering in the Heart of Jesus during the ordeal that brought us Redemption. Expectation of Passion and Death and of the convergence of evil upon Him; the immense inner struggle to maintain His redeeming love for those who crucified Him; and full anticipation of the horror of the Crucifixion—all these were present while He prayed to the Father.

When Love was to be crucified—in "the hour" (John 17:1) when Jesus was "obedient unto death" (Phil 2:8)—the radiance of the Father's love was made visible in the agony of the Son as the Father enabled the Son to go through with the ordeal and still to extend His redeeming, pleading, transforming love to us, His murderers. " 'And when I am lifted up from the earth, I shall draw all men to myself.' By these words He indicated the kind of death He would die" (John 12:32-33).

We ought to try to hear our Lord's priestly prayer to the Father while remembering this tension (Mat 26:36-46) and what was to happen before the evening of the day. It all was done that He might "share [His] joy with them to the full" (John 17:13), *in* them, Father and Son, drawn into the divine life by that Love which is both source and fruit of their union, the Holy Spirit.

Our Lord's priestly prayer is a prayer of the humanity that belongs to One equal to the Father, asking for what has been determined by Divine Providence. The goals of Crucified Redemption motivated the human Heart of the Savior in the dreadful hours that were to follow soon after. God, in His Providence, has preserved for us these words of Jesus, that we may by meditation enter into the Son's relationship to the Father. We are to share this relation, to become "sons in the Son," (*Pastoral Constitution*, 22) now and eternally.

The revelation of the Son—who is eternally the invisible Image of the invisible Father, and historically the visible image of the invisible God (Col 1:15)—took place in His words, His actions, and the several stages of His human life, culminating in His sacrifice. The priestly prayer is the deepest glimpse granted us of the eternal relation of Son and Father, now translated, extended, and revealed in the journey through torture and murder to Resurrection into Lordship. The mystery of obedience of the Son to the Father shines through these words, that are to be listened to in the light of what was to come, the horror of Passion and Crucifixion. Only then can we hope to see fulfilled in us the final words of this priestly prayer: "I have made your name known to them and will continue to make it known, so that the love with which you loved me may be in them, and so that I may be in them" (John 17:26).

13. The Son's Eternal Gifts to Us

"We believe in our Lord Jesus Christ, Who is the Son of God."

"We believe in Jesus Christ," with the faith that proves "the existence of the realities that at present remain unseen" (Heb 11:1). This faith assures us of the fact that Jesus, the Son of Mary, lives *now*. This belief expands our awareness of reality beyond creation, beyond that world we can see, can explore, and can experience, into the divine, into God—Father, Son, and Holy Spirit. The Good News, the Gospel of our faith, is the revealed fact that Jesus Christ—who "for us men and for our salvation came down from Heaven" (Nicene Creed), though not accepted by His own people (John 1:10-11), and though murdered by men (by all men, by us, by me)—remained faithful in His rejected love, pleading, "Father, forgive them; they do not know what they are doing" (Luke 23:34; see also Is 53:11-12). The Good news is that on the Cross He drew *all* men to Himself (John 12:32); that now, at the right hand of the Father, He continues to do so—at this very moment, and till the end of history. Faith gives us a living awareness of this reality, that Jesus Christ, once crucified and buried, rose, ascended, and now has been "highly exalted . . . [so] at the name of Jesus" all being must bend the knee, acclaiming "Jesus Christ is Lord" (Phil 2:8-11). This is our Faith, our Hope, and an invitation to respond with Love. "This is the love I mean: not our love for God, but God's love for us when He sent His Son to be the sacrifice that takes ours sins away" (1 John 4:10).

The five statements about Christ we here profess (*Credo*), are all united in the Person of the Son, who is the Image of the invisible Father. Eternally He is the Son, "Light from Light" (Nicene Creed), one in substance with the Father. In that mysterious obedience of God-the-Son to God-the-Father—an obedience which consists in the coming of the Son into His resisting world in the vulnerable nature of Man—redeeming love was offered to a world otherwise lost. Thereby, God-the-Son became, in His human nature, helpless; he could be threatened (Luke 4:28-29; John 8:59), and in free obedience could allow the Sin of the World to find in Him its true target and make Him its victim, the Lamb of God (John 1:29).

Jesus is His human name (Mat 1:21). It means "Yahweh saves." *Christ* means "the Anointed" of "the Messiah"—anointed by being the humanity of God the Son, because God "had anointed Him with the Holy Spirit and with power, and because God was with Him" (Acts 10:38). Certainly all during His life on earth, Jesus possessed, as God, divine power, yet He "did not count equality with God a thing to be grasped at" (Phil 2:6). But when the victory of His love was accomplished at the moment of His death (John 19:30), His rejected, yet faithful love had swept over all mankind whom He saw in His immediate vision of God, when He had drawn men to Himself (John 12:32). All the rejections of men throughout their history, He had suffered: He absorbed—and thereby absolved—them in His redeeming love, in an inconceivable inner struggle. Thereby, He merited the power to extend His divine power to each one of us (Mat 28:18). At the disposal of His human Heart, now glorified in Heaven, His divine power would extend salvation and growth in sanctity "to all who [would] accept Him"(John 1:12). To them He would give "power to become children of God" (John 1:12). This is the "power of His Resurrection" (Phil 3:10, that Jesus, by the promptings of His Sacred Heart, "by His divine power . . . has given us all the things that we need for life and for true devotion" (2 Pet 1:3). Through these gifts, willed by Jesus, given by His divine power, we are "able to share the divine nature and to escape corruption in a world that is sunk in vice" (2 Pet 1:4).

Truly, Jesus now is Lord. For to Him is given now "all authority in Heaven and on earth" (Mat 28:18). And that this redeemed existence, this transformation of hearts of men, is meant to overflow into Redemption for the times (Eph 5:16), is stated by the Church: "Constituted Lord by His Resurrection and given all authority in Heaven and on earth, Christ is *now* at work in the hearts of men by the power of His Spirit; not only does He arouse in them a desire for the world to come but He quickens, purifies, and strengthens the generous aspirations of mankind to make life more humane and conquer the earth for this purpose" (*Pastoral Constitution*, 38). And we believe that He is *our* Lord—as the Father is *our* Father. All, both friends and enemies, are sought by the redeeming love of the Son of God and the Son of Mary, by the Messiah, the Good Shepherd (John 10:1-18), seated at the right hand of the Father. All this, and much more, is meant when we profess our faith "in our Lord Jesus Christ who is the Son of God."

14. The Incarnation

"He is the Eternal Word, born of the Father before time began, and one in substance with the Father, homoousios to Patri, and through Him all things were made."

It is He who less than two thousand years ago began to exist as a human being. He did not cease to be God the Son. "The Word, who is life," "has existed since the beginning"—"this is our subject"—Him "we have heard . . . seen . . . watched . . . and touched" (1 John 1:1). By and in Him, we are drawn into the life which He is as God, which He shares as Man, "because God wanted all perfection to be found in Him" (Col 1:19). "In His body," that is, in His humanity of human soul and human body, "lives the fullness of divinity" (Col 2:9). And this divinity, this divine power, of which Jesus the Man is the created extension into the world of man, is the creative source of all redeeming gifts and transformations, of all grace and living truth which Jesus' Heart wills for us.

Not the Father, the Origin without Origin, but His Eternal Word, His distinct and perfect likeness, through whom all things were (and are) spoken into existence, He it is who began, in historical time, at the time of King Herod and the Emperor Augustus, to exist *in* and *as* a created nature, as Man. "Now all this took place to fulfill the words spoken by the Lord through the prophet: 'the virgin will conceive and give birth to a son and they will call him Immanuel,' a name which means 'God-is-with-us' '' (Mat 1:22-23).

We all are asked: "Do you not believe that I am in the Father and the Father is in Me?" (John 14:10). Jesus told us that we must believe it (John 14:11). "The Father and I are one" (John 10:30), we are told. Here is the *exemplar* of our own redeemed unity—that we may be one *as* they are one (John 17:22). Here is the *source* of our redeemed unity—*that we may be one in them*, Father and Son, as the Father is in the Son and the Son in the Father (John 17:21). Herein lies the cause of our unity: Jesus in us, the Father in Jesus (John 17:23). And as their Love, the Holy Spirit is their mutual bond, it is He who draws us into this unity, unity with God, unity in God. This is growth in holiness, union with God. Therefore the Holy Spirit is called "the Sanctifier." That is why we pray: "Come, Holy Spirit: fill the hearts of your faithful; and kindle in them the fire of your love." We also pray, "through [Jesus Christ], with Him, in Him, in the unity *of* the Holy Spirit, all glory and honor is yours, almighty Father" (end of Canons of the Mass; emphasis added); the glory and honor are given to the Father by our return into divine love and by our growth into this divine life.

The *Credo* speaks here of the One who would, in historical times, begin to exist as man, to dwell among us (John 1:14). This we *must* remember; it is a fact that must be a living part of our faith. It is the enormity of this event, of that wisdom of God that is foolishness to men (1 Cor 1:27), that the Creator of the universe—the Eternal Son, who is "true God from true God" (Nicene Creed), through whom "all things came to be" (John 1:3; see also Col 1:15-17), who sustains "the universe by His powerful command" (Heb 1:3)—would really begin to exist *in* and *as* a second, created, human nature, and will continue eternally to be true Man while remaining, as God, one in substance with the Father. If we recall the dimensions in time, mass, and energy of the universe, and the marvelously coordinated complexities of all living things, all due to the creative intelligence of God, the Incarnation is liable to stagger the mind and tear at the Credibility of revelation. But the total absurdity of the alternative—consistent atheism—supports our faith in the ways of God as they have become known by revelation and by faith ever since the first Pentecost, when the true meaning of Christ shook the first Christians—and should continue to shake us. Because what our Lord predicted was then beginning to come true: "When the Spirit of truth comes He will lead you to the *complete* truth" (John 16:13; emphasis added). And He will do this also for us who share the faith of the Church. And that we may not falter, we will pray, "I believe; help my unbelief" (Mark 9:24).

15. The Blessed Virgin Mary

"He was incarnate of the Virgin Mary by the power of the Holy Spirit, and was made Man. . . ."

(Read Luke 1:26-30.)

"Son of the Eternal Father, when you took our nature to save mankind you did not shrink from birth in a Virgin's womb" (*Te Deum*). And who but she, the Virgin, could have prayed in flawless harmony with God's will these words of the Psalm: "As a doe longs for running streams, so longs my soul for you, my God. My soul thirsts for God, the God of life; when shall I go to see the face of God?" (Ps 42:1-2). "I waited and waited for Yahweh, now at last He has stooped to me" (Ps 40:1).

A crystal-clear intelligence, formed by the sacred books of Israel and the service of the Temple, she knew better than anyone of the continuing rebellion of the world, and even of her own people, against God and against truth—the rebellion which obliterates even the very first urgings of love. She knew better than anyone the brutality of the Roman Empire: public crucifixions, the horrors of slavery, a paganism with few redeeming features—a life filled with despair for most, alternating with presumption in the few who were living at a privileged distance. Mary knew a civilization "immersed in this world, without hope and without God" (Eph 2:12), where even the faith of Israel was bearing dim and doubtful witness to the God whose names are Being and Love (*Credo*). Her yearning for the Messiah, her hope for the salvation of Israel, for the delivery of all mankind—her freedom from sin giving her a boundless capacity for compassion for sinners and their victims—she was to be the Mother of Him who would "give light to those who live in darkness and the shadow of death" and who would "guide our feet into the way of peace" (Luke 1:79).

She and St. Joseph were the first to see the face of God, in answer to their longing and prayer. They were the first to receive "the knowledge of God's glory, the glory on the face of Christ" (2 Cor 4:6). God's glory in the helplessness and innocence of the Child in Bethlehem, an innocence which He would retain, added the horror of the murder of a Child to the horrors of torture and crucifixion, the hatred of innocence and purity striking out against God Incarnate. And thus it would rend the heart of the Mother in her flawless compassion, through her power of vicarious suffering, rooted in that love that since her Immaculate Conception was always growing to the limit of her expanding capacity for love.

Did she know that the Servant of Yahweh was a prophecy of the One she was aked by God to give the world? Did she know that her Child would be "a thing despised and rejected by men, a man of sorrows . . . despised"(Is 53:6); that Yahweh would burden "Him with the sins of all of us" (Is 53:6); that He would be "like a lamb that is led to the slaughterhouse" (Is 53:7)?

The flawlessness and readiness of her obedience were the perfection of her love. For she knew that love of God is commanded (Deut 6:5-6), and therefore an obedience. "I am the handmaid of the Lord . . . let what you have said be done to me" (Luke 1:33).

And so she was ready for the time when the Holy Spirit would come upon her "and the power of the Most High [would cover her] with its shadow" (Luke 1:35), when the Eternal Son would begin to exist as Man in her. "By the power of the Holy Spirit He became incarnate from the virgin Mary and was made man" (Nicene Creed).

"No one has ever seen God; it is the only Son, who is nearest to the Father's heart, who has made Him known" (John 1:18). But now, since He came to exist as one like us, through His human mother, Mary, we can see "His glory, the glory that is His as the only Son of the Father, full of grace and truth" (John 1:14).

16. Christ's Human Freedom

"He . . . was made Man: equal therefore to the Father according to His divinity, and inferior to the Father according to His humanity, and Himself one, not by some impossible confusion of His natures, but by the unity of His Person."

(Read John 1:1-18; Col 1:15-20; Heb 1:1-4; and observe while reading that statements that can only pertain to a divine Person, and statements that can only pertain to Jesus as Man, alternate without thereby confusing us. These passages deal each with Jesus Christ, true God and true Man, One Person existing in two natures.)

How did the unique union of humanity with the Divine Person of the Eternal Son affect the freedom of Jesus Christ the Man? Did His inability to sin make Him, the "sinless one" (2 Cor 5:21), less human? Is freedom rooted in the choice between sinning and choosing the will of God? Does true devotion to Jesus Christ consist of identifying with Him, as is frequently asserted? Are we to identify with Him, or is it not He, rather, who identifies with us, having suffered all and thus having become capable "of feeling our weaknesses with us . . . [He] who has been tempted in every way that we are, though He is without sin" (Heb 4:15)?

Jesus-the-Man is the instrument of God. In Him we see the Father (John 14:9), whose visible Image He is (Col 1:15). In His obedience, He was the perfect instrument of the Father; because of this, He was able to bring about what He predicted He would do: draw all men to Himself (John 12:32). He did so while on the Cross, and continues to do so as the Risen Lord now in Heaven. But both tasks—to reveal the Father and to restore men to redeemed existence—or in the beautiful words of the *Pastoral Constitution*: "manifesting and actualizing the mystery of God's love for men" (section 45)—both tasks require His own divine power, which is His by His divine nature.

It is in this interdependence and blending of His human mind and will with His divine power that the ineffable union of the two natures—human and divine—is manifested. Jesus Christ the Man is the only mediator between the Father and mankind (1 Tim 2:5). It is by His Sacred human Heart that the Lord exercises the authority in Heaven and on earth that has been given to Him (Mat 28:18). But His human will has at its disposal—one may almost say as His instrument—"His divine power" by which He gives us "all things that we need for life and for true devotion, bringing us to know God Himself" (2 Pet 1:3). As we pray in the Preface for the fifth Sunday of Lent: "As a Man like us, Jesus wept for Lazarus His friend. As the Eternal God, He raised Lazarus from the dead."

The unity of humanity and divinity in the Person of the Eternal Son is at the very heart of the continuing work of Redemption. His human Heart maintained on Good Friday, and continues to maintain now in Heaven, its love for us, His torturers and murderers. His human Heart continues to plead for us at God's right hand (Rom 8:34). "He is living forever to intercede for all who come to God through Him" (Heb 7:25). But all that which is needed to draw us to Himself requires the creative and transforming power of God. As Man, He wills it; as God, He accomplishes it. "It is God, for His own loving purpose, who puts both the will and the action" into us (Phil 2:13). And by His divine power, He transforms our theoretical knowledge of divine revelation into that living faith which enables us to hope and invites us to love. "It is the same God that said, 'Let there be light shining out of darkness,' " namely God the Creator, "who has shone in our minds to radiate the light of the knowledge of God's glory, the glory on the face of Christ'' (2 Cor 4:6). And this light is the light of faith.

Both the human and the divine natures are involved in all that leads us to union with God and turns us "into the image that we reflect" (2 Cor 3:18). This, our transformation into a likeness of Christ, is willed by Jesus, by His redeeming, tested, and victorious human love, in harmony with His divine will. But "this is the work of the Lord who is Spirit" (2 Cor 3:18), of His divine power. The functions of the two natures are distinct, though complementary. But both natures, the human and the divine, belong to the One Lord Jesus Christ, our Brother and our Lord, "not by some impossible confusion of His natures, but by the unity of His Person" (*Credo*).

The supreme freedom of God is the unity of infinite knowledge, love, and mercy, in complete simplicity, in God's creative and sustaining power. All of these, as it were, form His power as it makes possible the humanity assumed by the Eternal Son, or Word, of the Father; the human Heart of Jesus, in His freedom of love, seeking even those of us who are defying Him. Herein lies the mystery of God's being immutable in His being, yet infinitely flexible in His creative and loving power, flooding the soul of Jesus, enabling Him in His human life to be the Good Shepherd, to seek what is lost—"for the Son of Man has come to seek out and save what was lost" (Luke 19:10). This is the freedom of Jesus Christ—the Lord who emptied Himself into obedience, into the freedom of love, into a love that is freedom—the freedom that brought Jesus to suffer "outside the gate to sanctify the people with His own blood" (Heb 13:12). And *our* freedom is to be able to "go to Him, then, outside the camp, and share His degradation" (Heb 13:13).

17. Our Vocation as Ambassadors for Christ

"He dwelt among us, full of grace and truth."

(Read *Dogmatic Constitution*, 5-8; *Decree on the Church's Missionary Activity*, 4; 2 Cor 5:17-20.)

And He continues to dwell among us. Among the manifold ways by which Jesus Christ continues to be among us—in the Eucharist, as head of the Church, in the inspired words of Scripture (above all in the Gospels where we find His actual words), dwelling in the souls of men who have been baptized into Him (Gal 3:27; 2:19-20)—we will here reflect only on Christ as He continues His presence and His work now and through those who are fellow workers with God (1 Cor 3:9), who by doing the will of the Father, by their obedience of Love, are "ambassadors for Christ" (2 Cor 5:20)—in other words, His presence among us through each one of us.

The *Decree on the Apostolate of Lay People*, paragraph 2, states: "The Christian vocation is, of its nature, a vocation to the apostolate as well." An *apostle* is "one who is sent." Through baptism and confirmation, we are placed as Christ's members into a world that is largely hostile. We are to be "innocent and genuine, perfect children of God among a deceitful and underhand brood, and [to] shine in the world like bright stars" (Phil 2:14-15). "Being sent" does not necessarily involve a change of place; it is rather a new kind of presence. We are baptized into sharing "the divine nature" (2 Pet 1:4); we are confirmed into the unifying love which is the Holy Spirit, as His temples (1 Cor 6:19), rendering Him present in the world, both hidden and active: "by the Holy Spirit which has been given us," "the love of God has been poured into our hearts" (Rom 5:5). And both the ability to love and the actualization of this ability are totally God's work "who puts both the will and the action" into us (Phil 2:13), and it is totally ours, accomplished by us through the enabling, transforming, creative power of God.

What St. John wrote—that "the Word was made flesh, He lived among us," and that he, John, as well as the new believers, "saw His glory, the glory that is His as the only Son of the Father, full of grace and truth" (John 1:14)—continues, now through the Church and through everyone who, by baptism, helps to constitute the Church. Thus each one of us shares in the task of bringing about that continuing presence of Christ that He promised before ascending into Heaven. "And know that I am with you always; yes, to the end of time" (Mat 28:20). "The Christian vocation is, of its nature, a vocation to the apostolate as well" (*Decree on the Apostolate of the Lay People*, 2).

Here lies the glorious and exciting vocation of each Christian. It is not a joyless pursuit of personal reward, sought in isolated effort. It is the search for a God whose name is Love (1 John 4:8, 16), a search which is already the beginning of finding Him with whom we shall enter into even greater union, if we only keep asking, searching, knocking (Mat 7:7-11), as He, in whom we hear the Father, assured us (John 14:9; 12:44; 18:37; 8:31; 12:49-50; 13:10).

Every apostolate, every assuming of responsibilities within the Church's task of giving Christ to men, is essentially hidden. It is a life, a task of prayer and expiation, and not necessarily of visible activity with the reward of visible results. It is accessible to all, young and old, well or dying. It is a readiness to speak, to keep silent, to act, to cooperate, to serve, to suffer. But these opportunities may never arise. "The fruitfulness of the apostolate of lay people depends on their living union with Christ" (*Decree on the Apostolate of Lay People*, 4). "Whoever remains in me, with me in him, bears fruit in plenty; for cut off from me you can do nothing" (John 15:5), because we "have died, and now the life [we] have is hidden with Christ in God" (Col 3:3).

How difficult to renounce the vanities of visible success, praise, acceptance, popularity. The apostolate is to follow Him who "suffered outside the gate to sanctify the people with His own blood. Let us go to Him . . . and share His degradation" (Heb 13:12-13). His Cross and Resurrection were the source of our Redemption. They remain for each of us the form of our apostolate. "If anyone wants to be a follower of mine, let him renounce himself and take up his cross and follow me" (Mark 8:34). It is for each Christian to decide whether he wants to drown in utter mediocrity and self-seeking (Gal 5:19-21; Rev 3:14-22) or go with Christ through many crucifixions to eternal life. And if we find ourselves actively engaged in apostolic activities we must listen to the injunction of Jean Cardinal Danielou: "The moment an apostolate becomes personal, that it begins to have a personal influence, that it is carried forward by personal influence, that it is carried forward by personal views, that we seek to hold on to souls and not simply to lead them to Christ, from that very moment everything collapses and we are no longer doing Christ's work"(*The Salvation of the Nations*, p. 115).

18. The Kingdom of God: Praying for it Unconditionally

"He proclaimed and established the Kingdom of God. . . ."

(Read Mat 13; *Dogmatic Constitution*, 5 and 6.)

The Kingdom of God is: "a Kingdom of truth and life, a Kingdom of holiness and grace, a Kingdom of justice, love, and peace" (Preface of the Feast of Christ the King). Often we pray "Thy Kingdom come, Thy will be done." In expressing this desire we also pray *for* this desire, that it may come to grow stronger in us. To pray for this desire should be to pray for it without reservation: we should be prepared to accept God's response, God's 'hearing' our prayer, whatever the cost. This requires us to accept our Lord's proclamation in faith and hope, so that *hearing* and *desiring* it would make it possible for Him to establish the Kingdom of God in us and through us.

How do we establish His Kingdom? "If we live by the truth and in love, we shall grow in all ways into Christ, who is the head" (Eph 4:15). But "to live by the truth" is to discover Him who is the Truth (John 14:6). It is to renew again and again the realization that in Him "the Kingdom of God is close at hand," and that therefore we are to "repent, and believe the Good News" (Mark 1:15).

Repentance is a turning away from that all-pervasive, truth-distorting self-indulgence, by which our pride and vanity and resentments continue to dominate and poison even our objectively correct thoughts and actions (see Gal 5:19-21). Repentance is a turning to Him who is the Way, the Truth, the Life, and the Resurrection (John 14:6; 11:25); it means to "put on a new self which will progress towards true knowledge the more it is renewed in the image of its Creator" (Col 3:10). Repentance is the radical (going to the roots) discarding of all self-seeking, the pruning (John 15:2; read verses 1 to 17) of us, His branches. To repent is to discover that God's foolishness is wiser than human wisdom, and God's weakness is stronger than human strength" (1 Cor 1:25), to discover, in short, the wisdom of the Cross. It is to acquire the mind of Christ, which was revealed when the Eternal Son emptied Himself in becoming Man and servant, and was crucified by the Sin of the World (Phil 2:1-8). To repent is to submit, however reluctantly, to being "persecuted in the cause of right," because then ours will be "the Kingdom of Heaven" (Mat 5:10). It is that poverty in spirit, without which there is no Kingdom of God (Mat 5:3).

As God's Kingdom takes root in us, we are gradually incorporated into this Kingdom. As God comes to prevail in us, as Jesus Christ becomes truly our Lord, as the veil is lifted, "we, with our unveiled faces reflecting like mirrors the brightness of the Lord, all grow brighter and brighter as we are turned into the image that we reflect" (2 Cor 3:18). As we reflect the image of Jesus Christ, we become manifestations of Him who Himself reflects the image of the Father. Then, God's "presence and His face" (*Dogmatic Constitution*, 50) will be revealed through us. As in Christ Jesus, in whom that glory was seen that belongs to Him as the only Son of the

Father (John 1:14), this glory is now reflected by us and turns us into "children of light [as] the effects of the light are seen in complete goodness and right living and truth" (Eph 5:9). "Anything exposed by the light will be illuminated and anything illuminated turns into light" (Eph 5:13-14).

Christ "proclaimed and established the Kingdom of God" (*Credo*, above) while He was on earth. He drew all men to Himself on the Cross (John 12:32). Now, from Heaven, He continues to draw all men, but He does so through His Church. And every one of us is meant to be the Church, and it is to the Church—to us, and to everyone in the Church, *as* the Church—that He "gave . . . the work of handing on this reconciliation" (2 Cor 5:18). "So we are ambassadors for Christ; it is as though God were appealing through us" (2 Cor 5:19).

Christ proclaimed His Kingdom by His word, and established it by His sacraments. He continues to do so, turning us into non-verbal manifestations of Himself by what, in our redeemed unity, we have become through our union with God. When our prayers become unconditional, a genuine seeking and longing, when we remain in Christ and His words have transformed us and remain in us, we may ask what we will, and we shall get it (John 15:7). When we are crucified with Christ, and we live with the life of Christ who lives in us (Gal 2:19-20), we will become instruments of expiation, we will love as He loved (John 13:34). And then, through us, the Kingdom of God will be in the world, for we will share in the Church's being " 'the universal sacrament of salvation,' at once manifesting and actualizing the mystery of God's love for men" (*Pastoral Constitution*, 45).

19. Christ Reveals the Father

"He . . . made us know in Himself the Father."

"To have seen me is to have seen the Father" (John 14:9). Here it is revealed that God, the infinite, "whose home is in inaccessible light, whom no man has seen and no man is able to see" (1 Tim 6:16), is not unapproachable. Christ the Man can actually reveal something of Him "who is," exists essentially. In God all exists in total unity and simplicity. His attributes, His will with regard to us, His limitless flexibility in response to our fickleness and infidelities, are "absolutely one in His infinitely holy essence" (*Credo*). And yet this "one only God" is heard, seen, watched, and touched, and therefore revealed (1 John 1:1), in all that we can know of Jesus Christ the Man. Jesus is the visible "Image of the invisible God" (Col 1:15), "today as He was yesterday, and as He will be forever" (Heb 13:8).

Aspects of God's love, and thereby of God Himself, were revealed in Jesus' lament for Jerusalem when "He shed tears over it" (Luke 19:41-44). He whose "two names, Being and Love, express ineffably the same divine reality of Him who is . . . in Himself above every name...and above every created intellect" (*Credo*) is revealed in the Child in the manger and in the hidden life of Nazareth. "Where did the man get this wisdom and these miraculous powers? This is the carpenter's son, surely?" (Mat 13:54-55). And yet, God the Son chose to remain indistinguishable in the drab town of Nazareth for more than thirty years. He who spent time eating and drinking with tax collectors and sinners (Luke 5:30) is the revelation of God.

He saw the large crowd and He took pity on them because they were "like sheep without a shepherd" (Mark 6:34). This is divine pity flooding the human Heart of Jesus. And teaching the love of enemies, He made it clear that in following this command, we share the very perfection of God (Mat 5:43-48), which in turn was shared by Him in His human Heart, especially when He said, "Father, forgive them; they do not know what they are doing" (Luke 23-24).

The prayer of Gethsemane, "let it be as you, not I would have it" (Mat 26:39), is a revelation of Jesus being truly human. But His lifelong unconditional obedience, even to "death on a cross" (Phil 2:8) is a revelation of that eternal unity and harmony of Father and Son—rooted in love and eternally productive of Love, which is the Holy Spirit ("who proceeds from the Father and the Son"—Nicene Creed)—which we profess as belief in "one only God, Father, son and Holy Spirit" (*Credo*). His obedience is the revelation and actualization of the eternal total self-giving of the Son to the Father, extended through the Incarnation into the world of man, a world that "did not accept Him (John 1:11). In Jesus' priestly prayer spoken to the Father in the presence of the Apostles (John 17), there is given to us the deepest and most sublime revelation through words of the eternal, immutable, and yet historically active dialogue between the Father and the Son, between the Speaker and His Word, a revelation surpassed as revelation of love only in the deathly silence on the Cross, interrupted seven times by His seven words.

We hear again and again Christ's priestly prayer, and by the grace of God, we may come to discern, in God's own time, something of the transverbal and ineffable reality of the Triune God. All our hope is rooted in the desire of Jesus and His promise that He would continue to make known to us the name of the Father—of whom He is eternally the invisible, and historically the visible Image (Col 1:15)—so that the love with which the Father loved Him (the Son) may be in us; so that Jesus Christ, the Father's Son, our Savior, may be in us (John 17:26).

20. The New Commandment: Extending Christ's Love

"He gave us His New Commandment to love one another as He loves us."

It is revealed to us that love can be commanded, and is therefore an act of obedience (Deut 6:4-6; Lev 19:18). This alone should make us seek the nature of this commanded love outside of common human experience. It is a love that is revealed in commandment, and by the example of Christ and of saintly—that is, Christlike—men and women. It is described in words and evoked through great art. This love surpasses natural efforts. The inner power of love is a divine gift, as is its exercise, since "both the will and the action" are put into us (Phil 2:13). And we read that "the love of God has been poured into our hearts by the Holy Spirit which has been given us" (Rom 5:5).

To love one another was commanded in the Old Law. If Christ's love is something new, and is to be the pattern for human love, it is vital to discern its newness. Does its newness lie in the revelation of the love of the Father for the Son, an entirely divine mystery, and yet one that fills the human Heart of Jesus? For as the Father has loved Him, He has loved us (John 15:9). And is our loving one another not a channeling of divine love to, and through us; is it not a divine power enabling us, from the mysterious depth of our union with God, to become, as individuals, what the Church is, namely, the "universal sacrament of salvation, at once manifesting and actualizing the mystery of God's love for men" (*Pastoral Constitution*, 45)?

What is new in Christ's human love is that this is a love coming totally from divine love (which is the name of God—1 John 4:8,16), and that it was maintained for us even when we were torturing, mocking, and murdering the "Holy One of God" (Mark 1:24). It was, and continues to be, that redeeming, creative, forgiving love which, from the Cross and now from

Heaven, is able to "draw all men to" Christ (John 12:32). This love is the achievement of the constant desire in Christ's human Heart that man be redeemed—a desire maintained even while being the target and victim of the sin of man; a desire achieved, in fact, precisely because, despite torture and murder, it was maintained. Thus again as Man He merited our Redemption and by His divine power He brought it about. For "by His divine power He has given us all the things that we need for life and for true devotion, bringing us to know God Himself, who has called us by His own glory and goodness" (2 Pet 1:3), "the glory on the face of Christ" (2 Cor 4:6).

But how can this love be ours, since we do not possess the creative power of Christ's divinity, and so remain powerless with regard to the transformation of others? Is it by extending the revelation and promise of God's love—the soul of prayer—to one another? Love of neighbor is, and always must be, hope for the other, for his conversion, if needed; for his salvation and growth in holiness. This desire is learned and expressed in prayer, as we acquire the mind of Christ (Phil 2:5). It is translated into act as we bear one another's burdens and thus fulfill the Law of Christ" (Gal 6:2). This desire is tested when we are rejected, and is victorious when our love is upheld in obedience to God who "wants everyone to be saved" (1 Tim 2:4), and who "has imprisoned all men in their own disobedience" (that is, allowed them to rebel) "only to show mercy to all mankind" (Rom 11:32).

The New Commandment is included in the *Credo* because it is embeded in the realities revealed and realized by living faith. It is the commandment to extend Christ's redeeming and crucified love into the world. It is our task as members of Christ. It is that without which Christian existence cannot be. All must be in its service. By attempting to obey the New Commandment, and by fulfilling it with the help of God's grace, we will become true Christians, that is, followers of Christ crucified; and we will be found worthy to "share His degradation" (Heb 13:13; see also, John 15:18-16:1; Mat 10:16-39).

21. The Beatitudes: The Heart of Christ

"He taught us the way of the Beatitudes of the Gospel: poverty in spirit, meekness, suffering borne with patience, thirst after justice, mercy, purity of heart, will for peace, persecution suffered for justice sake."

(Read Mat 5:3-12; Phil 3:7-10.)

Besides the new Commandment, the Beatitudes are the only teachings pertaining to Christian life that are found in the *Credo* of Pope Paul VI. They are absolutely central to Christian existence. The New Commandment to love one another as Christ loved us, to be obeyed with the dispositions of the Beatitudes, requires the Church—to become, in the words of Vatican II, manifestations and actualizations of "the mystery of God's love for men" (*Pastoral Constitution*, 45). God's love for sinners, for us who helped to crucify Him, flooded His human Heart, the Heart which remained faithful to us and pleaded for us, even as He was suffering the effects of all our sins. Thus His love for us must find an echo in us and an extension through us; it must become our love for each other. But without the Beatitudes forming our lives, this love cannot be, nor can it grow. For the Beatitudes are Christ's description of His own Heart (Mat 11:29). And since to see Jesus, to learn of Him, is to see the "Father of our Lord Jesus Christ, a gentle Father and the God of all consolation" (Cor 1:3), the Beatitudes give the eyes of faith a glimpse of God "whose home is in inaccessible light" (1 Tim 6:16), whom no one has ever seen. "It is the only Son, who is nearest to the Father's heart, who has made Him known" (John 1:18).

So, the Beatitudes *are* Christ; they are "the glory that is His as the only Son of the Father" (John 1:14). As a revelation of the unseen God, and a description by Christ of Himself (and His Mother), the Beatitudes are approaches through accessible dispositions to the imitation of God, "as children of His that He loves"; they enable us to "follow Christ by loving as He loved" (Eph 5:1). In the Beatitudes, divine charity, hidden in the mystery which is God, becomes visible and accessible.

To be poor in spirit is the foundation of the Christian life and the means of attaining life's goal of dying with Christ. "If in union with Christ we have imitated His death, we shall also imitate Him in His Resurrection" (Rom 6:5). It is to have the mind of Christ who, in His Godhead, "did not cling to His equality with God, but emptied Himself" (Phil 2:6-7). His first emptying of Himself, His becoming Man, was an emptying totally on the part of God the Son. The continuing emptying, becoming a servant, and being "humbler yet, even to accepting death, death on a cross" (Phil 2:8), was an emptying of Jesus Christ, in His Divine Person, but in human obedience—"let it be as you, not I, would have it" (Mat 26:39). It is poverty in spirit, first and exclusively on the part of God the Son, and then of the Son through and in His humanity.

Without poverty of spirit, there can be no life of hope—no attaining to

Christ's promises that we are called "to escape corruption in a world that is sunk in vice" (2 Pet 1:4), and that "by His divine power . . . [we] will be able to share the divine nature" (2 Pet 1:3-4). Hope finds its goal in growth in meekness—in the breaking down of the hardness and self-assertion which so easily becomes brutal domination, however disguised by the appearance of gentility. Without this meekness, there can be no suffering borne with patience. Nor can there be thirst after justice in a hardened heart barren of all generosity. "There will be judgement without mercy for those who have not been merciful themselves" (James 2:13). To sense God in this life and to see Him in the next requires that purity of heart (like all the Beatitudes, a gift from God) which can become ours only if, in poverty of spirit, we are willing to overcome all self-seeking. And to will peace for others and for all would remain mere fantasy if not sustained by a readiness to suffer persecution for justice sake.

We seek the Kingdom of God and His holiness (Mat 6:33) in poverty of spirit—in willingness to leave everything and follow Him (Mat 4:20). We achieve poverty of spirit when "we have been crucified with Christ," letting ourselves become targets and victims of sin. Only then do we cease to live with our own unredeemed, selfish and grasping life. Then in true poverty of spirit, clothed in the spirit of all the Beatitudes, we will live "with the life of Christ who lives" in us (Gal 2:20).

22. The Target and Victim of Sin

"Under Pontius Pilate He suffered, the Lamb of God bearing on Himself the sins of the world."

At one time, all across the Roman Empire the common entertainment was the mutual slaughter of gladiators, and throwing men to beasts to be killed, for the amusement of emperors, high officials, poets, rich and poor. At the same time, there was born in Bethlehem a Child named Jesus, which means "Yahweh saves," a Child who is eternally the Son of God, historically the Son of Mary. More than thirty years later, "under Pontius Pilate," He became the target and the victim of all man's sin, of the "Sin of the World" (John 1:29), channeled against Him by those directly involved in His destruction. But they all—chief priests and Pharisees (John 11:45-53), Herod and

Pilate, Judas, soldiers, the shouting (Mat 27:21-26) and sneering (Mat 27:39-44) mob, and even Peter the Rock when he was denying him (Luke 22:54-62)—though involved in the sin, were mainly instruments of man's sin. Through them, all the sins of man, from the first Original Sin (Gen 3:1-7) to the fearful sins and apostasies of the last days—when "false Christs and false prophets will arise . . . to deceive the elect, if that were possible" (Mark 13:22) and when "love in most men will grow cold" (Mat 24:12)—all sins found their target and victim in Him, "the Lamb of God" (John 1:29).

To bear the sins of the world, He, the sinless one, was "made . . . into sin" (2 Cor 5:21), "being cursed for our sake" (Gal 3:13). Does this mean that Jesus, the Son of God and the Son of Mary, had to bear a punishment on our behalf that was inflicted or providentially designed by the Father, so that "justice" could be done by brutal suffering, so that "satisfaction" might be rendered by sheer pain and agony? One wonders whether perverted thinking about God, which projects on Him man's own beastliness in justification of man's evil, had a bearing on this sort of monstrous, chilling interpretation of God's way.

Could not the words from the *Credo* quoted above be seen as expressions of what really happened—that Jesus Christ became the humble, sacrificial Lamb of God by drawing upon Himself the "Sin of the World" (John 1:29)? That by His living a human destiny (Romano Guardini, *The Lord*, p. 15) Sin, all sins, even those still to be committed, found in Him their ultimate target? The rejection of truth which is a constituent of sin, an existence of "lived lives"; the rejection of God, who is the source of our being; the rejection of Him who is the Resurrection and the Life (John 11:25)—is not this opting for the destruction of any revelation of truth, goodness, and love? And is not the rejection of the source of everything true and holy in us necessarily destructive of our very being, of our capacity for God; is it not indeed a choice of death?

God, by assuming man's nature, became capable of suffering, of literally becoming the target and victim of sin. God no longer can be thought of as the remote observer and judge. He now has suffered the destruction wrought by sin whenever sin—and this includes dispositions, thoughts, acts, and omissions—has sought and found its target in Him. Now God in Christ is no longer only the target of sin as our Creator, but also as Man, as our Brother. As Man, He could drink the cup (Mat 26:42). He could offer Himself as victim to sin (Eph 5:2; 1 John 3:16), so that Sin, reaching its intended goal in Him, could now be conquered by His crucified love. God in Christ could suffer the effect, the intention of evil. "Insofar as you neglected to do this to one of the least of these, you neglected to do it to me'' (Mat 25:45). And what is true of sins of omission is certainly true of all sins—they have God as their target, and have found their target in Christ, in whom God could be insulted, tortured and murdered. ''Christ did not think of Himself: the words of Scripture—'the insults of those who insult you fall on me'—apply to Him'' (Rom 15:3; see also Ps 69:9).

23. The Mystery of the Cross

''. . . He died for us on the Cross, saving us by His redeeming Blood.''

''How rich are the depths of God—how deep His wisdom and knowledge—and how impossible to penetrate His motives or understand His methods!'' (Rom 11:33). Without this conviction we cannot hope to enter into the mystery of God and the mystery of His ways. Instead of listening to God when we are confronted by His revelation we will impose on it our own narrow and distorted views. Instead of hearing the Father's ''beloved Son with whom [the Father is] well pleased'' (Mat 17:5), to whom we are called to listen, we will slide into that delusion so fearfully described by St. Paul: ''They will keep the outward appearance of religion but will have rejected the inner power of it'' (2 Tim 3:5).

With sharp honesty we must meditate on the words of Pope Paul's *Credo* given above. If the revealed facts of history pointed to by these words are not seen as the ground of our hope and the only source of our Redemption, then we cannot hope to come to any theology, to any ''understanding sought by faith'' (St. Anselm). We must face the question: Why would man's Redemption be brought about by a death of the utmost horror and brutality, a death apparently caused by political opportunism, though actually accused by resentment and hatred of goodness and holiness, hatred of that which comes from God and manifests Him?

We must not hesitate to ask, out of fear that the answer may embarrass us. Repression, covered up by a false notion of mystery derives not from incongruity but from the inexhaustible infinity of God, from absolute transcendence. But all creation somehow points to God. Truth, reality, is always something thought by God and given existence by Him. The more noble the reality, the more it speaks of the Creator. ''Ever since God created the world His everlasting power and deity—however invisible—have been there for the mind to see in the things He has made" (Rom 1:20).

The words of the *Credo* we are considering, like the words of the Creed, speak of divine reality in terms of such intense human reality, so deeply of the mystery of God's love, that they could be sung. Jesus' Way, of, with, and to the Cross, was the obedience to the Father, who did not answer Jesus' prayer: "My Father, if it be possible, let this cup pass from me." But the totally unconditional prayer, "nevertheless, not as I will, but as Thou wilt" (Mat 26:39), was heard. "My grace is enough for you: my power is at its best in weakness" (2 Cor 12:9), the Lord said to St. Paul.

Christ's death was the consummation of the eternal Son's self-giving to the Father extended into a world largely in rebellion against God. Death on the Cross was the victory of Sin. But as "death and life were locked together in a unique struggle," now "the Prince of Life, who died, reigns immortal" (Sequence, Mass for Easter). The Crucifixion became the lasting victory of redeeming love. To perfect this love, the consummation of all of mankind's rebellion from Adam to the end of history, had to be conquered "with good" (Rom 12:21). Christ's death *for* us had to be first a death *through* us. "Yahweh burdened him with the sins of all of us" (Isa 53:6). The fidelity of His love, a love upheld in obedience to the Father, transformed the consummate rebellion of mankind—the Crucifixion—into the ever great victory of divine love achieved by the same human Heart which was broken by this sin, "the Sin of the World" (John 1:29). "He was bearing the faults of many and praying all the time for sinners" (Isa 53:12; see also Heb 9:28; 1 Pet 2:24).

From Jesus' human heart came forth a two-fold obedience—love of the Father in His obedience to the Father, and the channeling of the Father's love for us sinners by pleading for us, His executioners, by showing us "how perfect His love was" (John 13:1). "What proves that God loves us is that Christ died for us while we were still sinners" (Rom 5:8), while we were still rebelling against God and found our victim in Him, when "He lived among us" (John 1:14) and when we should have seen "His glory, the glory that is His as the only Son of the Father" (John 1:14), but "did not accept Him" (John 1:11).

His death *through* us became a death *for* us by the redeeming love, by His redeeming obedience, by the obedient shedding of His Blood, the giving of His life; by letting Sin do what it always intends to do: eliminate God whose name is Love (1 Tim 2:5), He was able to die "for us on the Cross, saving us by His redeeming Blood" (*Credo*).

24. The Resurrection and the Sacred Heart

"He was buried, and of His own power, rose the third day, raising us by His Resurrection to that sharing in the divine life which is the life of grace."

(Read Eph 1:17-23; 3:14-21; Acts 2:36; Phil 2:5-11; Rev 19:11-18.)

The Resurrection of Jesus Christ is essentially the giving to Him, to His human Heart, the power and authority (Mat 28:18) to accomplish by His divine power, whatever His human Heart, His human mind and will, determines for the extension of the Redemption—that is, the Kingdom of God—into the hearts of men. This is what our Lord said He would do when "lifted up from the earth" on the Cross—that He would draw all men to Himself (John 12:32). This He can now continue to do from Heaven, till the end of time. Already on the Cross, He was able to envelop all mankind, even those still to be born, in His human love, because "hardly was He conceived . . . when He began to enjoy the vision of the blessed, and in that vision all the members of His Mystical Body were present and He embraced them with His redeeming love" (*Mystici Corporis*, Pius XII).

The first two aspects of the Resurrection, "He rose . . . He ascended . . . ," find their meaning in the third aspect, "He is seated at the right hand of the Father" (Nicene Creed). He received the power and authority to continue to draw all men to Himself (John 12:32), that is, to be *Kyrios*, "Lord," (Phil 2:9-11; see also Eph 1:20-23; Acts 2:33, 36): this is the glory of the Resurrection. Thus St. Paul preached not himself, but "Jesus as the Lord," and himself as servant "for Jesus' sake" (Cor 4:5).

"If your lips confess that Jesus is Lord and if you believe in your heart that God raised Him from the dead, then you will be saved" (Rom 10:9). At every moment of our lives we co-exist with the Risen Humanity of Jesus Christ, the "one mediator between God and mankind, Himself a Man, Christ Jesus" (1 Tim 2:5). He, "the Word of God," is "the King of kings and the Lord of lords" (Rev 19:13, 16). It is He to whom we turn when "we adore the most Sacred Heart of Jesus Christ" in which we adore "the uncreated love of the Divine Word and His human love" (Pius XII, *Haurietis Aquas*, 55).

St. Paul wrote: "All I want is to know Christ and the power of His Resurrection" (Phil 3:10). We see the Resurrection primarily as Jesus' Lordship. It was accomplished by the power of the "Father of glory," who would "enlighten the eyes of [our] mind" so that we might see "how infinitely great is the power that He has exercised for us believers . . . the strength of His power at work in Christ, when He used it to raise Him from the dead and to make Him sit at His right hand, in Heaven." It was the power of the Father's glory that "He has put all things under His feet, and made Him, as the ruler of everything, the head of the Church" (Eph 1:17-23). The Resurrection is the gift of the Father to the humanity of Jesus, a gift by which He can continue to use His human love, a love crucified and yet adhering to us who crucified Him, a love put to the test and yet victorious on Good Friday, a love that became the target of the world's hatred (of God, of truth, of holiness, of justice, and of love) and yet a love kept alive while we crucified Him. He extends this love to men of all times, at all times, to draw all men to Himself (John 12:32)—first from the Cross, then from Heaven.

All the divine gifts are given to arouse us, to attract us, to give us "the will and the action" (Phil 2:13) that enable us to believe, to hope, and to love Him who loved us first (1 John 4:19); all these gifts derive from the divine power which is at the disposal of His human Heart. It is that divine love filling the human Heart which is now translated into human love. Jesus, "by His divine power . . . has given us all the things that we need for life and for true devotion" (2 Pet 1:3). All that is noble and selfless in the world comes to us as God's gift through Jesus Christ, by the intercession of His Sacred Heart. "Constituted Lord by His Resurrection and given all authority in Heaven and on earth, Christ is now at work in the hearts of men by the power of His Spirit; not only does He arouse in them a desire for the world to come, but He quickens, purifies, and strengthens the generous aspirations of mankind to make life more humane and conquer the earth for this purpose." (*Pastoral Constitution*, 38).

What our Lord did for all while dying in torment on the Cross, victim of man's sin—to draw all men to Himself (John 12:32)—He continues to do now in Heaven, as Lord, thereby "raising us by His Resurrection to that sharing in the divine life which is the life of grace" (*Credo*). Coming, therefore, to realize the situation as described here, "let us be confident, then approaching the throne of grace, that we shall have mercy from Him and find grace when we are in need of help" (Heb 4:16).

25. The Second Coming

"He ascended to Heaven, and He will come again, this time in glory. . . . "

"The Father, who is the source of life, has made the Son the source of life" (John 5:26), so that, once He was lifted up, He could draw all men to Himself (John 12:32). We must never think of the Crucifixion as simply a victory of evil. As a historical fact, if by history we mean what can be witnessed and verified, the Cross was a terrifying instrument of torture, humiliation, and murder. But we know that, during the ordeal, hidden from the world, His human love went forth to all, to all men and women and children that ever have existed and will exist, from Adam and Eve to those who would actually witness "the Day of the Lord . . . [when] with a roar the sky will vanish, the elements will catch fire and fall apart, the earth and all that it contains will be burnt up" (2 Pet 3:10).

He, who is the Word or Son of the Father, is "the true light that enlightens all men" (John 1:9). Therefore He could say, "I, the light, have come into the world, so that whoever believes in me need not stay in the dark anymore" (John 12:46). Those who have not been able to hear and to learn of Jesus Christ, but "endeavor to do His will as recognized through the promptings of their conscience, they, in a number known only to God, can obtain salvation" (*Credo*). Thus He continues to draw all men to Himself, in ways known only to Him.

The testing and the victory of Jesus' redeeming love on the Cross had to be accomplished before "all authority in Heaven and on earth" would be given to Him (Mat 28:18), before He "was taken up into Heaven: [where] at the right hand of God He took His place" (Mark 16:19). The journey that began with the conception of the Son in Mary's womb, found its end in His ascent into Heaven "to be seated at the right hand of the Father" (Creed of the Mass) in that seat of universal power from where He now continues to draw all men to Himself (John 12:32), as our lives unfold here on earth. The Father "has put all things under His feet, and made Him, as the ruler of everything, the head of the Church which is His Body, the fullness of Him who fills the whole of creation" (Eph 1:22-23). "On his cloak and on His thigh there was a name written: the King of kings and the Lord of lords" (Rev 19:16).

The Ascension is the consummation of the Paschal Mystery. "Christ, the mediator between God and man, judge of the world and Lord of all, has passed beyond our sight, not to abandon us but to be our hope. Christ is the beginning, the head of the Church; where He has gone, we hope to follow'' (Preface I for the Ascension).

Him we hope to follow. When history comes to an end, "He will come again, this time in glory" *(Credo)*. Only with Christ's Second Coming will all history find its completion. This is revealed truth. It will be the time of triumph and reward, but also the time of sealing for eternity the exclusion of those whose hearts have so hardened in their rebellion against God that they will perish in final impenitence. But for the others it is the time when God "will wipe away all tears from their eyes" (Rev 21:4). It is the consummation of Creation and Redemption, when Christ will allow those "who prove victorious" to share His throne, just as He, having been victorious Himself by the fidelity of His redeeming love on the Cross, took His place with His Father on His throne (Rev 3:31).

The Second Coming of Jesus Christ is the time when equity will be restored. The victory of love, crucified by the Sin of the world, will then be fully revealed. It will be the moment which constitutes the content of our hope—for ourselves, for our own salvation, worked for "in fear and trembling" (Phil 2:12), without presumption or despair (the two sins against hope), because we know that nothing "can ever come between us and the love of God made visibile in Christ Jesus our Lord" (Rom 8:39). It is the moment which constitutes the content of our apostolic hope, a hope that is the very heart of love of neighbor, the hope for the salvation of others and of all. For we are called upon to share the desire of God, who "wants everyone to be saved and reach full knowledge of the truth" (1 Tim 2:4). Thus we must hope, in fear and trembling, without presumption or despair, for the "crown of righteousness . . . which the Lord will give to me on that Day; and not only to me but to all those who have longed for His Appearing" (2 Tim 4:8). Till that day we will pray: "Come, Lord Jesus" (Rev 22:20).

26. Our Response to the Promise of Joy

" . . . He will come again . . . to judge the living and the dead: each according to his merits—those who have responded to the Love and Piety of God going to eternal life. . . . And His kingdom will have no end."

(Read Mat 25:31-46; 2 Pet 3:8-13; Rev 21:1-8)

The Church, in Vatican II, speaks of "the time of the renewal of all things" when "together with the human race, the universe itself, which . . . attains its destiny through [man], will be perfectly reestablished in Christ" (*Dogmatic Constitution* 48, first paragraph). And this day will come at the end of time and the end of history, the end of man's earthly existence when "the Son of Man [will come] in His glory [and] all the nations will be assembled before Him" for judgment (Mat 25:31-32). Then all creation will be made new (Rev 21:5), and there will be "a new heaven and a new earth" (Rev 21:1) and God will be "all in all' (1 Cor 15:28). All this and more is crystallized in the credal words, "He will come again to judge the living and the dead" (*Credo*; see above).

Although we are to "work for [our] salvation in fear and trembling" (Phil 2:12), would it not be well to "want to be gone and be with Christ" (Phil 1:23); would it not be well, in short, to desire eternal rest, eternal life, to desire to see God "as He really is" (1 John 3:2), to see God "face to face" (1 Cor 13:12), when "He will wipe away all tears from [our] eyes, [when] there will be no more death, and no more mourning or sadness" (Rev 21:4)? Is not the firmness of our faith determined by the firmness of our hope for eternal life? Does not the "Our Father" receive its inner life and urgency from this expectation? What is Jesus Christ, in whom all the sins of men found their ultimate target and their victim, if He is not our Savior from eternal slavery and from isolation in consummate selfishness, but above all the bringer of light, Himself the light of the world (John 8:12), the only way to the Father (John 14:6), whose visible Image He is (Col 1:15)? What is our life if we are not among "those who have longed for His Appearing" (2 Tim 4:8)? It is certainly not Christian; rather it is a life lived "in darkness and the shadow of death" (Luke 1:79), unredeemed, and on the brink of despair, however often we escape into presumption: it is life without hope.

To respond now "to the love and piety of God" (*Credo*) is the way to that life which is holiness—union with God—and which becomes, irrevocably, eternal life, through death and Resurrection. But how can we look forward to the eternal joy which our Lord wishes to share with men (John 17:13; 15:11), unless we have tasted true joy in this life? When the difference between joy and fun has largely been obliterated; when Heaven is conceived, if at all, in terms of Las Vegas or Disneyland, when anti-values and addiction to costly escapes have become a vital part of our economy and life, how much remains of those things that reflect Heaven? Love of

-53-

spouses for each other, of parents, of children; the warmth and security of the family, of neighborhood; the common life and task of community and nation; the beauty and freshness of God's creation; great music, great writing, painting, architecture—are any of these considered even as possibilities for joy and gratitude by many people today?

Here lies the tremendous responsibility of our apostolate: to become visible presences of Christ—and, as the Church, "manifesting and actualizing the mystery of God's love for men" (*Pastoral Constitution*, 45) in our own lives. We must do this in a world full of "wickedness and ill will [where we are] hating each other and hateful ourselves; (Tit 3:3), that through us, too, "the kindness and love of God our Savior for mankind" will be revealed (Tit 3:4). And since the visible life of the Church in many places has become anemic, if not actually defiled, by sacrilegious theologies and liturgies defacing the face of Christ, we are too often left to our own resources. So we will have to make humble new beginnings, we will seek the face of love as splendor or gentleness in Bach or Mozart, as generosity and courage in Beethoven, as compassion in Dostoevsky; we will look for the Catholic spirit in Scripture and the teaching of the Church, in Newman or Guardini, while waiting for a rebirth of the visibility of the Faith, which is a promise and foretaste of Heaven. Meanwhile we pray: "Come, Lord Jesus" (Rev 22:20).

27. Hell: The Rejection of Love

"He will come again . . . to judge the living and the dead: each according to his merits . . . those who have refused [God's love and piety] to the end going to the fire that is not extinghished."

(Read Mat 23:13-39; Luk 6:24-26; John 8:21-59; Gal 5:19-21; Col 3:5-11; 2 Tim 3:1-5; *Pastoral Constitution* 13 and 37.)

"And at his gate there lay a poor man called Lazarus, covered with sores, who longed to fill himself with the scraps that fell from the rich man's table" (Luke 16:20-21). "Go away from me, with your curse upon you, to the eternal fire prepared for the devil and his angels. For I was hungry and you never gave me food. . . ." (Mat 25:41-42). A life of self-indulgence dries up all capacity for love, understanding, and generosity. This is described by St. Paul: "When self-indulgence is at work the results are obvious: for-

nication, gross indecency, and sexual irresponsibility . . . feuds, jealousy
. . . factions, envy, drunkenness . . . those who behave like this will not
inherit the Kingdom of God'' (Gal 5:19-21).

The point may come when our Lord, the Good Shepherd, will no longer
speak to me. Pilate ''said to Jesus, 'where do you come from?' But Jesus
made no answer'' (John 19:9). When Jesus was asked, ''What authority
have you for acting like this?'' (Mat 21:23), He knew that they would not
be disposed to trust and to learn, and He refused to answer: ''Nor will I
tell you my authority for acting like this'' (Mat 21:27). St. Paul teaches:
''If our gospel does not penetrate the veil, then the veil is on those who
are not on the way to salvation, the unbelievers whose minds the god of
this world has blinded, to stop them seeing the light shed by the Good News
of the glory of Christ, who is the Image of God'' (2 Cor 4:3-4).

If we consider the crimes committed in the name of religion out of self-
righteousness—a specific form of pride that erupts in ''religious'' people;
if we consider that Christ met with opposition, even unto death, on *religious*
grounds—is not refusing ''God's love and piety to the end'' (*Credo*, above)
a very real and a very frightful possibility? Perhaps we, too, ''will keep
up the outward appearance of religion but will have rejected the inner power
of it'' (2 Tim 3:5). If we constantly sin and therefore live a lie, nourishing
various illusions, of which self-righteousness is perhaps the most perverse
and perverting, can the ''love of God our Savior for mankind'' (Tit 3:4),
rooted in His compassion alone, find entrance into our hearts? Can the
wisdom of God, which is foolishness to man (1 Cor 1:20-25), possibly find
any resonance? Can the invitation of the Lord, with its inescapable condition for following Christ to be ''fools for the sake of Christ, [to be] treated
as the offal of the world . . . the scum of the earth'' (1 Cor 4:10, 13), be
considered even as a possibility? Are we willing to take up our cross to follow
Him?

In the refusal of the cross, a refusal which is an essential element of
all sin, there is the frightening possibility and even likelihood of a growing
refusal of God, a refusal that may become more pervasive as time goes on.
Lying to ourselves by rationalizing our failings can become habitual. We
will ''keep truth imprisoned in [our] wickedness'' (Rom 1:18). Our ''empty minds'' will be darkened (Rom 1:21). We will be ever more ''immersed
in this world, without hope and without God'' (Eph 2:12).

The incredible disorders and consequent sufferings men inflict upon men
can only be the result of sin, of men letting themselves be led by the Prince
of the Prince of this world, for ''evil cannot come from his good Creator''
(*Pastoral Constitution*, 13). Evil and suffering in the world of man reveal

the extent and destructive power of sin. The nature and extent of evil seem to give the lie to God's goodness and omnipotence. It is a world in which we are called to be "perfect children of God among a deceitful and underhand brood" (Phil 2:15). Or am I among the latter?

The possibility of our becoming enveloped in total selfishness, in resentment and in hatred of truth, life, justice, love, sanctity, and existence itself (all these are names of God), the possibility of becoming hateful ourselves and of hating one another (Tit 3:3) is very real. But we should not despair, for all things "are possible for God" (Luk 18:27); in Him, mercy has infinite power, knowledge, and wisdom at its disposal. A human Heart beats for us in Heaven. Could Christ condemn? "No! He not only died for us— He rose from the dead, and there at God's right hand He stands and pleads for us" (Rom 8:34).

· Hell is real, a real possibility to which we can damn ourselves, and we are to take St. Paul's warning as God's word, that we are to "work for [our] salvation in fear and trembling" (Phil 2:12).

George Bernanos wrote in his *Diary of a Country Priest* (p. 127):

> Hell is not to love any more. . . . To a human being still alive, it means to love less or love elsewhere. . . . The error common to us all is to invest these damned with something still inherently alive, something of our own inherent mobility, whereas in truth time and movement have ceased for them, they are fixed forever. . . . Truly, if one of us, if a living man, the vilest, most contemptible of the living, were cast into those burning depths, I should still be ready to share his suffering, I would claim him from his executioner. . . . To share his suffering! The sorrow, the unutterable loss of those charred stones which once were men, is that they have nothing more to be shared.

Holy Mary, Mother of God, pray for us sinners, now, and at the hour of our death.

28. The Holy Spirit: The Spirit of Love and Unity

"We believe in the Holy Spirit, Who is Lord, and Giver of life, Who is adored and glorified together with the Father and the Son."

Love unites and, in turn, flows from unity. At least this seems to be so among men, wherever genuine love—that is unselfish love—abides, whether spousal love, love of parents, or children, of friends, or some form of professional or civic friendship. Spouses after many years of marriage know that it was love that brought and held them together, and that their blessed union, tested by circumstances and their own defects, grew as their tested love became victorious through the divine gifts of faith, hope, and charity. Here the Law of Christ, "to bear one another's burdens" (Gal 6:2), is at work. The divine gift of charity, by which God enables us to be manifestations and actualizations of "the mystery of God's love for men" (*Pastoral Constitution*, 45), is the source of unity. Actualized and victorious love enlarges the capacity for love, augmenting our share in the growth of charity, which then is "poured into our hearts by the Holy Spirit which has been given us" (Rom 5:5).

Does it thus become clear that charity is both the source and foundation of unity, and in turn proceeds from this unity? Can we see in this charity the kind of created reality which, in the light of the revelation of the divine mystery of the Blessed Trinity, is shown to be a created, God-given reflection of God's inner mystery? With the caution of the Fourth Lateran Council that in divine analogies (when the same concept is applied to God and to man), "between the Creator and the creature so great a likeness cannot be noted without the necessity of noting a greater dissimilarity between them," can we see in true human love a reflection of the Holy Spirit? Dare we, knowing the inadequacy of human concepts, liken the Holy Spirit to the bond of Father and Son, while the same Holy Spirit in turn "proceeds from the Father and the Son" (Nicene Creed), and contemplate the Holy Spirit both as presupposition and fruit of this uncreated unity of Father and Son?

Many of us may be in the position of the disciples in Ephesus who "were never even told there was such a thing as a Holy Spirit" (Acts 19:2). We may be able to recite statements about Him, but still be somewhat embarrassed by our ignorance of the living reality. Rather than wasting time blaming ourselves or others, is there a possible remedy? We know that all divine gifts are given by the one God, three Persons. Why not then appropriate some to the Holy Spirit? Perhaps meditation on true unity among men, on living in unity and working and suffering in charity for restoration and deepening of unity may dispose us for the grace of growing in knowledge of the Holy Spirit as the Spirit of Unity.

As we seek to overcome what is divisive in our lives and what thereby keeps charity out of our hearts, we enable the healing and restoring power of the Holy Spirit to help us into the life of the Spirit, which brings "love, joy, peace, patience, kindness, goodness, trustfulness, gentleness, and self-control." This is so because we "cannot belong to Christ Jesus unless [we] crucify all self-indulgent passions and desires" (Gal 5:22, 24). "Since the Spirit is our life, let us be directed by the Spirit. We must stop being conceited, provocative, and envious" (Gal 5:25-26). *Our* share is to let ourselves be "crucified with Christ" (Gal 2:19). Then we will become free to adore the Holy Spirit, who will draw us more deeply into sharing the divine nature (2 Pet 1:4), so that we may enter into the redeemed unity by His power as the root of the uncreated unity, which in turn "proceeds from the Father and the Son."

To share in the divine life, to "become sons in the Son" (*Pastoral Constitution*, 22), is to belong to a "people brought into unity from the unity of the Father, the Son, and the Holy Spirit" (*Dogmatic Constitituion* 4; quoted from St. Cyprian). When the "Spirit of Truth" (John 16:13) is sought in adoration, He will enable us to "live by the truth and in love, [and] we shall grow in all ways into Christ" (Ep 4:15). It is the obedience of love, the fulfillment of the greatest commandment, to love the Lord our God also "with all [our] mind" (Mat 22:37), by the power of the Holy Spirit, the "Spirit of Truth," by putting our intelligence in the service of God. Then for me, too, "the hour will come" when I will be among the true worshippers who "will worship the Father in spirit and truth" (John 4:23). And the great doxology, the ending of the Canon of the Mass, summing up the Sacrifice of Christ rendered present by the Mass, leading to the strengthening of redeemed unity in Holy Communion, will be said with growing intensity and understanding. Slightly paraphrasing, we say: Through Christ, with Christ, in Christ, in the unity into which Christ wills to draw us by giving, by sending us the Holy Spirit, all glory and honor is yours, almighty Father, for ever and ever. Amen.

29. The Holy Spirit and the Church

"He [the Holy Spirit] spoke to us by the prophets; He was sent by Christ after His Resurrection and His Ascension to the Father; He illuminates, vivifies, protects, and guides the Church."

(Read Mat 13:4-23; *Dogmatic Constitution* 4.)

The prophets spoke words of power and authority, words of God. "The word of God is something alive and active" (Heb 4:12). It carries with it the power of God by which men can grasp and obey God's commands, and come to live by His truths in obedience—that is, in love (Eph 4:15). And yet, "Yahweh, the god of their ancestors, tirelessly sent them messenger after messenger, since He wished to spare His people and His house. But they ridiculed the messengers of God, they despised His words, they laughed at His prophets, until at last the wrath of Yahweh rose so high against His people that there was no further remedy" (2 Chron 26:15-16; see also Mat 23:33-39).

It would seem that when God was rejected by Israel, and is now rejected by Christians, evil prevails. Then expiation—acceptance of the destructive and bitter consequences, out of love for those who sinned and thus caused the victory of evil (Rom 12:21)—is called for. If this expiation goes beyond suffering the deprivation which sin produces, and becomes persecution "in the cause of right," on account of Jesus Christ (Mat 5:10-11), as they persecuted the prophets before (Mat 5:12), then we are to rejoice! (Mat 5:12). It is this last of the Beatitudes, redeeming love and expiation, for which the other Beatitudes prepare us. For without the dispositions of poverty of spirit, meekness, patience, thirst after justice, mercy, purity of heart, and will for peace, redeeming love cannot survive and our faith becomes harsh, self-righteous, a false zeal, and in turn, destructive. Religious conflicts through the ages, even, and especially, between Christians, constitute some of the most disgusting chapters of history.

For us to discern the Voice of God through human words and actions, or even in the very bearing of Christ, requires a two-fold action on the part of the Holy Spirit. First, as in the time of the prophets and more so in the time of Christ, in the present time of the Church the Holy Spirit provides the inspiration and power for the Voice coming to us through human means. But second, the Holy Spirit not only "illuminates, vivifies, protects, and guides" the prophets and teaching Church (*Credo*): He likewise acts directly upon the people of God who are called upon to hear and understand the Voice of God in the prophets, in Jesus Christ, and now, in the Church.

First, the "veil" that prevents men from "seeing the light shed by the Good News of the glory of Christ, who is the Image of God" (2 Cor 4:3-4), this veil must be removed. A life of self-indulgence nourishes dispositions of the heart that are hostile to truth, blind to God's call, a shield against His grace. Pride, vanity, sensuality, resentment, hatred, snobbery, arrogance, addiction to power, jealousies, and other vices simply imprison the will and the power to judge ever more deeply in lies. It is the Holy Spirit, the

Advocate, who, "when He comes, . . . will show the world how wrong it was, about sin, and about who was in the right, and about judgment" (John 16:8). He will do so as the "Spirit of Truth" (John 14:16). After such surgery, conversion becomes possible, and the spirit of conversion must continue as a constant corrective, as an integral part of the spiritual life. It is the Holy Spirit, who, in the sacrament of penance, is sent "among us for the forgiveness of sins" (Form of Absolution).

After the cleansing action of the Holy Spirit, the Sanctifier, which gives our souls a new disposition, the Holy Spirit draws us into redeemed unity by His gifts, transforming us into adopted sons—nourishing our spiritual life and growth to a likeness of Christ—so that intimate friendship with the Father may find utterance in the cry "Abba, Father" (Gal 4:5-7; see also Rom 8:14-17). And the life of the Spirit will dispose and enable us to lead a life guided by the Spirit. And "what the Spirit brings is very different" from a life of self-indulgence. It will be a life of "love, joy, peace, patience, kindness, goodness, trustfulness, gentleness, and self-control" (Gal 5:22-23). The beauty of holiness which is the beauty of the Triune God, will shine in us and through us, and allow us to manifest and actualize the mystery of God's love for men in this world (*Pastoral Constitution*, 45). In this way, as the Church, as a member of Christ, as a Christian, I will contribute to the "one sole purpose" of the Church—"that the Kingdom of God may come and the salvation of the human race may be accomplished" (*Pastoral Constitution*, 45). Therefore we pray: "God our Father, let the Spirit you sent on your Church to begin the teaching of the Gospel continue to work in the world through the hearts of all who believe" (Oration, Mass for Pentecost). We say "through the hearts of all who believe," because "anything exposed by the light will be illuminated and anything illuminated turns into light" (Eph 5:13-14).

30. Our Search for God: The Holy Spirit's Role

> "*[The Holy Spirit] purifies the Church's members if they do not shun His grace. His action, which penetrates to the inmost of the soul, enables man to respond to the call of Jesus: Be perfect as your Heavenly Father is perfect*" (Mat 5:38).

"From the heart come evil intentions: murder, adultery, fornication, theft, perjury, slander" (Mat 15:19). Hidden in our inmost soul lie the obstacles to transformation into the "true image of His Son" (Rom 8:29). It is in the hidden depths of the heart, where the God-given powers of faith, hope, and charity are rooted, that the cleansing and transforming actions of the Holy Spirit take place. The transformation is hidden, for we "have died, and now the life [we] have is hidden with Christ in God" (Col 3:3). In the deepest recesses of the heart we are to be "renewed by a spiritual revolution so that [we] can put on the new self that has been created in God's way" (Eph 4:23-24). Thus by the God-given powers or virtues and by the gifts of the Holy Spirit there will grow in us the capacity to "live by the truth and in love," and thus "we shall grow in all ways into Christ" (Eph 4:15).

In His teaching on Divine Providence (Mat 6:25-34) our Lord clearly described our own task. He told us: "Set your hearts on [God's] Kingdom first, and on His righteousness, and all these other things will be given you as well" (Mat 6:33). It is the promise that if we search, we will find; that if we knock, the door of His Kingdom will be opened (Mat 7:7). It is the very heart of the Lord's Prayer, that His will be done, and thus His Kingdom come, to and through us. This we must learn to pray ever more unconditionally.

We profess, we hold onto, the divinely revealed truth, that the Holy Spirit by His unifying power "enables man to respond to the call of Jesus" (*Credo*, above) to share, and thus render present, the very perfection of the Father (Mat 5:48), namely the redeeming love that is willing to be crucified and yet to remain faithful to those who crucify us—as God remains always faithful, even when we are unfaithful (2 Tim 2:11-13; Ps 118). Because here lies the mystery of Redemption—that Christ continued loving us with His redeeming love while His love was being crucified. "Father, forgive them" (Luke 23:34).

To die with Christ, to boast about nothing but "the cross of our Lord Jesus Christ, through whom the world is crucified to me, and I to the world" (Gal 6:14) is the royal road to dying to the grasping, unredeemed self. As God the Son emptied Himself by His Incarnation, in His obedience even to "death on a cross" (Phil 2:5-8), ours is to be the same mind (Phil 2:5). We must set our "hearts on . . . His righteousness"—the source of all holiness. "All . . . holiness comes from you . . . by the working of the Holy Spirit" (Third Canon). The righteousness or holiness of God is the source and exemplar of all holiness. Contemplative seeking of God and His Kingdom is our share, so that in response to our seeking God's Kingdom and holiness, God may shine "in our minds to radiate the light of the knowledge of God's glory, the glory on the face of Christ" (2 Cor 4:6).

The Holy Spirit disposes and enables us to see the glory of God "on the face of Christ," "the glory that is His as the only Son of the Father" (John 1:14). His gifts of understanding and knowledge create in us that sort of resonance, which allows us to vibrate in harmony with the revealed realitites that constitute the content of our faith. It may be likened to the wooden part of a violin, without which the vibration of the strings would be thin and empty. The music in the soul of the performer finds and elicits in the wood the response which allows him to convey to the listener the music that fills his soul. Conditioned reflexes alone do not produce music, just as in so many of our sermons, in which "material" is scraped together, and handed out under the pretense of preaching, nothing but emptiness of mind and heart is conveyed. Because, as Urs von Balthazar wrote, "He who does not listen to God, has nothing to say to the world" (*Who is a Christian?*). And these gifts cannot be ours if we do not seek. The divine promise that he who seeks always finds (Mat 7:8; cp. Luke 11:13), also warns us that we will not find God if we do not seek. We will remain burdened with verbalized religion, without understanding or knowledge. Without these, the other gifts remain dead, and the Spirit of Truth will not come to lead us to the complete truth (John 16:13; 14:17). We are commanded to love God with all our mind, with all our intelligence (Mat 22:37).

When we do invoke the Holy Spirit, we should pray above all for bishops, the chief teachers in the Church, and for their priests, who are their appointed helpers in this task, asking: "Come, Holy Spirit, fill the hearts of your faithful; and kindle in them the fire of your love."

31. Mary the Mother of God

"We believe that Mary is the Mother, who remained ever a Virgin, of the Incarnate Word, Our God and Saviour Jesus Christ. . . ."

"My thoughts are not your thoughts, my ways not your ways—it is Yahweh who speaks. Yes, the heavens are as high above earth as my ways are above your ways, my thoughts above your thoughts" (Isa 55:8-9). We must keep this pronouncement in mind when we deal with the extraordinary mystery of the Incarnation, and when we consider that Mary is the only link between mankind and the Eternal Son through whom "all things came to be" (John 1:3), who "is the radiant light of God's glory and the perfect copy of His nature, sustaining the universe by His powerful command" (Heb 1:2). Only by being born of a human being could God become Man, become flesh (John 1:14), and dwell among us as our Brother. The central fact of our existence and the ground of our hope is that, now and forever, the Eternal Son exists also as Man, now in glory in Heaven, as He was seen by St. John (Rev 5:6-14) and St. Stephen (Acts 7:55-56). This could not have come to be without God's having assumed a human nature and having come forth from mankind. By God's wisdom, a woman was chosen to be Mother, the Mother in and through whom the Eternal Word would begin to exist also as Man. God's word, spoken by the Angel, tells it all: "The Holy Spirit will come upon you . . . and the power of the Most High will cover you with its shadow. And so the child will be holy and will be called Son of God" (Luke 1:35).

Consider the enormity of the Incarnation: God actually needing someone through whom He could both empty Himself to become as men are, and also enter upon His journey through life to death, Resurrection, and Lordship; the enormity of the Incarnation: not clinging to His equality with God, yet being God while living a human destiny. And thus Mary became, and remains forever, Mother of the One who emptied Himself through her in order to share her, and our, nature—Mother of God, Mother of men.

Not only was the Eternal Word, the Eternal Son of the Father made flesh, but men also saw His glory, "the glory that is His as the only Son of the Father" (John 1:14). As Man, He was, and continues to be now in Heaven, the visible "Image of the invisible God" (Col 1:15). Mary's gift to the world, the visible humanity of the invisible Son, was the way in which the Father could be seen (John 14:9), heard (John 8:28), and literally become the target and the victim of the Sin of the World. It was in His human Heart—the gift of Mary, the Immacualate Heart—that His love for men was tested (Wisdom 2:10-20) and victorious (Luke 23:34).

"The Almighty has done great things for me," (Luke 1:49) said the Mother of God, of our Savior, when invited to give to mankind its Redeemer. And when she heard this invitation to obedience, to the ultimate extension of love in faith and hope, her flawless intelligence and memory brought to her mind the sign to be given: that a virgin would be with child, a child whom she would call "Emmanuel, a name which means 'God-is-with-us'" (Mat 1:22-23; see also Is 7:14). But frightening prophecies must also have occurred to her: "Ours were the sufferings He bore, ours the sorrows he carried. . . . He was pierced through for our faults, crushed for our sins.

-63-

. . . Yahweh burdened Him with the sins of all of us" (Is 53:4-6). Yet when called by God she responded, for obedience is pure hope without presumption, safe against the pressure of despondency and despair. Like the faith of Abraham, the Father of Faith, her faith was required in ways that are strictly ways of God, according to the wisdom of God, clearly not the ways of men, but encouragement for later generations. (Is 55:8-9). We read of many examples of the testing of Mary's faith. One was the flight into Egypt, while innocent children were murdered, a flight which only saved Him for the later converging of all murderous designs of men upon Him, when His hour had come (John 12:23). There was the agony of losing and seeking the twelve year old; the apparent rebuke at Cana (John 2:4); three years of observing Him from a distance during His public life; the growing opposition, and this coming from her (and his) own people; and the sadness of her Son which she shared in a special way: "As He drew near and came in sight of the city He shed tears over it" (Luke 19:41), knowing of Jerusalem's growing infidelity and blindness and its eventual destruction, foretold by prophets (Micah 3:12; Jer 26:18), as Mary also knew.

As Mother of the Redeemer, as handmaid of the Lord, she would finally suffer the birthpangs of the Church, when she stood under the Cross, helpless, yet extending in faith, love, and hope her compassion to us all (who at that moment were crucifying Him who was "destined to be a sign that is rejected") while a sword pierced her own soul (Luke 2:34-35). On the Cross, "lifted up from the earth," He drew all men to Himself (John 12:32), while His Mother, fitted for this task by the Immaculate Conception, shared the Cross by her flawless compassion. By her compassion, she became the Mother of those to be redeemed.

32. Mary's Untainted Faith

"We believe that Mary . . . by reason of this singular election . . . was, in consideration of the merits of her Son, redeemed in a more eminent manner, preserved from all stain of Original Sin and filled with the gift of grace more than all other creatures."

(Read Wisd 7:22-30; *Dogmatic Constitution* 55, 56)

" . . . Mary had not been subjected to Original Sin but entirely preserved from its stain and, because of this, redeemed in a more sublime manner" (from the *Definition of the Dogma of the Immaculate Conception*). And thus there was found in her an intelligence of crystal-clear receptivity to the word of God, receptivity both to the world or creation which is "God's word to man" (Romano Guardini, *The World and the Person*, p. 143), and also to the revealed Word of God: to Him who is the Truth (John 14:6) and would be her Son. The Great Commandment—to love, to obey, to serve the Lord with all one's heart and soul and mind (Mat 22:37)—found within her no obstacle. No interior temptations clouded the freshness of her intelligence; in her heart there never rose "evil intentions: murder, adultery, fornication, theft, perjury, slander" (Mat 15:19). The "Praise of Wisdom" in the Book of Wisdom (Wis 7:22-30) is a perfect description of her who gave to the world the One who is the Way, the Truth, and the Life, and became thereby our Resurrection, by that tested and victorious love in His human Heart that drew all men to Himself (John 12:32), "by His divine power" (2 Pet 1:3).

Our vision of the content of our faith is so often tainted, reduced, and unbalanced by pragmatism and an almost compulsive concern with God the Bookkeeper and Bureaucrat, that the splendor of God, the beauty of His gifts of truth and life, which should "shine in our minds to radiate the light of the knowledge of God's glory," is often dimmed. And yet, this glory is "the glory on the face of Christ" (2 Cor 4:6). The drabness that has come into our speaking of God, and into our celebration of His healing power and His sacrificial presence, confirms us in our imbalance and impoverishment so that we can hardly say with St. John, "we saw His glory, the glory that is His as the Only Son of the Father, full of grace and truth" (John 1:14). Praying Mary's Magnificat, we hardly feel as if we are speaking of our own perception of revealed divine reality—proclaiming the greatness of the Lord and expressing exultation in God our Savior (Luke 1:46-55).

There was nothing in Mary that could limit her capacity for joy and exultation. Adoration grew from her total self-effacement (Phil 2:3). Her mind was that of Christ, ready for any task, uncertainty, suffering, because there was no reservation in her knowing herself the "handmaid of the Lord" (Luke 1:38), and because she knew that it is God who "puts both the will and the action into [us]" (Phil 2:13). After the pattern of her Son's life, in imitation of His daily crosses and expiations, she, as handmaid and Mother, emptied herself to be a servant, to suffer death vicariously while standing under the Cross (Phil 2:5-8). With the great clarity of her mind, totally consecrated to God's service, and formed by the books, by the traditions, and by the Temple of Israel, she had set her heart "on God's kingdom first and on His righteousness" (Mat 6:33) (holiness), seeking to learn of God's holiness in adoration and to share it (2 Pet 1:4), knowing that all else needed would then be added (Mat 6:33). Was she not told by the Angel that "nothing is impossible to God" (Luke 1:37)?

Her gifts, flawlessly unfolding, being "full of grace" (Luke 1:28), she had a clear perception of evil and sin, of its spread through and into the hearts of men; of the brutalities of the Roman world; and of the staleness and often misguided expectations of the faith of her people Israel. She knew the prophecies about the Messiah, she knew the words of Moses, calling his people "a deceitful and underhand brood" (Deut 32:5), among whom we are called to be "innocent and genuine, perfect children of God . . . [to] shine in the world like bright stars" (Phil 2:15). This is the vocation of Christians, whose Mother she was to become. But she also knew that God's "mercy reaches from age to age for those who fear Him" (Luke 1:49), and that in her Son "the kindness and love of God our Savior for mankind" (Tit 3:4) would be revealed to lead us from a life of despair alternating with presumption, a life "immersed in this world, without hope and without God" (Eph 2:12) to a life in which we would be "adopted as sons," by God's sending "the Spirit of His Son into our hearts," the Spirit that cries, 'Abba, Father' " (Gal 4:5-6).

To live by the God-given power of hope is to realize the hopelessness of our situation (as heirs to the original rebellion and as people involved in its continuation through history) and yet to hold on to the promises of God; it is to see the relative absence of God from the world and the hearts of so many and yet to know that He will be with us till the end of time (Mat 28:20); it is to know that God "wants everyone to be saved" (1 Tim 2:4); it is to believe that "God has imprisoned all men in their own disobedience only to show mercy to all mankind" (Rom 11:32). It is to trust in her, untouched by sin, in whom God made a new beginning in the world, whose untainted will was in flawless harmony with her crystal-clear intelligence, full of grace. It is to ask our Lady of Wisdom to pray for us sinners now and at the hour of our death.

33. Mary's Assumption into Heaven

"Joined by a close and indissoluble bond to the Mysteries of the Incarnation and Redemption, the Blessed Virgin, the Immaculate,

was at the end of her earthly life raised body and soul to heavenly
glory, and likened to her risen Son in anticipation of the future
lot of all the just. . . ."

St. Paul's blessed dilemma must have been also that of Mary. For him,
as for her, "life . . . is Christ, but then death would bring . . . something
more. . . . I want to be gone and be with Christ, which would be very much
the better" (Phil 1:21, 23). For Mary "to stay alive in this body [was] a
more urgent need" for the sake of the young Church (Phil 1:24). But the
day came when her maternal power of intercession had to be extended to
the entire expanding Church. This meant that she had to be called by her
Divine Son to enter into the blessed vision of Heaven, into the splendor for
which her inconceivable capacity for loving God was ready, a capacity which
the Beatific Vision would fill. Now, from Heaven, she sees the hearts of
all men, and pleads for them in the measure of their need and their capacity
in answer to prayers to her. Her concern for man's Redemption did not come
to an end by the transition of death, but continues in Heaven, where she
is able to extend her intercession to every human being here on earth.

Since the rebellion of our first parents, death has come into the world—the
violent tearing apart of the soul from the body, when the latter can no longer
function. Death is not simply a transition into eternal life. It is a violent
deprivation, and the fate of all men, irrespective of personal holiness. It
is the consequence of penalty for repudiating God, who is the source and
goal of every human life. It is God's withdrawal of a special gift that would
have provided for a peaceful transition of the whole man to heaven. It is
the organic consequence of defiance of the Creator. Now, however, it gives
us an opportunity for expiation if we accept death as our Lord accepted
death—an obedience allowing us to fulfill the Law of Christ by bearing one
another's burdens (Gal 6:2). Mankind's solidarity in this destiny has no exception. But now "death is swallowed up in victory" (1 Cor 15:54) by the
fidelity of Christ's love, a love stronger than the converging evil of mankind
seeking His destruction. His redeeming love prevailed. And this universal
expiation is to be shared by us in facing and suffering the consequences of
man's initial and continuing rebellion, as victims of sin, in expiation of sin—
ours and others (Col 1:24). And Mary was no exception. Whether death
comes peacefully, as hers must have come, or with signs of violence, it remains the supreme testing of our faith, hope, and trust. If desire for God
is completely pure, self-effacing, and single-minded, it will find fulfillment
in God's own time and way. "If you remain in me and my words remain
in you, you may ask what you will and you shall get it" (John 15:7). And

as Mary must have longed to extend her maternal intercession in answer to men's trust in her, her own death and resurrection or Assumption into Heaven must have been in answer to her growing longing.

It would be strange if her transition from a life of faith to a life of vision, to seeing God "face to face" (1 Cor 13:12), would still leave her deprived of the body to be glorified in Heaven. In her and for her, God had been "all in all" (1 Cor 15:28) during her entire existence—this was the purpose and meaning of the gift of the Immaculate Conception. Her flawless responses to all demands and graces of the Father, guided by her sharp and sanctified intelligence—totally in the service of God, like her whole being—enabled her to be always "full of grace" to the extent of her constantly growing capacity for God. Her longing for the eternal home, after her principal task was done, must have grown until the blessed day of her transition into Heaven—the day of her death and Assumption. And we are grateful that the fact of the completion of her journey through life with its many crosses and expiations, placing her by her Assumption above all creatures, is revealed to us and has been reaffirmed in her honor by the Solemn Declaration of the Assumption as Dogma by Pope Pius XII in 1950.

Our Lord said, at the last Supper, "It is for your own good that I am going because unless I go, the Advocate will not come to you" (John 16:7). Likewise, Mary knew that it was for the good of the Church that she would go, because from Heaven she would be able to penetrate the hidden secrets of the hearts of all men, and she would intercede for all men on their hazardous journey and receive their prayers when they ask her to pray for them, now, and at the hour of their death.

34. The Queen of Heaven

"We believe that the Blessed Mother of God, the New Eve, Mother of the Church, continues in Heaven her maternal role with regard to Christ's members, cooperating with the birth and growth of divine life in the souls of the redeemed."

"Jesus Christ is the same today as He was yesterday and He will be forever" (Heb 13:8). Therefore she, who became His Mother, is His Mother today and forever. It is to be expected that the dispositions, the achievement, what today we call "personality," will be identical in the risen, glorified state as they were at the moment of death. But in this new state, nothing will be hidden and the person in his innermost being, now glorified, will be part of the visible glory of Heaven. All the victories of love maintained under opposition (Mat 5:10-12, 43-48), all the faith that overcame the world—"the victory over the world" (1 John 5:4)—will be a glorious achievement, an integral part of the person in glory.

The great prayers of St. Paul in the third chapter of his Letter to the Ephesians (Eph 3:14-21), describing supernatural life on earth, foreshadow its fruition in Heaven. The hidden self, will then be clearly seen, will have grown strong (Eph 3:16); Christ will live irrevocably in the heart, no longer in the obscurity of faith, but seen in vision (Eph 3:17). Love will be no longer obedience and mystery, but the clearly perceived total unconditional response to God whose name is Love (Eph 3:19; 1 John 4:8, 16); God will be seen face to face (1 Cor 13:12; see also Rev 22:4), "the breadth and the length , the height and the depth," then seen in their divine source and essence (Eph 3:18); and the love of Christ, though eternally beyond full comprehension, will be then the very heart of the beatific vision, and the redeemed then "filled with the utter fullness of God" (Eph 3:19). And all this exists in supreme intensity and fullness in the Mother of God, whose capacity for God was never limited by any trace of self-seeking. Flawless discovery and fulfillment of God's will, unconditional trust in faith and hope, with a charity of the utmost delicacy and strength, a sharing and channeling of God's redeeming love by compassion—in varying degrees these are possessed by all the blessed, but supremely, beyond human reckoning, by Mary.

What we are at the moment of death we will be eternally. If we die in union with God, we will enter eternal life, which is to know the Father, "the only true God, and Jesus Christ whom [He has] sent" (John 17:3)—a knowledge rooted in love, a love rooted in the beatific vision of the Blessed Trinity. As we have shared God's desires, directed to the gathering of all men into the redeemed unity which is Heaven (John 17:21,22; 1 Tim 2:4), we will continue to share His desires in the measure of each one's capacity for holiness. Missionaries such as Patrick, or Boniface, or Bishop Shanahan of Nigeria will continue to plead for their spiritual descendents for whose evangelization they labored. St. Joseph, once protector of the Child and the boy Jesus, continues as protector of the Body of Christ, the Church during her perilous journey (Mat 10:16-42; John 15:18-16:4).

It is in the light of the eternal life, as the perfection toward which life on earth is tending, that "we believe that the Blessed Mother of God . . . continues in Heaven her maternal role" (*Credo*). If Heaven is a completion and perfection, it must, in a new and mysterious mode, be a continuation of one's vocation or task on earth. It is really unthinkable that in Heaven one will be cut off from that which gave meaning to life or from that which required the bearing of the cross. Only "when everything is subjected to [the Father] then the Son Himself will be subject in His turn to the One who subjected all things to Him, so that God may be all in all" (1 Cor 15:28). The interplay between Heaven and earth will have come to an end. Then, all will be glory.

In a fallen world, every apostolate is a sharing in the work of Redemption, participating in Christ's task of drawing all men to Himself (John 12:32), begun on Calvary and continuing now in Heaven. Mary shared in the Cross on Calvary through her compassion, her "suffering-with." With it she also extended, in the darkness of faith, her hope to all whose sin had caused the Passion and Death of her Son, that is, to all of us. Now in the beatific vision, she continues to pray, in answer to the many prayers asking her for her maternal prayer. Mother of the Redeemer, Mother of the redeemed, her vocation on earth continues now in the glory of Heaven. As Queen of Heaven she shares in the "rejoicing in heaven over one repentent sinner" (Luke 15:7). Like the redeeming love of her Son, her compassionate love was tortured and tested by the Sin of the World, and she, too, was victorious, she, too, continued to pray for her Son's murderers, for us. The fidelity of her love under the Cross established her tested and victorious love as a continuing instrument of salvation for the mighty and growing multitude, in Heaven and on earth, of those who have proven victorious and are allowed to share God's throne, as Jesus Himself was victorious and took His place with the Father on His throne (Rev 3:21). And in this growing multitude of Heaven, her power as the Immaculate Mother of God is supreme, continuing "in Heaven her maternal role . . . cooperating with the birth and growth of divine life in the souls of the redeemed" (*Credo*, above).

35. Original Sin and Hope

"We believe that in Adam all have sinned, which means that the original offense committed by him caused human nature, common to all men, to fall to a state in which it bears the consequence of that offense. . . . "

Considering the condition of man, "the defeat of good, the success of evil . . . so fearfully yet exactly described in the Apostle's words, 'having no hope and without God in the world' [Eph 2:12], " Cardinal Newman goes on to say, "either there is no Creator, or the living society of men is in a true sense discarded from His presence. . . . And so I argue about the world: if there be a God, since there is a God, the human race is implicated in some terrible aboriginal calamity. It is out of joint with the purposes of its Creator" (*Apologia pro Vita Sua*, Ch. 7).

This fact, this reality of such all-pervasive evil, the consequence of Original Sin, profoundly determines the nature of man's hope. It may at times stretch man's hope to the breaking point, and the temptation to despair or escape into presumption (as in some forms of atheistic humanism) becomes more pressing with the weakening of faith. To live in Christian hope is to realize ever more deeply our inherited deprivation of the original gifts of God and the force of evil, and at the same time to hold on in living faith (in living realization of revealed realities) to the promises of God—knowing in faith that God's infinite power, knowledge, and wisdom are supporting His boundless mercy, and that this constitutes Divine Providence. But this would deteriorate into fantasy if we did not hold onto the revealed truth that God's ways are not our ways (Isa 55:8), that it is "impossible to penetrate His motives or understand His methods" (Rom 11:33), and that "God's foolishness is wiser than human wisdom, and God's weakness is stronger than human strength" (1 Cor 1:25). There can be no Christian hope unless we hold onto the revealed fact that "God's grace has been revealed, and . . . has made salvation possible for the whole human race" (Tit 2:11), that Christ "has abolished death, and . . . has proclaimed life and immortality through the Good News" (2 Tim 1:10).

The ocean of suffering that surrounds us, brought into our homes by the media, constantly tears at our hope. In the period we have entered in the Western world "loneliness in faith will be terrible. Love will disappear from the face of the public world" (Romano Guardini, *The End of the Modern World*, p. 132; see also Mat 24:12). The rapid brutalization of society, and the destruction of genuine bonds among men, accelerated by the legalized and common practice of abortion, forces the Church into ever greater isolation. In addition to this isolation, we have also to contend with betrayals from within, and again, too often, a great silence where we have the right to hear the truth spoken with authority. It is to us the Lord spoke these fearful words: "Many false prophets will arise; they will deceive many, and with the increase of lawlessness, love in most men will grow cold; but the man who stands firm to the end will be saved" (Mat 24:11-13).

Without the divine revelation of Original Sin, we could not believe in the God of Abraham, the God Whom we see and hear and are commanded to love, in and by our Lord Jesus Christ. In Him alone, who suffered all the brutalities and indignities we inflict and will inflict upon each other, is victory. In Him alone, Who cried, "My God, why have you forsaken me?" (Mat 27:46) can we find the strength to hold onto hope, knowing that "nothing . . . can come between us and the love of Christ" (Rom 8:35). As Church, we hear the assurance of Christ through His Church, to us, His Church, in St. Paul's words: "I am certain of this: neither death nor life, nor angel, nor prince . . . nothing still to come, not any power . . . nor any created thing, can ever come between us and the love of God made visible in Christ Jesus our Lord" (Rom 8:38-39).

36. Hints of Joy to Come

"We believe that Original Sin "caused human nature . . . to fall to a state . . . which is not the state in which it was at first in our first parents, established as they were in holiness and justice, and in which man knew neither evil nor death."

The enormity of the Original Sin of Adam can be seen in the devastation it has brought about in the human hearts and, in consequence, in the human condition throughout history. "What revelation makes known to us is confirmed by our own experience. For when man looks into his own heart he finds that he is drawn towards what is wrong and sunk in many evils which cannot come from his good Creator" (*Pastoral Constitution*, 13). The integrity and balance of our knowledge of God hinges on a profound and all-pervasive conviction that man was originally meant to know "neither evil nor death" that he was established "in holiness and justice," and that we are no longer what we were intended to be (*Credo*).

This original condition has become for us something beyond comprehension. For us evil and sin seem to be an integral part of human existence and seem to belong to our very nature. And although sporadically the battle against more evil—and more often against its results: suffering and social injustice—is found in human history, men remain largely determined by "the sensual body, the lustful eye, pride in possessions" which could not come from the Father, "but only from the world" (1 John 2:16; see also James

4:16-17). Strong faith is needed to believe in a lost Paradise. And yet, if we would yield to the pressure of present reality and simply take it for granted that man's present condition was willed by God, belief in "the God and Father of our Lord Jesus Christ, a gentle Father and the God of all consolation" (2 Cor 1:3) would become impossible, because "a gentle Father" revealed in Him who is "gentle and humble in heart" (Mat 11:29) could not be the origin of the present human condition with all the injustices and brutalities of a "deceitful and underhand brood" (Phil 2:15; see also Deut 32:5).

Dim realization of a lost Paradise and hope of deliverance from present madness has found expression in myth and fairy tale. Because this life cannot constitute the total meaning of human existence, above all if meaning is sought for every individual life, from that of a middle-class American to those of victims of concentration camps or the Gulag Archipelago (Soviet labor camps, designed to dehumanize, drive to despair and destroy), because of this, man keeps dreaming and hoping. There are those who paint, sculpt, write, or sing of joys, tasted now, passing yet promising, and pointing to an eternal reality. We are made for joy, and the Lord Jesus came and spoke and suffered brutal rejection to share His joy with us to the full (John 17:13; 15:11). And the real artist is one who reassures us of the reality of joy. When hearing Mozart we know that once "the Lord God [was] walking in the garden in the cool of the day" and that now it is we who are hiding in guilt from the presence of the Lord God (Gen 3:8).

It is not too difficult to realize that mankind has lost its innocence and that, if there is a God, God cannot have willed for us to be as we are now. Also, if there is a God, there must be eventual restoration of joy. And since this is obviously not the case in this life, there must be an afterlife of eternal joy. If not, if guilt can only remain and grow, if there is no release, despair is the only thing left, even if the affluent can find temporary escapes.

For all those who have not received the Good News of salvation, beauty is a reminder of the possibility of joy, of salvation. If many an atheist finds consolation in art and nature, in friendship and unselfish service, is that not hope, promise, that there must be a Love whose gifts we are allowed to taste, that there is Someone whose name is Love (1 John 4:8 16)? Is it not preparation for the time "when the kindness and love of God our Savior for mankind" will be revealed (Tit 3:4)? And when sanctity is met in the midst of all the brutalities of the world, in the midst of its growing coldness (Mat 24:12), then actually the presence and the face of God are revealed, in the hidden saints, in those "who are more perfectly transformed into the image of Christ" (*Dogmatic Constitution*, 50; see also 2 Cor

3:18).

Beauty and sanctity are a revelation and a promise that contradict the absence of God from man's world, that reveal to all "God's presence and His face" (*Dogmatic Constitution*, 50). Through them "it is as though God were appealing" to man (2 Cor 5:20). Our call, our task, and our goal is to achieve sanctity (a foretaste of eternal life) which inspires all the "generous aspirations of mankind to make life more humane" (*Pastoral Constitution*, 38), aspirations that find their source in the love of God overflowing toward those whom God loves. Here lies our twofold obedience in response to the Great Commandment to love God with our whole strength and intelligence, and to the New Commandment to love as Christ loved us with His redeeming love (John 13:24). This is our true life. And this life will have no end.

37. The Human Struggle

> *"It is human nature so fallen, stripped of the grace that clothed it, injured in its own natural powers and subjected to the dominion of death, that is transmitted to all men, and it is in this sense that every man is born in sin."*

(Read Gen 3:1-19; Rom 1:18-32)

Sin wounds the sinner above all. Choosing what pride in its varied forms makes attractive is at the same time ignoring or rejecting humility—that disposition which corresponds to the truth of our position before God. Disdain for others—whether from snobbery, or conceit, or pride in one's achievements, or gifts, or wealth—destroys our capacity to make any sense of the Crucifixion, "to the Jews an obstacle . . . to the pagans madness" (1 Cor 1:23). And yet, "God's foolishness is wiser than human wisdom, and God's weakness is stronger than human strength" (1 Cor 1:25).

Having accepted Satan's lie, that God lied when He told our first parents they would die if they defied Him, they ate of the forbidden fruit to usurp God's place, to dethrone Him who is both their Creator and the very goal of their lives, whom they were intended to see face to face eternally. Then they found themselves naked, helpless (Gen 3:4-7). They had rejected God's gentle, Fatherly love, His trust; they had ridiculed the unity of God's infinite power and His intensely personal love and friendship. Their rebellion was the will that truth, love, justice (in other words, the names of God) would derive from their own autonomous and arbitrary will. In their pride, they now viewed God as competition rather than as the source of life and freedom. And thus they committed themselves and all their offspring to a life rooted in the total lie that God is really not God and must yield to them. It is only because man is so blessedly inconsistent, that they did not become completely incapable of truth and redemption. Their pride collapsed when they discovered their helplessness. They "hid themselves from the Lord God" (Gen 3:8), and humbly accepted the inevitable consequences of their rebellion. It was then that they came to realize that acceptance of the consequences of their sin could become a way of expiation and return to God. Redeeming hope came into the world, because God "wants everyone to be saved and reach full knowledge of the truth." (1 Tim 2:4). "God has imprisoned all men in their own disobedience only to show mercy to all mankind" (Rom 11:32). "The gift itself considerably outweighed the Fall" (Rom 5:15).

"Only faith can . . . prove the existence of the realities that at present remain unseen" (Heb 11:1). Man's present condition, "immersed in this world, without hope and without God" (Eph 2:12), living "in wickedness and ill will, hating each other and hateful ourselves" (Tit 3:3), needs no faith to be recognized. The mystery is not that evil gives rise to evil, it is not "that it should never have an end, but that it should ever have had a beginning," as Cardinal Newman wrote in *Grammar of Assent* (Ch. 10).

The dreadful consequences of Original Sin have, from the beginning, been counteracted by the redeeming grace of God. During the Crucifixion, Christ drew all men to Himself (John 12:32), and He continues to do so now. But we must not consider the drawing power of the Risen Lord and the world— "world" here meaning "a spirit of vanity and malice whereby human activity from being ordered to the service of God and man is distorted to an instrument of sin" (*Pastoral Constitution*, 37)—we must not consider this conflict merely in terms of two opposing forces. In this conflict, there cannot be a compromise. It is rather a profoundly mysterious struggle in which the decision and responsibility are entirely man's—God's omnipotence having emptied itself (Phil 2:6) to maintain man's freedom—a struggle between freedom and grace and the mystery of iniquity in all its fury. Faced with this struggle, we must hold onto the revealed fact that "grace is enough" for us (2 Cor 12:9).

To maintain balanced knowledge about God, knowledge penetrating ever more deeply into the eternal mystery of Being and Love, the Triune God, certain facts of revelation must remain in mutual resonance. We must recall that man is not what he was intended to be (having been established originally "in holiness and justice," knowing "neither evil nor death"—*Credo*); that he is now heir to Adam's sin (the original temptation still active in all, demanding frequent decisions for or against God); that Christ redeemed us by drawing all men to Himself (John 12:32) (while being tortured and murdered by the converging Sin of the World); and that now, at the right hand of the Father, He continues to draw all men to Himself, through the promptings of His human heart, yet by His divine power (2 Pet 1:3). And thus our Redemption is realized, after Original and personal sin have "imprisoned all men in their own disobedience" that God, through the wounded Heart of Jesus, may continue to "show mercy to all mankind" (Rom 11:32). For God, whose name is Love (1 John 4:8, 16) "wants everyone to be saved and reach full knowledge of the truth" (1 Tim 2:4).

38. Solidarity in Sin and Salvation

"We therefore hold, with the Council of Trent, that Original Sin is transmitted with human nature, 'not by imitation, but by propagation' and that it is thus 'proper to everyone.'"

(Read Phil 2:1-11; *Decree on the Apostolate of Lay People*, 2-4)

Solidarity in sin and in salvation are difficult for us to discover, to grasp, to live, unless we break through the isolation which so much of our culture imposes on us by its commercialized individualism and by our fear of listening and speaking. *Loneliness* and *alienation* are words that almost make us swoon in self-pity and self-importance. But how do I become self-effacing (Phil 2:3), how do I acquire the Mind of Christ (Phil 2:5)? If we follow Him who in obedience emptied Himself even to death on the Cross (Phil 2:6-8), then we will discover solidarity in sin and in salvation, our own contribution to the apostolate (*Decree on the Apostolate of Lay People*, 3).

In our selfishness we resent being at a disadvantage through the sin of others, and we resent the apparently undeserved spiritual advantages of others, the sheer gifts. We resent both the gratuitousness of God's gifts and the absence of such gifts, presuming to sit in judgment on God. What would we make of these words of St. Paul: "When God wants to show mercy He does, and when He wants to harden someone's heart He does so. You will ask me, 'In that case, how can God ever blame anyone, since no one can oppose His will?' But what right have you, a human being, to cross-examine God?'' (Rom 9:18-20).

How can we reconcile these apparently harsh words of St. Paul with these words of his: God ''wants everyone to be saved and reach full knowledge of the truth'' (1 Tim 2:4)? Or with this promise of mercy for all: ''God has imprisoned all men in their own disobedience only to show mercy to all mankind'' (Rom 11:32)?

The words of the *Credo* we are considering remind us of our initial solidarity in the deprivations due to the sin of Adam. It is a solidarity rooted in a common misfortune, namely in the failure of the first man, father of the human race, whose rebellion made him and his descendants incapable of friendship with God and of living with the gifts of holiness and justice, of freedom from death and from any part in evil, of the gifts of integrity and harmony. In other words, Adam's descendants would come into this world as deprived as Adam found himself and made himself by his rebellion against truth and reality—by his refusal to be a child of God, by his attempt at usurping God's powers. Evil in mankind immediately began to bear fruit: murder (Gen 4:1-16), and a growing incapacity to communicate (Gen 11:1-9) were two of the first results, although grace (God's redeeming and transforming creative love), for the most part invisibly, was also at work, becoming a visible historical fact only with the call of Abraham, the promise made to him (Gen 12:1-3; Acts 7:1-8) and the gradual fulfillment of this promise, the history of Israel (résumé: Acts 7:2-49).

The people of Israel ''were adopted as sons, they were given the glory and the covenants; the law and the ritual were drawn up for them, and the promises were made to them . . . from their flesh and blood came Christ'' (Rom 9:4-5). As they heard God's special call, they became His people, forever, ''still loved by God . . . for the sake of their ancestors'' (Rom 11:28). The Redeemer would be forever ''the glory of [God's] people Israel'' (Luke 2:32).

Whether we are descended from those first called by God in Abraham, or whether we have entered ''the posterity of Abraham'' (Gal 3:29) through being called to faith and baptism into Christ, where all distinctions cease (Gal 3:26-29), we have thereby, as Church, been called to ''manifesting and actualizing the mystery of God's love for men'' (*Pastoral Constitution,* 45). As Church, we have been entrusted with extending the call to all—''it is as though God were appealing through us, and the appeal that we make in Christ's name is: be reconciled to God'' (2 Cor 5:20). ''The Christian vocation is, of its nature, a vocation to the apostolate as well'' (*Decree on the Apostolate of Lay People*, 2). For us all, it is an apostolate of prayer and expiation, of sharing in the redeeming Cross of Christ (Luke 9:23), by suffering "to make up all that has still to be undergone by Christ for the sake of His body, the Church" (Col 1:24). This will continue till the end of history, when "finally, the intention of the Creator in creating man in His own image and likeness will be truly realized, when all who possess human nature, and have been regenerated in Christ through the Holy Spirit gazing together on the glory of God, will be able to say 'Our Father' " (*Decree on the Church's Missionary Activity*, 7).

Our solidarity in sin, all men being imprisoned in their own inherited and implemented disobedience, will then have been dissolved by the mercy of God. It is now for each one of us to decide daily whether we wish to be among those who, by sin, reject the Cross, shifting it to others, and thus continue to crucify Christ, or whether we are among the followers of Christ, each one of whom renounced himself and takes up his cross every day (Luke 9:23). Then, as fellow workers of God (1 Cor 3:9), we will raise the spiritual level of the world, and thus contribute, in union with Christ, and, in solidarity with all who are seeking God's kingdom and holiness (Mat 6:33), to bring that day closer when "God may be all in all" (1 Cor 15:28).

39. The Redemption

> *"We believe that our Lord Jesus Christ, by the Sacrifice of the Cross redeemed us from Original Sin and all the personal sins committed by each one of us. . . ."*

"Let our strength be our norm of justice. . . . Let us beset the just one, because he is obnoxious to us. . . . His life is not like other men's. . . . He judges us debased. . . . With revilement and torture let us put him to the test. . . . Let us condemn him to a shameful death" (Wis 2:11, 12, 15, 16, 19, 20). Hatred of justice, of holiness, of the very reflection of God was the first fruit of the first rebellion (of Original Sin) and the motive of the first murder. Cain, having just murdered his brother, upon whom God looked with favor, when asked by God about him, cynically lied: "I do not know; am I my brother's keeper?" (Gen 4:9). The seeds of destruction spread quickly, as the lives and the history of men reveal. Man is no longer what

God intended him to be, "established . . . in holiness and justice," knowing "neither evil nor death" (*Credo*). For now we are "subjected to the dominion of death" (*Credo*), death of body and all-pervasive danger of sickness and death of soul. But Redemption is now offered us, having been achieved by our Lord through His Sacrifice of the Cross.

The uncanny description in the Book of Wisdom given above, describes how the hatred of the rebellious for justice and holiness is translated into sadism, torture, and murder—how can they be redeemed by the very sufferings of the just which they caused, prophetically described in those words? What transformation must we undergo from these evil dispositions, before our hearts become capable of being transformed, so that the likeness of Christ (Rom 8:29) may begin to grow again in us?

All sin—all evil intentions and acts flowing from the dispositions of the heart (Mat 15:19-20)—have God as their target. The original temptation of our first parents (Gen 3:4-5), often so fearfully alive in us (Rom 7:14-23), if accepted, becomes a blow against God. And when God was heard, seen, and watched among us (1 John 1:1), hatred and resentment of holiness found their target, and eventually their victim (John 11:47-53) in Him—the One who was "gentle and humble in heart" (Mat 11:29)—"because he is obnoxious to us" Wis 2:12).

And yet, when the coverging sins of all times, the Original Sin of Adam and its manifold and still multiplying fruit throughout man's history, would find Him and render Him helpless on the Cross, He would draw all men to Himself (John 12:32). His human-divine love reached out to all men, past, present, and future, in divine pity and compassion, enveloping them (in a victory over all His human revulsion) by that strange human love that has its origin in the Father, filling His human Heart—"As the Father has loved me, so I have loved you" (John 15:9). By His divine, creative, transforming power, He seeks entrance into men's hearts. He awakens our longing and our conscience, and invites us to seek Him, promising that we will then find Him (Mat 7:7-8). And the slightest response, the merest flickering of hope of repentance drawn forth by the manifestation of God's love, enables Christ, now in glory, to draw us more to, and into Himself. If we choose to remain faithful to the working of divine grace, Jesus will continue to draw and transform us "by His divine power . . . bringing us to know God Himself, who has called us by His own glory and goodness" (2 Pet 1:3). Faith will arise in us, and God will "radiate the light of knowledge" of His very own glory, the glory His grace enables us to discover "on the face of Christ" (2 Cor 4:6). And thus we will come to "be able to share the divine nature and to escape corruption in a world that is sunk in vice" (2

-79

Pet 1:4).

And Jesus, who has already drawn us to Himself on the Cross, is now continuing to draw us—seated as He is at the right hand of the Father—away from "wickedness and ill will," from "hating each other and [being] hateful ourselves" (Tit 3:3), into becoming "children of [God's] that He loves," following Him by loving as He loved us (Eph 5:1; see also John 13:34).

Allowing Himself, through Israel, then mankind's representatives, to become the target and victim of all sin, He drew all men to Himself while on the Cross (Jn 12:32). This victory—His loving us while we were rejecting Him by inflicting on Him the horrors of His Passion and Crucifixion—made it possible for His victorious redeeming love to continue now to be "at work in the hearts of men by the power of His Spirit" (*Pastoral Constitution*, 38), to redeem us "from original sin and all personal sins" (*Credo*) until "God may be all in all" (1 Cor 15:28).

40. God's Power

"We believe that our Lord Jesus Christ . . . redeemed us . . . in accordance with the word of the Apostle, 'where sin abounded, grace did more abound' [Rom 5:20]. "

(Read Ps 103; Luke 15:11-32; 22:54-62)

The more the power and knowledge of the Creator is revealed to us, the more amazing is the love of this one only God for us, for all of us. The fidelity of God's love was maintained when we smugly enjoyed the spectacle of His degradation and death, mocking Him (Mark 15:29-32) during

His agony. "We may be unfaithful, but He is always faithful, for He cannot disown His own self" (2 Tim 2:13). "These two names, Being and Love, express the same divine reality of Him . . . who 'dwelling in light inaccessible (1 Tim 6:16), is Himself above . . . every created intellect" (*Credo*). Infinite Power and infinte Love: this is the One Living God—Power at the disposal of Love, Love directing the use of His creative, forgiving, transforming Power, which also sustains the "universe by His powerful command" (Heb 1:3). He is the same God of infinite Power who revealed His Love in the tears Christ shed over Jerusalem, because the city, the nation "did not recognize [its] opportunity when God offered it!" (Luke 19:41-44).

Lightly we say, "Creator and Redeemer." But this really constitutes the very essence of the Good News, the Gospel, that He through whom "all things came to be" (John 1:3) is also "gentle and humble in heart," Creator and Redeemer, Being and Love, offering rest for our souls (Mat 11:29-30). He is the Oneness of Being and Love, the living God, without whom, as it is revealed, we can do nothing (John 15:5; James 1:16-18), yet to whom all things are possible (Luke 1:37; Mat 19:26). But we must be on our guard not to see God's power as diminishing our abilities and freedom, as if we could shift our responsibility to Him. The infinite power and knowledge (Ps 139) of God are creative, enabling powers, creating, sustaining, and actualizing in us the very abilities that constitute our freedom. God's uncreated enabling power creates and sustains in us the power to initiate thought and action, to set and to change goals, and to order things not only in accord with priorities, but to order and revise the priorities themselves. "It is God, for His own loving purpose, who puts both the will and the action into you" (Phil 2:13).

We will consider two cases: one historical, Peter's denial and repentance; the other a parable, the Return of the Prodigal Son.

In Luke we read of St. Peter, when the cock crew after his third denial, "the Lord turned and looked straight at Peter, and Peter remembered what the Lord had said to him. . . . And he went outside and wept bitterly" (Luke 22:61-62). When Peter the Rock (Mat 16:18) fell, through his regard for human opinion, he was given the grace to repent, the gift of tears, and a new hope to keep him from despair. One may account for his change, for the collapse of his presumption (John 13:37; Mat 26:33) and his deep sorrow in natural, psychological terms. One may attribute to the sad glance of Christ a certain influence. But we know that Peter's conversion, tears, and restored fidelity certainly had deeper roots, if we consider that Peter would soon be "Rock" again. Only two days later he and John would be running to see the tomb reported empty (John 20:3), finally understanding "the teaching of Scripture, that He must rise from the dead" (John 20:9). Soon after, recognizing the Lord at the lake, Peter would jump into the water to meet Him (John 21:7). Later, on Pentecost, Peter would preach the first Christian sermon with a courage and wisdom that gave witness to his having become a new man, a "new creation" of which St. Paul wrote, "it is all God's work" (2 Cor 5:18). And yet it was always the same Peter, now enabled by God's creative, transforming gifts to accomplish the superhuman, to live in faith, hope, and charity. Finally Peter would die a martyr, crucified upside down, to add to the humiliation. "Where sin abounded, grace did more abound" (Rom 5:20).

The Prodigal Son, having squandered his inheritance and being reduced to look after swine, unable even to eat the husks given to the pigs, was driven by hunger to return home. The beautiful words he planned to say to his father, "I have sinned against Heaven and against you; I no longer deserve to be called your son; treat me as one of your paid servants" (Luke 15:18-19) might at first have been mere rhetoric, somewhat put on for a purpose. But by the time he arrived, shaken to his depth by the completely unexpected welcome by his father, these same words had, by God's transforming pity revealed by his own father, become expressions of deep repentance and of a new love in response to God's love. This love of God was revealed and actualized by his human father. There was celebration, because "this son of mine was dead and has come back to life . . . was lost and is found" (Luke 15:24). "There will be more rejoicing in Heaven over one repentant sinner than over ninety-nine virtuous men who have no need of repentance" (Luke 15:7). "Where sin abounded, grace did more abound" (Rom 5:20).

As members of Christ, as His ambassadors (2 Cor 5:20), it is our apostolic task to reveal and channel, and thereby prepare for, God's redeeming love. Ours is to be an active hope for the salvation of others, of all, and thereby a sharing in the desire for the salvation of all (1 Tim 2:4) which God—the God who "is compassion and love, slow to anger and rich in mercy" (Ps 103:8)—has.

41. Baptism Into Christ

"We believe in one Baptism instituted by Our Lord Jesus Christ for the remission of sins."

(Read Mat 7:7-11; John 15:7; James 4:1-3; 1 John 5:14-15).

When the Sin of the World, the Original Sin of Adam, together with all the sins of men since, and those to be committed till the end of time enveloped the body and soul of Christ during His Passion and death on the Cross, His redeeming love went out to all of us, His murderers. His Heart, broken by us during the ordeal when our murderous intent found in Him its target and victim, continues to draw us to Himself. From then on, as soon as this drawing, redeeming love finds a response in us, it takes effect. Our interior opposition is cleansed away in accord with our change of heart. What is entirely beyond our power, the overcoming of our evil and destructive inclinations, is accomplished by the creative, transforming power of Christ. This power is His by the power of His divinity (2 Pet 1:3), but is willed and directed toward us by His human Heart. The restraining of our inclination to evil then makes it possible for us to be drawn by Him into Himself, to become "sons in the Son" (*Pastoral Constitution*, 22), to "be called God's children" (1 John 3:1), by His creative call to become God's children.

When we are baptized into the very life of the Blessed Trinity, we begin to "escape corruption in a world that is sunk in vice" and thus become able "to share the divine nature" (2 Pet 1:4). We are enabled "to be adopted as sons" and to become "heirs" even now by sharing His life, and to be drawn by the Holy Spirit into friendship and that kind of closeness to the Father which allows us to cry "Abba, Father" (Gal 4:5-7; Rom 8:14-17; John 15:13-16). In baptism, we begin "to share in the divinity of Christ who humbled Himself to share in our humanity" (Mass).

In baptism we receive the virtues, or gifts, or powers, of faith, hope, and charity. Through these, the new life becomes a dynamic power, a living relationship to God, and, through Him, our relation toward others becomes Christ-like. This is the foundation and invitation to leading a spiritual life. And this spiritual life, this seeking and finding of God, is first of all a listening to God, as He is seen, heard, and (sacramentally) touched in Jesus Christ. He is the Beloved Son to whom we were commanded by God to listen on the mountain of the Transfiguration (Mat 17:5). Him we are commanded to seek, with the promise that we shall find Him. We are also told to ask, so that we may become receptive to the gifts through which we grow in holiness. And we are asked to knock so that the door to an ever deeper entering into divine life will be opened (Mat 7:7).

If we are not heard—and this is almost impossible to know, unless we have the courage to face our self-indulgence, mediocrity, and disinterest in the things of God—if you are not heard, it may well be "because you have not prayed properly, you have prayed for something to indulge your own desires" (James 4:3). And our glorious beginnings in baptism may well end in keeping up "the outward appearance of religion [while having] rejected the inner power of it" (2 Tim 3:5). So we must "set [our] hearts on His Kingdom first, and on His [holiness]" (Mat 6:33), in order to get to and remain on the ascending road to God and to grow in self-effacing, emptying of ourselves, becoming servants on our journey to the cross and the resurrection. For this is the Mind of Christ, which is to be acquired by us (Phil 2:3-8). Like His life, our life is to be a progressive emptying of ourselves (Phil 2:5-8). "You cannot belong to Christ Jesus unless you crucify all self-indulgent passions and desires" (Gal 5:24).

These are our tasks rooted in baptism. We must develop a spiritual life, we must love God with our whole mind (Mark 12:30), applying our intelligence to know the Father, "the only true God, and Jesus Christ" whom the Father has sent (John 17:3). We must set aside every day some time for meditation, for reading, for prayerful listening to God as He speaks to us through the Church in Scripture, in liturgy, in her specific teaching, in the Christian tradition found in authentic spiritual writing speaking to us of God, but above all in the lives of saintly people whom we meet and of whom we read. And we must apply our mind to the planning of this our spiritual life.

Baptism is God's call to follow Christ. The goal during my pilgrimage on earth is to "live now not with my own life but with the life of Christ who lives in me." But this cannot happen unless "I have been crucified with Christ" (Gal 2:19,20). Having been "baptized into Christ" (Gal 3:27) is the beginning, the cross is inevitably found on the way, and resurrection to the eternal vision of God is the goal.

42. Infant Baptism

"Baptism should be administered even to little children who have not yet been able to be guilty of any personal sin, in order that, though born deprived of supernatural grace, they may be reborn 'of water and the Holy Spirit' to the divine life in Christ Jesus [John 3:5]."

Nothing exists, nothing continues to exist, nothing changes or happens, nothing grows and multiplies unless it is creatively thought and willed by God. The universe, of which the sciences give us an ever more amazing description, exists for the sake of man; it "attains its destiny through him" (*Dogmatic Constitution*, 48).

Meant to live "in holiness and justice, knowing neither evil nor death" (*Credo*), man fell into living "without hope and without God" (Eph 2:12). But Redemption restores us to union with God and to the capacity to believe, to hope, and to love. Ought we to delay the sacrament that restores the child to union with his Creator, his origin and his eternal goal?

God is the "Creator in each man of his spiritual and immortal soul" (*Credo*). Thereby we possess a created capacity for God, for sharing "the divine nature" (2 Pet 1:4), for becoming temples of the Holy Spirit (1 Cor 6:19): we are "being built into a house where God lives, in the Spirit" (Eph 2:22). And if we love Jesus, we will keep His word, and the Father will love us, and the Father and His Son Incarnate, Jesus, will come to us and make their abode with us (John 14:23). And all this is initiated when we are baptized "into the name of the Father and of the Son and of the Holy Spirit" (Mat 28:19—"into" is the translation of the Greek word that indicates the beginning of that real union, of that mutual indwelling of God and us, spoken of by our Lord and quoted above).

All this is the beginning and growth of Redemption, of holiness, which through death is transformed into eternal life. And eternal life is to know the Father, "the only true God, and Jesus Christ" whom that Father has sent (John 17:3)—a knowledge rooted in love, as the love is rooted in that knowledge which is to see God "face to face" (1 Cor 13:12), to "see Him as He really is" (1 John 3:2), and thereby to complete our transformation "into the image that we reflect" (2 Cor 3:18).

This glorious destiny, for which we are created, and which alone gives meaning to our lives (and to the lives of all men, however frustrated and unhappy their lives on earth may be), this purpose is already achieved by baptism. And that moment we become "children of God" (Rom 8:16), as we are "baptized into Christ" (Gal 3:27). Union with God is restored, and the little child has become a "temple of the Holy Spirit" (1 Cor 6:19).

It is true that the child could not be asked to make his commitment at the time of baptism. But Saul on the road to Damascus was not asked (Acts 9:1-7), nor was Mary when she was immaculately conceived, nor St. John the Baptist when "he leapt for joy" in Elizabeth's womb (Luke 1:44). Must we insist on having earned and deserved divine gifts? Is this not contradicting the very nature of grace? God, who "wants everyone to be saved" (1 Tim 2:4), told Moses: "I have compassion on whom I will, and I show pity to whom I please" (Ex 33:19). We have no claim on God. All is mercy. "God has imprisoned all men in their own disobedience only to show mercy to all mankind" (Rom 11:32).

If we see sorrow or bliss in the face of a little child, a few weeks old, would we not want the child to be a temple of the Holy Spirit? Who are we to delay, until a person can compare notes, study a list of respectable religions like a menu, and then graciously reward God for His invitation by selecting baptism in the Catholic Church?

God, "Creator in each man of his spiritual and immortal soul" (*Credo*), desires to take full possession of each person born into the world, to make His home with Him (John 14:23). This consecration of the newly born, this assurance of eternal life, is now the responsibility of the Church. "Deprived of supernatural grace" (*Credo*), as we come into this world, we must not delay baptism, so that those born into this world "may be reborn of water and the Holy Spirit to the divine life in Christ Jesus" (*Credo*).

43. The Four Marks of the Church

"We believe in one, holy, catholic, and apostolic Church."

Unity of the Church. Vatican II, quoting St. Cyprian, states that "the universal Church is seen to be a people brought into unity from the unity of the Father, the Son, and the Holy Spirit," (*Dogmatic Constitution*, 4). It is the answer to Christ's priestly prayer, that we may be one as He and the Father are one, with the Father in Him and Jesus in us (John 17:22). This redeemed unity to which we are called and drawn (John 12:32? is what will make the world realize that Jesus was sent by the Father (John 17:23).

Holiness of the Church. Union with God restored to men who are torn apart by sin is holiness. To "be able to share the divine nature and to escape corruption in a world that is sunk in vice" (2 Pet 1:4) is holiness, "which is simply the unity of Morality with Doctrine" (Humbert Clerissac, O.P., *The Mystery of the Church*, p. 19). Holiness is restored as "we live by the truth and in love, [growing] in all ways into Christ, who is the head" (Eph 4:15). Our "mind must be renewed by a spiritual revolution so that [we] can put on the new self that has been created in God's way, in the goodness and holiness of the truth" (Eph 4:23-24).

Catholicity of the Church. All nations are to be made disciples and, through baptism, enter into the redeemed unity which restores our original condition and destiny—union with God—and to become "true images of His Son" (Rom 8:29). New birth, new life, and growing likeness to Christ, the "Image of the invisible God" (Col 1:15), means to become and to be children of God (Rom 8:16). To this all men are called, for this man was created, for this God creates our "immortal and spiritual souls" (*Credo*). It is God's loving will that everyone be saved (1 Tim 2:4). "There is one Lord, one faith, one baptism, and one God who is Father of all, over all, through all, and within all" (Eph 4:5-6). This is true catholicity: the Church is for all men. The enemy of catholicity is snobbery, elitism, in matters of the Faith. It is a repudiation of the one thing necessary (Luke 10:42); the "supreme advantage of knowing Christ Jesus [and looking] on everything [else] as so much rubbish" (Phil 3:8). The enemy of catholicity is the rejection of the basic equality among all men rooted in having been baptized into Christ, which erases all "distinctions between Jew and Greek, slave and free, male and female" (Gal 3:28). It is, in short, the refusal to love.

Apostolicity of the Church. "As the Father sent me, so I am sending you" (John 20:21). This sending constitutes the Church. *Sending* means a new presence, a new relation, a new responsibility, a new task. With the powers of the Apostles to send is given the power to communicate their powers to others, who thereby become their successors—the bishops of the Catholic Church. Revealed truths were first given to the Apostles. These truths constitute the content of the Faith of the Catholic Church that must be preserved and taught to the whole world (Mat 28:19-20). This is the bishops' responsibility.

The power to sanctify was given to the Apostles (and through them to their successors, the bishops, to the Church), as well as the power to forgive sins (John 20:22-23), the power to celebrate Mass (1 Cor 11:23-25), the power of all the sacraments, the power to pray as a Church, the power to rule and to teach all men "to observe all the commands" He had given them (Mat 28:20): His teaching, His truth, Himself as "the Way, the Truth, and the Life" (John 14:6).

Thus baptized into Christ (Gal 3:27), we become "part of a building that has the Apostles and prophets for its foundations, and Christ Jesus Himself for its main cornerstone" (Eph 2:20).

The four marks of the Church, in their mutual illumination, are the face of the Church, her personality, that which even in the individual Catholic (if his being a Catholic is a living reality) unmistakably indicates the presence of the Church. The face of the Church is seen in the greatest variety of saints:

Peter, Paul, Augustine, Francis, Thomas Aquinas, the two Theresas, and Pius X, for example. There is union with God and the mind of Christ manifested in that ultimate generosity to obey the Father unto death, even "death on a cross" (Phil 2:8). There is that holiness which reveals to us God's presence and His face (*Dogmatic Constitution*, 50). There is in all things that catholicity, that universality, which forms the Catholic's longing, his prayers, and an awareness of solidarity in sin and Redemption without which one cannot be really a Catholic, without which one cannot pray "in spirit and truth" (John 4:23), "Holy Mary, Mother of God, pray for us *sinners*, now, and at the hour of our death."

And there is an element of timelessness, knowing that the Jesus whom we know from the Gospels is the same Person (Heb. 13:8), who now in Heaven continues to draw all men to Himself (John 12:32), who will come again; in glory knowing that He who spoke through the Apostles continues to speak to us now. "Heaven and earth will pass away, but my words will not pass away" (Mark 13:31). Being Church means to be the recipient and channel of the gosepl, of Him who is the Way, the Truth, the Life, and the Resurrection (John 14:6; 11:25). "The Church is to be through us, what the Church is for us" (Henri de Lubac, *The Splendor of the Church*, p. 161). And through the Church, Jesus Christ is to be through us what He has been, and is now, for us.

44. The Vicar of Christ

"We believe in one, holy, catholic, and apostolic Church, built by Jesus Christ on that rock which is Peter."

" 'This person was with Him too.' But he denied it. . . . 'You are another of them.' But Peter replied, 'I am not, my friend.' . . . 'This fellow was certainly with Him.' . . . 'My friend,' said Peter, 'I do not know what you are talking about.' At that instant . . . the cock crew, and the Lord turned and looked straight at Peter, and Peter remembered. . . . And he went outside and wept bitterly" (Luke 22:57-62).

Peter was the man to whom Jesus said, "Get behind me, Satan! Because the way you think is not God's way but man's" (Mark 8:33). And yet, this was the same Peter, who spoke those magnificent words, which ought to remain ours, "Lord, to whom shall we go? You have the message of eternal life, and we believe; we know that you are the Holy One of God" (John 6:8-69). Now we go to Peter, to his successors as Bishop of Rome, upon whom, the rock, Jesus was to build His Church, if we want to hear infallibly the message of eternal life. For Peter the Rock was to learn of his own frailty, he was to learn that without Jesus the Lord we can do nothing (John 15:5), but that, while "for men . . . this is impossible; for God everything is possible" (Mat 19:26). This is the life of hope: to deeply realize our weakness, a weakness inherited and aggravated by personal sins and betrayals, but to realize also that "where sin abounded, grace did more abound" (Rom 5:20; see also *Credo*).

"It was to shame the wise that God chose what is foolish by human reckoning" (1 Cor1:27), so that "by God's doing, [Christ Jesus] has become our wisdom, and our virtue, and our holiness, and our freedom" (1 Cor 1:30). "It was those who are poor according to the world that God chose, to be rich in faith and to be the heirs to the Kingdom which He promised to those who love Him" (James 2:5). To have the Mind of Christ is to empty oneself "to assume the condition of a servant . . . even to obedience unto death, death on a cross" (Phil 2:5-8). It is to "learn to be a fool. . . . Because the wisdom of the world is foolishness to God" (1 Cor 3:18-19). And all this Peter had to learn, even after he was made "Rock," before he could function as rock on Pentecost—when he spoke the first Christian discourse (Acts 2:14-36) which cut to the heart of those who heard him (Acts 2:37)—and before he could stretch his hands, not only in prayer, but in that total prayer of crucifixion, and before being taken where he would rather not go (John 21:18), to be crucified upside down.

How embarrassing to be asked in the presence of the others whether he loved Him, the Risen Lord, more than the others loved Him. Could he forget the Lord looking straight at him, after he denied him three times? And yet, Peter, and his successors—whether weak or strong, whether politicians enjoying splendor and power, or saints in dread of betraying the Lord Jesus, whose Vicar they were called and enabled to be—they know in their hearts that "you can trust God not to let you be tried beyond your strength, and that with any trial He will give you a way out of it and the strength to bear it" (1 Cor 10:13). But at what cost—to day in and day out be "put on show in front of the whole universe, [to be a fool] for the sake of Christ . . . treated as the offal of the world . . . the scum of the earth" (1 Cor 4:9, 10, 13).

Being mocked by one's own, unable to correct the massive wall of lies which is being erected (with the applause of so many who were consecrated to the undivided service of God), and seeing the lies designed to poison the minds of children—how Pope Paul VI must have envied the clean martyrdom inflicted by professed opponents of the Church of Jesus Christ. But he was the Vicar of Him who had to say, "Someone who shares my table rebels against me" (John 13:18; see also Ps 41:9): and "A servant is not greater than his master" (John 15:20). And so the Crucifixion continues: some of the men who are supposed to lead the flock of Christ are liable to jeer at Him (Luke 23:35) in His Vicar, though they should know what was said of them—that they "would be better drowned in the depths of the sea with a great millstone round [their] neck" (Mat 18:6). For their jeering is meant for those children they are supposed to lead.

But as Peter was not to forget that his becoming the Rock of the Church against which the gates of hell would not prevail was immediately followed by being told that his way of thinking was not God's way but man's, his successors are not to forget it either (Mat 16:18, 23). Pope Paul VI knew what it is to be "treated as the offal of the world . . . the scum of the earth" (1 Cor 4:13).

45. The Mystical Body of Christ

The Church "is the Mystical Body of Christ. . . ."

Target and victim of the Sin of the World, of all the sins of men, Christ, "lifted up from the earth" on the Cross, drew all men to Himself (John 12:32). His redeeming love went out to all men, past, contemporary, and to those still to come, to extend to them the call and the capacity to become children of God (Rom 8:16) and to enter into union with God. It was the life long prayer of Christ, maintained while being tormented and murdered by our sins, that we might become one in Him and in the Father, drawn into this union by the Holy Spirit. "I have given them the glory you gave to me"—the glory which is the compassionate love, that comes from the Father and fills the human Heart of Christ—in order "that they may be one as we are one. With me in them and you in me" (John 17:22-23).

Thus the Mystical Body of Christ was formed. Jesus' redeeming love was tested and victorious on the Cross—never withdrawn, upheld by the gigantic effort of His human will, in obedience to the Father. And this constitutes love: one's will pressed into obedience, into conformity with the will of the Father for the ultimate good of those who have rebelled or drifted away, who have become aliens (Eph 2:19), if not enemies. Now they, we, are being called, and enabled to enter into friendship with Christ, to become His friends (John 15:15). The foundation is laid for the elimination of all human divisions that are but frozen enmities, rooted in lies. Now we can all be "baptized into Christ," can be "clothed . . . in Christ, and there are no more distinctions between Jew and Greek, slave and free, male and female, but all . . . are one in Christ Jesus" (Gal 3:27-28). Yet the Christian world hardly appears to have overcome these divisions, a terrible judgment on our mediocrity and cultivated blindness.

Verses 1 through 6 of chapter 4 of the Letter to the Ephesians could serve as a test and examination of conscience, of whether we have any intention at all of becoming members of Christ, "part of a building that has the Apostles and prophets for its foundations, and Christ Jesus himself for its main cornerstone," of whether we have any desire to be "built into a house where God lives, in the Spirit" (Eph 2:20, 22).

Paul implores us to lead a life worthy of our vocation—the vocation to become true children of the Father (by loving our enemies—Mat 5:44). We become His children by becoming "true images of His Son" (Rom 8:29), whom to see is to see the Father (John 14:9). It is to love as Christ loved and continues to love (see the New Commandment—John 13:34; 15:12)— to love our enemies with redeeming love, even while they are determined to destroy us (Luke 23:34; 1 John 4:10-11; 3:16). It is to lead the life of the Beatitudes (Mat 5:3-12), which are nothing less than a self-portrait of Christ. Without these dispostions, we could not "bear with one another charitably, in complete selflessness, gentleness, and patience" (Eph 4:2). Only in this spirit can we do all "to preserve the unity of the Spirit by the peace that binds" us together (Eph 4:3).

And here is the blessed vision of peace, of being Church, or becoming Church, that should draw us with irresistible power: "There is one Body" (Eph 4:4), as "all of us, in union with Christ, form one body, and as part of it we belong to each other" (Rom 12:5). There is "one Spirit" (Eph 4:4), the mutual love of the Eternal Father and the Eternal Son, who "proceeds from the Father and the Son" (Nicene Creed), who draws us ever more deeply into union with God, thereby making us ever more profoundly able "to share the divine nature and to escape corruption in a world that is sunk in vice" (2 Pet 1:4).

And so we "were all called into one and the same hope" (Eph 4:4), the twofold hope for our own personal salvation, and for the salvation of all, sharing thereby God's desire that everyone be saved (1 Tim 2:4). We were all called to know the full reality, invisible now, but revealed and grasped in faith (Heb 11:1) that "there is one Lord," Creator and Redeemer. We are called to the "one faith" (Eph 4:5), a faith with one content which we share with the whole Catholic Church across the earth, and across the ages, and which assures and promises resurrection, when we shall see God "face to face" (1 Cor 13:12). We are joined by the one baptism (Eph 4:5) by which we are drawn into the life of the Triune God (Mat 28:19). And so God is coming to be, and to be more and more exclusively, "Father of all" (Eph 4:6), so that as members of Christ's Mystical Body we become, in and as His Church, manifestations and actualizations of "the mystery of God's love for men" (*Pastoral Constitution*, 45). Then the Church, and thereby Christ, is for me—the Way, the Truth, and the Life (John 14:6).

And finally, God is Father "within all" (Eph 4:6), making us vessels of His redeeming love, so that the "grace and peace . . . from God our Father and the Lord Jesus Christ" may come to us and through us (2 Cor 1:2). Because we are called and enabled to be "ambassadors for Christ . . . it is as though God were appealing through us" (2 Cor 5:20).

46. The Visible Church

The Church is "at the same time a visible society instituted with hierarchical organs, and a spiritual community. . . ."

Our Lord spoke in a way that demanded trust, saying, "He who eats my flesh and drinks my blood lives in me and I live in him" (John 6:56). "After this, many of his disciples left him and stopped going with him. Then Jesus said to the Twelve, 'What about you, do you want to go away too?' Simon Peter answered, 'Lord, to whom shall we go? You have the message of eternal life ' " (John 6:66-68).

Would that Peter's words were ours—that we would, with like confidence, hear the words of Christ, now the words of the Church. That we would let ourselves be formed by the Church—now fed by Peter in his successors, the Vicars of Christ—till the Mind of Christ is formed in us (Phil 2:5). But this channel of truth and life, the Church, must be accessible and visible to all. The threefold task of teaching, sanctifying, and ruling must remain reliable and trustworthy. Does not unity among men come from sharing ultimate truths, from finding themselves on a journey to the same goal?

But how can this be achieved unless truths and the channels of supernatural grace are assured, unless the responsibility and power are utlimately rooted in one man, who has inherited the command to feed Christ's sheep (John 21:15-17), to be the Rock against which the "gates of hell" will never prevail (Mat 16:18)?

As Church, each one of us is called and is also an instrument of calling. We are recipients of Redemption, fruit of Redemption, but at the same time "ambassadors for Christ [and] it is as though God were appealing through us" (2 Cor 5:20). But how could there be a commandment to go to all the world, unless the Church is visible, unless, like "the Word, who is life," she can be "heard . . . seen . . . watched, and touched" (1 John 1:1), as was the Lord when "He lived among us, and we saw His glory" (John 1:14)? To be Church is to realize deeply the need for Redemption, to have followed the call to Redemption, and to have become "fellow workers with God" (1 Cor 3:9) in the continuing work of Redemption. Therefore, the Church without visibility is as unthinkable as Incarnation without it.

It is a sad fact that the need for Redemption often stands out more clearly than the flow of Redemption through the Church. "The Church . . . clasping sinners to her bosom, at once holy and always in need of purification, follows constantly the path of penance and renewal" (*Dogmatic Constitution*, 8). If this saddens us, so be it. We are also called to share the indescribable sadness of the Lord (Luke 13:34-35; 19:41-44; Mat 26:36-46; Heb 5:7-9). To refuse this sadness would be refusing the cross which the Church of necessity constitutes, inasmuch as the Church (while on earth) is composed of those in need of and called to Redemption. And if I exempt myself from a Church that always prays *Kyrie Eleison* "Lord have mercy," I must also hear these words of the Lord as meant for me: "Serpents, brood of vipers, how can you escape being condemned to hell?" (Mat 23:33). And how can I escape, if my self-righteousness, my conceit, my arrogance and spiritual snobbishness and smugness place me outside the redeeming love of God, of Christ? We know what our Lord thinks of those who are neither cold nor hot, who are lukewarm, who say to themselves that they are rich, have made a fortune, and have everything they want, never realizing that they are wretchedly and pitiably poor. "I will spit [them] out of my mouth," is the judgment of the Lord (Rev 3:15-17).

If to have seen Jesus Christ is to have seen the Father (John 14:9) if the Church, that is, if you and I, are to be manifestations and actualizations of "the mystery of God's love for men" (*Pastoral Constitution*, 45) how can this be unless the Church, like the Lord Himself, is visible? How can the apostolate be of the very nature of the Christian vocation (*Decree of the Apostolate of Lay People* 2) unless there is visible communication?

Whenever responsibility is shared, there must be a chain of command, and correspondingly a chain of obedience, otherwise there is chaos and destruction. There must be one to whom we can go who cannot err in matters of faith and morals, to whom the revelation of unseen realities is entrusted, and who administers the awesome, God-given power over the body of Christ and the power of the keys. Faultfinding and resentment against this hierarchical structure is always a temptation. Here, too, Christ's words hold: "If there is one of you who has not sinned, let him be the first to throw a stone" (John 8:7). Sin and rot in high places have been sad realities and are possibilities. But our response cannot but be that of Christ—tears and prayer (Heb 5:7; Luke 19:41), acceptance of the crosses which the Church of saints and sinners is so often made to bear, and also often causes. Christ was crucified by His own people, and as we are liable to be among those who crucify, we should also be among those who suffer this crucifixion.

We are on pilgrimage. May it be a journey from being an executioner of Christ to being crucified with Christ (Gal 2:19), "to make up all that has to be undergone by Christ for the sake of His Body, the Church" (Col 1:24).

47. The Responsibility of the Pilgrim Church

The Church is "the Mystical Body of Christ . . . the Church on earth, the pilgrim People of God here below, and the Church filled with heavenly blessings. . . ."

The first fruit of Redemption in our lives is baptism. But this is only the beginning of Redemption, of growth into union with God (John 17:21-23) and transformation into likeness of Christ (Rom 8:29). Through baptism we are justified, that is, restored to the right relationship with God, to the state of sanctifying grace, to sharing the divine nature (2 Pet 1:4). But this is only the beginning of sanctification, of growth in holiness (1 Thess 4:3). At the beginning of Christian existence, the life of faith, hope, and charity is still weak and precarious. Sin and sinful dispositions are still the prevailing realities. Self-indulgence is still very much at work and the results, as enumerated by St. Paul (Gal 5:19-21), are still a fearful possibility. The journey to sanctity, to that life eternalized at death into the beatific vision, is our task now.

This task has two aspects, for it is both personal and communal. The New Testament leaves no doubt that everyone is responsible for his own salvation: "What gain, then, is it for a man to have won the whole world and to have lost or ruined his very self?" (Luke 9:25). The description of the Last Judgment (Mat 25:31-46) is clearly based on the individual's personal behavior.

But we are also responsibly involved in the salvation and growth in holiness of others, of all others. The "Our Father" is in the plural. We are to pray for our enemies (Mat 5:44). To scandalize one child deserves drowning, "with a great millstone round his neck" (Mat 18:6). We are to be "fellow workers with God" (1 Cor 3:9), "ambassadors for Christ; it is as though God were appealing through us" (2 Cor 5:20).

Our pilgrimage is a common journey, and for better or for worse we do depend essentially upon one another. We are the Church. We are called to be the salt of the earth and the light of the world (Mat 5:13-16). The apostolate, that is, our active responsibility and work for each other's salvation, belongs essentially to our vocation as Christians (*Decree of the Apostolate of Lay People*, 2). Although there is a hierarchy of power and rank, there is another hierarchy of holiness, cutting across all visible order. And it is this latter hierarchy in which we all are to rise.

"The Church . . . clasping sinners to her bosom, at once holy and always in need of purification, follows constantly the path of penance and renewal" (*Dogmatic Constitution*, 8). We all are called to pray, "Forgive us our trespasses as we forgive." The world would soon turn into almost total hell, where, as Sartre wrote, hell would be "the other" (*Huis Clos*), almost all others, if mercy between men disappeared. And this hell-on-earth would become eternal, for "there will be judgment without mercy for those who have not been merciful themselves" (James 2:13).

And yet, "the Church is filled with heavenly blessings" (*Credo*). These come down upon us by the power of the sacraments, through the intercession of the Risen Lord (Heb 7:25) who becomes "for all who obey him the source of eternal salvation " (Heb 5:9). Grace is being pleaded for by the Mother of Christ and by all the other saints; by the prayers and continuing expiation of the Church on earth on her hazardous journey to Heaven. The members of the Church on Pilgrimage are recipients of the fruits of Redemption and, as "ambassadors for Christ" (2 Cor 5:20), they are "mediators of salvation" (Heinrich Fries, *Aspects of the Church*, p. 115). The more deeply Redemption brings about in us that redeemed unity for which our Lord prayed in His priestly prayer (John 17), the more we will "live by the truth and in love," and will be adding our own "strength, for each separate part to work according to its function. So the body grows until it has built itself up, in love" (Eph 4:15-16). What is true for the Church on Pilgrimage is true for each pilgrim, that "the fruitfulness of the apostolate . . . depends on our living union with Christ" (*Decree on the Apostolate of Lay People*, 4). "Whoever remains in me, with me in him, bears fruit in plenty; for cut off from me you can do nothing" (John 15:5).

As we grow in union with God and in likeness to Christ, we actually become revelations of God's "presence and His face" (*Dogmatic Constitution*, 50), and we become, in, and with the Church, "the universal sacrament of salvation"; we contribute to the Church's manifesting and actualizing the mystery of God's love for men" (*Pastoral Constitution*, 45). Therefore Guardini wrote: "Upon each one of us depends the degree of harmony achieved between the nature of the Church and her outward semblance, between her inner and outer aspects" (Romano Guardini, *The Church and the Catholic*, p. 116). Here lies our ultimate responsibility.

48. The Apostolate of Redemption

The Church is "the germ and the first fruits of the Kingdom of God, through which the work and the sufferings of Redemption are continued throughout human history. . . ."

Economic and political developments have made the whole world of men an interrleated whole. Whatever happens anywhere has repercussions somewhere else, often to the detriment of many. This happens on the visible level of human existence and can be studied by sociologists, economists, historians, and ecologists. The growing solidarity of mankind is increasingly recognized, leading us to question whether responsible action can sufficiently correct the prevailing massive irresponsibilities of selfishness and consequent thoughtlessness and stupidity to prevent chaos and destruction. Ultimately, however, man's life is determined by his freedom, by the possibilities that lie in his heart, from which on the one hand come "evil intentions: murder, adultery, fornication, theft, perjury, slander" (Mat 15:19), but from which also proceeds all that is noble, intelligent, generous— the things capable of redeeming the times. All this becomes discernible on the visible, natural level of history.

It is in and through the human heart that God in His Divine Providence seeks redeeming entrance into the world. "This may be a wicked age, but your lives should redeem it'' (Eph 5:16). And wherever God's creative, transforming graces are at work, wherever the birth of Christ in the heart of man is being prepared, the Church begins to exist in germ. If the germ takes root and grows upward into the light, faith becomes explicit and baptism is sought and received.

But at times, no credible contact with the Church is possible. Credibility may be lacking when true Christians are not known, when "innocent and genuine, perfect children of God" remain hidden "among a deceitful and underhand brood" (Phil 2:15) that is only pretending to be Christian. And yet, grace is everywhere. "Divine Providence [will not] deny assistance necessary for salvation to those who, without any fault of theirs, have not arrived at an explicit knowledge of God, and who, not without grace, strive to lead a good life" *(Dogmatic Constitution,* 16). Solidarity in grace is not confined to Catholics, but embraces all mankind. First comes the hidden germ, then the first fruits, then the "light of the world" (Mat 5:14; see also 5:16). Those who have received the light of faith in its Catholic integrity and are baptized into Christ (Gal 3:27) are thereby sent into the world (Mat 28:19) and given "the work of handing on this reconciliation" (2 Cor 5:18). "We are ambassadors for Christ; it is as though God were appealing through us" (2 Cor 5:20).

The Church is commissioned to reveal and actualize God's love for men *(Pastoral Constitution,* 45). When our Lord ended His priestly prayer to the Father with the words, "I have made your name ['the two names "Being" and "Love " expressing ineffably the same divine reality'—*Credo*] known to them and will continue to make it known" (John 17:26), He knew that He would be murdered the next day. The task of continuing to make the Father's name known is now done by Him through His Church, that is, through each Catholic. Each Catholic shares this responsibility. This apostolate, however hidden, is of the very nature of the Christian vocation *(Decree on the Apostolate of Lay People,* 2).

This apostolate is always and essentially a sharing in God's desire for "everyone to be saved and reach full knowledge of the truth" (1 Tim 2:4). It is also a sharing in Christ's expiation. It is the very heart of charity, this apostolic hope, actively hoping for the Kingdom of God to come and envelop all men. It involves all of us sharing in the patience of our God, who wants "nobody to be lost and everybody to be brought to change his ways" (2 Pet 3:9). Patience for us means waiting and suffering.

Prayer is the expression of our longing to become fit instruments of this apostolate. For we realize that "the fruitfulness of the apostolate . . . depends on our living union with Christ" *(Decree on the Apostolate of*

Lay People, 4). "Whoever remains in me, with me in him, bears fruit in plenty" (John 15:5). Prayer is also expression of this longing for the extension and intensification of God's Kingdom (where God prevails, to become finally and eternally "all in all" [1 Cor 15:28]. Expiation is to accept all suffering, all crosses as having their ultimate source in man's rebellion. As Christ always is the target of sin and became its victim in the Crucifixion, we, too, are to share, and thereby extend into the world, His response—one of redeeming love (John 13:34). It is our task to "resist evil and to conquer it with good" (Rom 12:21). With Him we share being the target and victim of sin accepted in loving expiation.

In our solidarity in sin and Redemption, we affect the spiritual level of the world, cutting across all distance of place and time. By sin, we lower it, by prayer and expiation we raise it. Prayer and expiation are the essential apostolate, the very heart of it. Without it, I am simply a "gong booming or a cymbal clashing" (1 Cor 13:1). It is the extension of God's Kingdom into, and through, the hearts of men which, in its growing solidarity, will transform history. Our longing for salvation for all, made real and effective by genuine prayer and the loving acceptance of expiatory crosses—this is how we become fellow workers of God (1 Cor 3:9) and true ambassadors of Christ (2 Cor 5:20). The outcome is hidden now: "What we are to be in the future has not yet been revealed; all we know is, that when it is revealed we shall be like Him because we shall see Him as He really is" (1 John 3:2).

49. The Splendor of the Faith

The Church looks for Redemption's "perfect accomplishment beyond time in glory."

"While She slowly grows to maturity, the Church longs for the completed Kingdom and, with all her strength, hopes and desires to be united in glory with her king" (*Dogmatic Constitution*, 5). The Church hopes with the hope rooted in love, the hope which is love unfulfilled. Therefore, although we are still on pilgrimage, we can still describe what it is to be a Christian, to long "for His Appearing" (2 Tim 4:8). "Come, Lord Jesus" (Rev 22:20) is our prayer for His Second Coming, but also a prayer that the longing the prayer expresses may increasingly be ours.

We must break out of the stifling prison of a spiritual vision that is confined to that narrow and disconnected sort of moralizing which destroys all joy and all anticipation of joy, a spirit not found in Scripture or liturgy, and which simply produces "mountains of boredom" (Alfred Delp, *Prison Meditations*, p. 113), if not an atheism of disgust with what is presented as the faith. The Incarnation, the Church, the Eucharist, all these are there for our sakes, to make us "partakers of the divine nature" (2 Pet 1:4). Jesus made it quite clear that His human-divine joy should become ours too. "I have told you this so that my own joy may be in you and your joy may be complete" (John 15:11). "While still in the world I say these things to share my joy with them to the full" (John 17:13).

Joy is the only reason for our existence; without it, human life would be a cruel absurdity. There is joy in the world, and to know, to seek, and to communicate joy is to nourish our longing for eternal life. To give joy is our supreme apostolic duty. To be given a glimpse of joy and innocence is a grace, an awakening of the memory of lost innocence and an invitation to regain this innocence, a promise that it can be regained.

How can we share in this longing for the blessed eternity for which we are created and which is the goal of our pilgrimage? Is it by accepting in the spirit of expiation the sufferings that come our way? St. Paul teaches us that "the troubles which are soon over, though they weigh little, *train* us for the carrying of a weight of eternal glory which is out of all proportion to them" (2 Cor 4:17; emphasis added). Is our effort to give joy and to alleviate suffering training us in that generosity and unselfishness without which we remain incapable of joy? In our own historic moment, is it not necessary to avoid, when seeking relaxation, the seduction of the stark ugliness that surrounds us, for example, to have simply no part in the obscene noises and gyrations which have become world-wide entertainment? Must we not consider escapes though drugs and sensationalism to be enemies of the Cross (Phil 3:18-21)? Purity of heart is to be sought because without it we shall not see God (Mat 5:9), nor would we want to see Him.

When beauty is little in evidence in the service of the liturgies, when resentment has injected into some celebrations what is obviously ugly, unworthy, even blasphemous, when fear and television have caused such great destruction of human relationships, human friendship, human love, the Christian is very much alone in seeking and finding glimpses of beauty that feed his longing for God, who is the source of all truth, goodness, and beauty. He may have to depend on his own reading, make the best of the liturgy if he has no access to worthy celebrations, and place his intelligence in the service of learning and contemplating divine truths by his own initiative. He must use his intelligence in the planning and revising of his spiritual life. In the liturgical texts (most of the time) and in carefully chosen reading, he will still find, the *Splendor of the Faith*, which he shares with the Apostles and the saints of all times. The wounds and warts in the appearance of the Church will be his cross, and he will remember that comfort is promised to those who mourn (Mat 5:5). He can be assured that holiness, the only thing that counts and lasts, will continue to flourish, "for nothing is impossible with God" (Luke 1:37). Our true life is hidden, because we have died, and now the life we have is "hidden with Christ in God" (Col 3:3).

50. The Sacraments

"In the course of time, the Lord Jesus forms His Church by means of the Sacraments emanating from His Plenitude."

It all begins with being baptized into the name—that is, into the very life—of the Father and of the Son and of the Holy Spirit (Mat 28:19; Gal 3:27). It is the beginning of sharing the divine nature (2 Pet 1:4). It is our becoming one with each other as we become one with the Son, who through baptism comes to dwell in us. And as the Son is eternally and immutably one with the Father in the Holy Spirit, baptism is the Blessed Trinity coming to live in me and I in Them (John 14:23). Baptism is the beginning of a union that is to grow in intensity, in its fruits of holiness, and in its apostolic, outreaching power.

The Church, "the Universal Sacrament of Salvation" (*Pastoral Constitution*, 45), is the instrument by which the Risen Lord now continues to draw all men to Himself (John 12:32), to draw us by a multitude of gifts or graces into that redeemed unity which will find its eternal consummation in the beatific vision. These gifts all involve inner transformations in man, transformations which can only be brought about by the creative power of God. Christ in His human Heart allots every grace to us (Eph 4:7). In His Sacred Heart "lives the fullness of divinity" (Col 2:9), as God possesses Jesus the Man in indestructible union, a union which nevertheless allows for dialogue between the Father and Jesus the Man, our only Mediator (1 Tim 2:5). Jesus prayed, "Father, I thank you for hearing my prayer. I knew indeed that you always hear me" (John 11:41-42); and "My Father . . . if it is possible, let this cup pass me by" (Mat 26:39). Therefore, because of His divine power, which is equally that of the Father and the Holy Spirit, "it follows then, that His power to save is utterly certain, since He is living forever to intercede for all who come to God through Him" (Heb 7:25).

And He is always heard (John 11:41).

It is this "power to save" which makes the sacraments visible manifestations and actualizations "of the mystery of God's love for men" (*Pastoral Constitution*, 45), a creative love that transforms and enables man on his journey to eternal life, love, and vision. "It is God, for His own loving purpose, who puts both the will and the action into you" (Phil 2:13).

It is grace that disposes and draws us toward the sacraments. It is by the gratuitous gifts of and through the sacraments that we, in turn, are enabled to believe, to hope, to love, since each sacrament in its specific effects is rooted in these three powers. In baptism, the three supernatural virtues are first infused. In confirmation, they are strengthened toward apostolic responsibilites, alerting and enabling us to meet apostolic needs and perform apostolic tasks. Confirmation is the Sacrament of Apostolic Hope.

In the Eucharist we are in vital, life-giving contact with the love of Christ, which was tested (Wis 2:10-20) once and for all when the Sin of the World found in Him its target and victim to do what sin intends—to destroy the God whose name is Love. The ordeal of the Crucifixion appears to the historical observer as the ultimate destruction of Jesus Christ. The victory of His redeeming love for us, His murderers, maintained in His Heart during the ordeal, in an inconceivable inner struggle, remained almost entirely hidden (Luke 23:34). And yet, while being crucified, He drew all men to Himself (John 12:32). His redeeming, transforming, forgiving, enabling, creative love went out to all men, even to those not yet born. And this love will continue to go out from the Heart of the Risen Christ until "everything is subjected to Him . . . so that God may be all in all" (1 Cor 15:28). Then His priestly prayer—that we may be one as He and the Father are one, with Jesus Christ in us and the Father in Him (John 17:22-23)—will have been fulfilled. This is how the Eucharist "forms [Christ's] Church" by the fullness of divinity" (Col 2:9), whose human Heart allots to each "his own share of grace" (Eph 4:7).

In the sacrament of penance and the sacred anointing of the sick, Christ, through His Church, repairs the destruction that sin continues to bring about in men's hearts whenever we accept the original temptation so fearfully alive in all of us—to rebel against the God whose names are Being and Love (*Credo*; Gen 3:1-5).

The sacraments of marriage and priesthood directly provide the power to build up the Church. The family, the "domestic Church" (*Dogmatic Constitution*, 11), is the foundation of the parish, of the diocese, of the Church, of a country; and these all together constitute the Church on Earth entrusted to the Vicar of Christ, to the bishops and priests, who obtain their necessary powers of building and repairing the Body of Christ from the sacrament of holy orders. Thus the seven sacraments nourish, replenish, and vivify the Church Militant.

51. A Share in the Paschal Mystery

Through the sacraments, the Church "makes her members participants in the Mystery of the Death and Resurrection of Christ, in the grace of the Holy Spirit who gives her life and movement."

"The divine design of salvation embraces all men" (*Credo*). "However great the number of sins committed, grace was even greater" (Rom 5:20). Grace is everywhere. But those who have already received the grace of faith and baptism can actually seek and request more grace through the sacraments, and likewise it is entrusted to men to administer and confer the sacraments. Whether these gifts place men into an irrevocable state, such as after baptism, confirmation, marriage, or holy orders, or whether they are infallible actualizations of transforming and redeeming graces, the sacraments make the recipients partakers of the Paschal Mystery, extending this life-giving Mystery both to them and through them.

The Paschal Mystery lies in this: In becoming Man, God in His Eternal Son became vulnerable in order to literally become the target of all sins and thus their victim. For sin desires the removal or destruction of God, of all traces of God in truth and goodness. This removal seemed to become possible when Christ revealed His identity and His mission. And when, finally, on Calvary, sin finished its task, God in Christ had thereby become totally involved in the Sin of the World, because sin found in Him its victim and could celebrate its triumph over God. Christ was slain by us. Evil had won its final victory. By our sins, we all share in the mystery of His death, since our sins helped to nail Him to the Cross in fulfillment of His mission. Sin is destruction of truth; it is lived falsehood. The Author of truth and life, dwelling among us as Man, became intolerable and had to be destroyed.

But the Paschal Mystery is above all the Mystery of victory and of Resurrection. After sin had been challenged and even as it achieved its goal, namely the death of Him who is "the Way, the Truth, and the Life" (John 14:6), sin was being conquered by the fidelity of God's love (2 Tim 2:13), a love that filled the same human Heart that Sin was allowed to break. This human-divine love, divine in its source, human in its vulnerability and in its lonely battle (Mat 27:46), was upheld in an inconceivable struggle "to the end" (John 13:1; see also 19:30). All this was accomplished in obedience to the Father (Mat 26:39, 42; Phil 2:8), out of Jesus' twofold love, for the Father and for sinners. The destruction brought about by sin and the apparent victory of sin coincided with the invisible, yet ultimate, victory of love—this is the Paschal Mystery. And thus the victorious love of Christ became the source of all Redemption through Resurrection and Ascension to Lordship. Now "all authority in Heaven and on earth" is His (Mat 28:18). "The last Adam has become a life-giving spirit" (1 Cor 15:45). Now Christ possesses the "power over all mankind" which the Father gave Him (John 17:2). Now the Risen Christ allots to "each one of us . . . his own share of grace" (Eph 4:7).

The unspeakable grace that we receive from faith and baptism—that is, the desire for the graces conferred by the sacraments—cannot be refused without upsetting the integrity of our spiritual life. This grace allows us to seek and infallibly find reconciliation and life directly at its source. But as already stated, the Paschal Mystery, extending its life-giving power to the recipient of a sacrament, draws him thereby more deeply into union with God and transforms him more profoundly into a likeness of Christ, and thereby into a more capable apostle. "The fruitfulness of the apostolate [of lay people] depends on their living union with Christ" (*Decree on the Apostolate of Lay People*, 4). "Whoever remains in Me, with Me in him, bears fruit in plenty" (John 15:5).

Here lies the road to eternal life for the Catholic. "The apostolate is lived in faith, hope, and charity poured out by the Holy Spirit into the hearts of all members of the Church" (*Decree on the Apostolate of Lay People*, 3). Being a Catholic is inseparable from being an apostle. It is always to share in the twofold movement—movement toward God and movement to carry God to men. "The Christian vocation is, of its nature, a vocation to the apostolate as well" (*Decree on the Apostolate of Lay People*, 2). The two commandments, constituting the dynamic of Christian life, to love God and to love each other as Christ loved us (John 13:34), make us active members of the Church. What Jesus Christ is for me He must also be through me. "We are ambassadors for Christ; it is as though God were appealing through us" (2 Cor 5:20).

We are called to be "participants in the Mystery of the Death and Resurrection of Christ" (*Credo*) through the transforming and enabling power of the Spirit of Christ. Through it we grow in union and in the apostolic capacity to receive and communicate truth and love. It all is said by St. Paul

"If we live by the truth and in love, we shall grow in all ways into Christ, who is the head by whom the whole body is fitted and joined together, every joint adding its own strength, for each separate part to work according to its function. So the body grows until it has built itself up, in love" (Eph 4:15-16).

52. The Church:
Holy, Yet Always in Need of Purification

The Church "is therefore holy, though she has sinners in her bosom, because she herself has no other life but that of grace: it is by living her life that her members are sanctified. . . ."

"The Church, clasping sinners to her bosom, at once holy and always in need of purification, follows constantly the path of penance and renewal" (*Dogmatic Constitution*, 8). It is a painful experience of those who have discovered the Catholic Church through the splendor of her saints, that the extent of evil seems to be as deep and as wide within the Church as outside of her. St. Paul's description of unredeemed man may well serve at certain times and in certain places as a description of Catholic regions, even of hierarchical, clerical, and religious life. These are his devastating words: "Remember, there was a time when we too were ignorant, disobedient and misled and enslaved by different passions and luxuries; we lived then in wickedness and ill will, hating each other and hateful ourselves" (Tit 3:3). But the actual amount of evil and good cannot be known, for holiness is self-effacing, while sin is loud and aggressive. The true Christian's life is "hidden with Christ in God" (Col 3:3). Salvation came into the world in the silence of the Annunciation and in the peace of Bethlehem, and the working of grace remains largely hidden, even from those in whom holiness is growing.

The members of the Church are not those who consider themselves perfect. The "perfect" could not pray *Kyrie eleison*, "Lord have mercy," for, according to their own judgment, they need no mercy. The "perfect," who do not really exist, would pray like the Pharisee: "I thank you, God, that I am not grasping, unjust, adulterous like the rest of mankind" (Luke 18:11). But the Pharisee could not pray the "Our Father" nor sing the *Agnus*

Dei. To him, Jesus could not come as Redeemer. He could not answer the call to repentance (Mark 1:15). If you say to yourself, "I am rich, I have made a fortune, and have everything I want," you do not realize that "you are wretchedly and pitiably poor, and blind, and naked too" (Rev 3:17), even less so if you think that you are spiritually successful. The "ninety-nine virtuous men who have no need of repentance" (Luke 15:7) do not exist. And the greater the purity of one's heart, the deeper one's knowledge of God (Mat 5:8), the greater is one's "unhappiness . . . not to be one of the saints" (Leon Bloy, *The Woman Who Was Poor*, p 356).

The Church on earth is an interplay of longing for God and of His coming. It is the asking and the being given, the seeking and the finding, the knocking and the door being opened (Mat 7:7). It is that poverty of spirit without which the Kingdom of Heaven cannot be entered (Mat 5:3). The Church is alive among the baptized when the Mind of Christ begins to grow in them when readiness to empty oneself begins to be their form of life (Phil 2:5-8), when all they want to know is "Christ and the power of His Resurrection and to share His sufferings by reproducing the pattern of His death" (Phil 3:10). And the pattern of His Death is to allow oneself, in obedience to God, to be target and victim of sin, to suffer and to mourn. This may be by being the object of persecution and calumny, because it is to those who suffer thus that the Kingdom of Heaven is promised (Mat 5:10, 11). It may be, and this is always with us in varying degrees unless we seek escape elsewhere, by being given the grace of compassion with the victims of sin, to "be sad with those in sorrow" (Rom 12:15). Because "if one part is hurt, all parts are hurt with it" (1 Cor 13:26). For "blessed are those who mourn, for they shall be comforted" (Mat 5:4). These are the birthpangs of the Church which we, as Church, are invited to share (John 16:20-21; Gal 4:19). For to be Church, to be members of Christ, we must follow Him to the Cross by a crucified life. We must share the grief of Christ weeping over Jerusalem because the city, like Christendom ever since, "did not recognize [the] opportunity when God offered it!" (Luke 19:41-44). We must learn to place ourselves within the history of man's rebellion and salvation—it is "the Cross of our Lord Jesus Christ, through whom the world is crucified to me, and I to the world" (Gal 6:14).

In this way we share in the redeeming Cross of Christ and increasingly become recipients of Redemption and instruments of Christ's victorious love now radiating from His glorified Sacred Heart. It is our call to expiation—to lovingly allow ourselves to be victims of sin—"to make up all that has still to be undergone by Christ for the sake of His body, the Church" (Col 1:24). It is our readiness to "fulfill the Law of Christ" by carrying each other's burdens and failures (Gal 6:2)—to pick up the crosses shifted onto Christ and His Church by every sin. For to commit sin always involves the refusal of a cross: the cross of not sinning. And every refusal of a cross is always leaving the cross still to be taken up in expiation by someone else, somewhere, sometime.

The Church emanates from Him who is the Truth and the Life (John 14:6). To Truth and Life, we, as Church members, are called, for "it is by living her life" of truth and expiation, "that her members are sanctified" (*Credo*).

53. Removing Ourselves from the Life of the Church

"It is by removing themselves from [the Church's] life that [her members] fall into sins and disorders that prevent the radiation of her sanctity."

There are innumerable ways of removing oneself from the life of the Church. Some "will keep up the outward appearance of religion but will have rejected the inner power of it" (2 Tim 3:5). Others will retain the name of Christian, but will break away from the Church, and thereby indicate their hostility or rationalize their breaking away in condescending benevolence. There is no lack of subtle prevarications. Some may simply find the Church incompatible with a life style they have chosen, or the Church may find the life style professed incompatible with continued membership. Whatever the reasons, whether honestly given or hidden in inner or outer confusion, the unhappy person is cut off from "the only genuine form of human existence, its way of life dictated at once by man's deepest nature and by divine revelation" (Romano Guardini, *The Church and the Catholic*, p. 68).

The heart of man is hidden, and it is utter presumption to assess degrees of guilt. The loss of an integral faith that includes the Catholic Church is an indescribable tragedy. The possibility of scandal given by Catholics, however, is greater than we care to admit. What Vatican II says of causes of atheism can well be involved in someone's leaving the Church: "Believers can have more than a little to do with the rise of atheism. To the extent that they . . . fail in their religious, moral, or social life, they must be said to conceal rather than to reveal the true nature of God and of religion" (*Pastoral Constitution*, 19). Self-righteous condemnation of one who has broken with the Church is really a denial of mystery and a presumption of knowledge that only God possesses. Even psychological analysis, unless done in great humility, is harmful, if not outright insolent. And if this kind of insolence reduces its victim to the level of a biological specimen to be analyzed, it could be equivalent to that form of contempt which is close to hatred. "To hate your brother is to be a murderer" (1 John 3:15).

When we ourselves are tempted to part from the Church, we must cling to the revealed fact that God's grace is sufficient (2 Cor 12:9). But who are we to condemn others for not acting on the level of heroic sanctity? Who knows the wounded heart of man? Rather, we must allow ourselves to be wounded and mourn with St. Paul when he thought of the blindness of his own people. "My sorrow is so great, my mental anguish so endless, I would willingly be condemned . . . if it could help my brothers of Israel, my own flesh and blood" (Rom 9:2-3). And is not everyone my brother, my own flesh and blood?

It can require heroic fidelity, a thorough purification of our hope, to remain a Catholic. For to remain a Catholic is to hold onto the belief in Divine Providence, the belief that to those who set their heart "on His kingdom first, and on His righteousness [holiness], all these other things will be given . . . as well" (Mat 6:33). The "other things" are in this case the strength to remain faithful, without sliding into presumption or despair.

At times our fidelity may be tested because the Church cannot really take sides in a struggle where both sides are committed to immoral means, where brutality is part of the program, where terror is a policy accepted by both sides. "The Church has but one sole purpose—that the Kingdom of God may come and the salvation of the human race may be accomplished" (*Pastoral Constitution*, 45). Divine Providence works in hidden ways, and time is really unimportant, since the ultimate outcome lies beyond time. "With the Lord, 'a day' can mean a thousand years, and a thousand years is like a day. The Lord is not being slow to carry out His promises, as anybody else might be called slow; but He is being patient with you all, wanting nobody to be lost and everybody to be brought to change his ways" (2 Pet 3:8-9). Divine Providence is the blending, in the utter simplicity of the divine essence, of omnipotence, infinite knowledge, and wisdom, in the service of God's mercy. And this mercy, now filling the Sacred Heart of Jesus, the glorified Lord, takes its initiative from this human Heart, which was broken by our sins, and yet remained faithful, continuing to draw all men to Himself (John 12:32) while sustaining the murderous onslaught of the Sin of the World. "His power to save is utterly certain, since He is living forever to intercede for all who come to God through Him" (Heb 7:25). And He is always heard by the Father (John 11:41).

When tempted to give up on the Church, we must recall that nothing "can ever come between us and the love of God made visible in Christ Jesus our Lord" (Rom 8:39). Then, in us "Loyalty reaches us from earth and Righteousness leans down from heaven" (Ps 85:11); and with regard to the Church we will say to the Church what Peter said to our Lord: "To whom shall we go? You have the words of eternal life" (John 6:68). For the Catholic Church alone is "the universal sacrament of salvation, at once manifesting and actualizing the mystery of God's love for men" (*Pastoral Constitution*, 45).

54. Sin and Expiation

"This is why [the Church] suffers and does penance for these offenses, of which she has the power to heal her children through the Blood of Christ and the Gift of the Holy Spirit."

Identification of all morality with sexual morality has encouraged us to remain blind to the realm of evil in other areas of life. And since crime and sin make it easier to succeed in life, we have further crippled our moral sense by accepting a corrupted version of the Puritan tradition that success is a sign of God's approval. How else can we explain our litanies of thanks embellishing our public rhetoric, thanking God for our wealth? Is this not preferring this world, of which the Lord's kingdom is not (John 18:36)? Is it not cultivating the wisdom of this world, which "is foolishness to God" (1 Cor 3:19)? Is it not the theology of Satan which was offered to our Lord on a mountain, when Satan showed Him the kingdom of the world, saying, "I will give you all these . . . if you fall at my feet and worship me" (Mat 4:9)? And so we Christians have cultivated the art of rationalizing our crimes—calumnies, murder with and without actual killing (1 John 3:15), envy and greed on the personal and national level, priviledge, ambition, power for its own sake, vanity, intrigue. And who would dare to say that the "world" has not entered the Church? This was already evident in the first century (1 Cor 5:1-13; 2 Cor 12:20; Gal 1:6-9). And is not even the history of the Church at times a depressing account of the apparent victories of man's selfishness and treason—visible as was the victory of evil on Calvary? Is not the church's history full of monuments to vanity, the seduction of power attained through compromise—while sanctity largely remained as invisible as the victory of Christ's redeeming love on Calvary when sin had its hour. "This is your hour; this is the reign of darkness" (Luke 22:53).

In recent years the spirit of nagging, of mocking the sacred, and of public rebellion has become a sad fact in the Church in the United States. Authority, meant for the protection of the faith and of the weak, has largely been suspended. Some Catholic educational institutions have accepted deception in the teaching of doctrine, have allowed defiance of the teaching of Christ in His Church, and have helped in the destruction of the consciences of the students entrusted to them by tolerating such options as co-ed housing or by presenting abortion as a valid option, along with many other sins. As Msgr. George Kelly wrote, *The Battle for the American Church* is not yet decided. The fact that silence is replacing the voice of authority points to the working of powers of evil beyond human capacity. The hidden suffering this continues to cause must be enormous. The grief of believing parents, friends, priests, and religious at what has happened is deep. Perhaps it is the beginning of an expiation to bear fruit now and in the future.

To commit sin always involves the refusal of a cross, the cross of not sinning. Divine justice, the mystery of God's mercy, requires that every cross that is inflicted find a victim, even if the cross is at first rejected. To become expiation, the cross must by taken up, either by the sinner in a spirit of penance and expiation, or by someone else out of love for the sinner, even if unknown. Christ has taken on every cross refused by sin throughout the entire history of mankind, and all sins committed and still to be committed have already found their intended target and victim in Him. But the historical implementation of Christ's expiation, achieved through the absorption of sin by goodness (Rom 12:21) still requires that men, in their own bodies, accept the necessary suffering "to make up all that has still to be undergone by Christ for the sake of His Body, the Church" (Col 1:24). Christ's expiation of Sin, carried out through the expiation of His members, must permeate all human history.

Romano Guardini wrote: "Christ lives on in the Church, but Christ Crucified. One might almost venture to suggest that the defects of the Church are His Cross." And the purpose of these defects "is perhaps this—they are permitted to crucify our faith, so that we may sincerely seek God and our salvation, not ourselves'' (*The Church and the Catholic*, p. 55).

As all human suffering has its ultimate source in sin, acceptance of suffering in love as expiation is always possible. It is the Law of Christ that we are to bear the burden of one another's failings (Gal 6:2, Knox translation). In this manner, all can become ''ambassadors for Christ'' the Redeemer (2 Cor 5:20). Is this not the love Christ had, and continues to have, for us and for all, and which we are commanded to practice (John 13:34, 15:12)? Does not this love require us to take up our cross and thus to follow in His footsteps (Mat 10:38)? Is this love not exemplified in the last Beatitude, to be ''persecuted in the cause of right'' (Mat 5:10)? Is it not the Mind of Christ, to empty oneself even to the point of ''accepting death, death on a cross'' (Phil 2:8)?

And here we may see a possible light in the darkness of suffering of an ever growing part of humanity—in gulags, by starvation, by suffering indignities, in hopelessness, through human design or simply unintended circumstances. Even if they do not know of the Sin of the World having already crucified the Living God in His humanity, as they linger on and die, hoping against hope, are the suffering and long-suffering masses not expiating the ocean of sin that torments them? What can be said? ''How impossible to penetrate [God's] motives or understand His methods!'' And in faith and hope all we can do is to adore, for ''all that exists comes from Him; all is by Him and for Him. To Him be glory forever! Amen'' (Rom 11:33, 36).

55. The Church and the Jewish People

The Church is "heiress of the divine promises and daughter of Abraham according to the Spirit, through that Israel whose Scriptures She lovingly guards, and whose Patriarchs and Prophets she venerates. . . ."

The most shocking and explicit revelation of the potential for sin is the latent and often flowering anti-Semitism among Christians throughout the centuries of Christian history. It prepared the ground for the Holocaust, possibly the vilest of all planned and organized crimes in the history of mankind, and committed largely by baptized people in the very heart of Christendom. And this happened despite the fact that St. Paul assures us that the Jews, "as the chosen people . . . are still loved by God, loved for the sake of their ancestors" (Rom 11:28). "They were adopted as sons, they were given the glory and the covenants; the Law and the ritual were drawn up for them, and the promises were made to them. They are descended from the patriarchs, and from their flesh and blood came Christ who is above all, God forever blessed! Amen" (Rom 9:4-5). "Anti-Semitism . . . is the most horrible blow yet suffered by our Lord in His ever continuous Passion, it is the bloodiest and the most unforgivable because He receives it upon His Mother's face and at the hand of Christians" (Leon Bloy, *Pilgrim of the Absolute*, p. 268).

The *Catechism of the Council* teaches: "Should anyone inquire why the Son of God underwent His most bitter Passion, he will find that besides the guilt inherited from our first parents, the principal causes were the vices and crimes wich have been perpetrated from the beginning of the world to the present day and those which will be committed to the end of time." The catechism continues by saying that "those who wallow in sin and iniquity crucify themselves again the Son of God, as far as in them lies, and make a mockery of Him. This guilt seems more enormous in us than in the Jews" who were involved in the actual Crucifixion.

The *Catechism of the Council of Trent* was quoted by a Jewish scholar who approached Pope John XXIII to ask him to do something to stop Christians from calling Jews "Christ-killers"—and his request was successful.

Jacques Maritain saw "the deepest impulse toward that monstrosity—Christians who are anti-Semites. They are seeking an alibi for their innermost sense of guilt, for the death of Christ of which they want to clear themselves: but if Christ did not die for their sins, then they flee from the mercy of Christ! In reality they want not to be redeemed. Here is the most secret and vicious root, by virtue of which anti-Semitism dechristianizes Christians, and leads them to paganism" (*The Range of Reason*, "The Christian Teaching of the Story of the Crucifixion," p. 132).

Perhaps we may add another reason. In the Jews, the Christian meets the victims of Christian persecution; he meets a people wounded, crucified for centuries. The Jews, in bearing the marks of crucifixion, marks that do not lend themselves to ingratiate them in a hedonistic, arrogant world, remind Christians of their own frequent refusal to live the eighth Beatitude. Called to be "crucified with Christ" as the necessary condition for living now, not one's own self-seeking life, but living "with the life of Christ" who then can live in them (Gal 2:19-20), as St. Paul teaches us all, many a Christian has refused the Cross and preferred to join Christ's executioners by crucifying Him in His brothers—"Insofar as you neglected to do this to one of the least of these, you neglected to do it to me" (Mat 25:45). What holds in this context for sins of omission, holds equally for all sins committed against others.

St. Paul ends his meditation on the mystery of Israel and on their mysterious blindness with the amazing revelation that "God has imprisoned all men in their own disobedience only to show mercy to all mankind" (Rom 11:32). Yet Christians dare to give reasons for their crimes against the people from whose "flesh and blood came Christ who is above all" (Rom 9:5)—the Jews did or do or are or were or caused or control this or that. These Christians imply that they themselves are without sin. God's judgment on them was pronounced long ago: "If there is one of you who has not sinned, let him be the first to throw a stone. . . ." (John 8:7).

And St. James has these fearful words: "There will be judgment without mercy for those who have not been merciful themselves; but the merciful need have no fear of judgment" (James 2:13).

56. The Church:
Teaching, Sanctifying, and Ruling

The Church "is founded upon the Apostles and [hands] on from century to century their ever-living word and their powers as pastors in the Successor of Peter and the bishops in communion with him."

"The Church has but one sole purpose—that the Kingdom of God may come and the salvation of the human race may be accomplished" (*Pastoral Constitution*, 45). To restore fallen and still rebellious man to union with God through the Father's Eternal Word extended to us by the Incarnation, to intensify our sharing in "the divine nature," and to enable man "to escape corruption in a world that is sunk in vice" (2 Pet 1:4)—these are the tasks of the Church. It all began with the Apostles, chosen, initiated, empowered, and sent, "so that sharing in Christ's power, they might make all people His disciples and sanctify and govern them" (*Dogmatic Constitution*, 19). They became His disciples when He, the Truth, came to live in them as truth. He made them capable of grasping revealed truth and living by it, so that the teaching of truth would find its necessary illumination in their lives, which, if holy, show to men God's presence and His face (*Dogmatic Constitution*, 50).

They became administrators of the channels of sanctification, the sacraments, by a true sharing of Christ's human-divine power. Thus He, who is *the Life*, becomes uniquely present in the Apostles and their successors. "In the person of the bishops . . . the Lord Jesus Christ, supreme high priest, is present in the midst of the faithful" (*Dogmatic Constitution*, 21).

Christ gave the Apostles the duty and power to rule, to make laws, and to impose sanctions; this commission to govern extends Christ as *the Way*, through them. Whatever Peter (or His successor) and the bishops in union with him "bind on earth shall be considered bound in Heaven" (Mat 16:19). This is the power of the keys. The bishops are to administer the Law so that they can be educators and protectors of the weak. Also they are to create and strengthen the structures that form the foundation of the Christian community.

To the Church Teaching corresponds the light of *faith*; to the Church Sanctifying, the dynamism, the reaching out to God in *hope*; to the Church Governing, the leading of the people into Christian communities, the defense of these communities, the maintenance and strengthening of these communities that are the building blocks of the living Church—all of which requires *charity* of both those governing and those governed. For charity is the foundation and fruit of all community. The smallest community, the family (*Decree on the Apostolate of Lay People*, 11) is rooted in love, and is the source of the love that is meant to radiate into the wider communities.

These are the powers and responsibilities given to the Apostles: first, the power to proclaim Truth, that is, revelation of realities hidden in God and His Providence. These are to be proclaimed and lived by the Apostles. When they "live by the truth and in love, [they will] grow in all ways into Christ" (Eph 4:15). From this union flows their apostolic power, and the power of their prayer, to which they are bound—the Divine Office. It is eminently true of them—the foundations of the building which is built on "the Apostles and prophets" (Eph 2:20)—that if they remain in Christ, and His words remain in them, they may ask what they will, and they will get it (John 15:7). But as history, past and present, so painfully reminds us, infidelity and spiritual rot and gross neglect of duty can exist among the successors of the Apostles. Cut off from Christ they can do nothing (John 15:5), and are liable "to be thrown in the fire and burnt" (John 15:6).

The second power and responsibility given to the Apostles is to extend, cultivate, and protect the Church's sacraments and her life of prayer.

Together, these are the Sanctifying and Worshipping Church. Through the liturgy, the Church receives "a foretaste of that heavenly liturgy which is celebrated in the Holy City of Jerusalem toward which we journey as pilgrims, where Christ is sitting at the right hand of God" (*The Constitution on the Sacred Liturgy*, 8). The liturgy is the celebration of hope, the apostolate in which all apostolic power and zeal finds its strength. It is worship of "the Father in spirit and truth" (John 4:23). It is of some significance that two of the greatest works of music, Bach's B-Minor Mass and Beethoven's *Missa Solemnis*, are glorifications of the majestic texts of the Common of the Mass, asking for mercy (*Kyrie*), expressing pure adoration (*Gloria*), professing the faith (*Credo*), and asking for peace (*Agnus Dei*).

The third power of the Church is to rule by proclaiming Christ's Law, to "refute falsehood, correct error, call to obedience" (2 Tim 4:2). Rulership is an aspect of Christ, and is now the Church's mission that provokes the most intense opposition, both within and without. It is the occasion of witnessing, or martyrdom.

This threefold function of Christ, to be Priest, Prophet, and King, is now given to the bishops if they are in union with Christ's Vicar, the Bishop of Rome. The reality of the Church's threefold power and task is revealed. It is an article of faith and demands our adherence in faith. That human failings at times may test this faith has been the bitter experience of many. But our faith is not to "depend on human philosophy but on the power of God" (1 Cor 2:5). We must hold onto the fact that "God's foolishness"—His entrusting Himself to men as much in need of Redemption as those whom they shepherd—"is wiser than human wisdom, and God's weakness"—which allowed us to crucify Him—"is stronger than human strength" (1 Cor 1:25). And with Peter we ask and profess, "Lord, to whom shall we go? You have the message of eternal life" (John 6:68). But now He teaches, sanctifies, and rules through and in the Church.

57. The Teaching Church

"Perpetually assisted by the Holy Spirit, [the Church] has the charge of guarding, teaching, explaining, and spreading the Truth which God revealed in a then veiled manner by the Prophets, and fully by the Lord Jesus."

(Read Mat 13:4; Heb 4:12-13; Rev 3:14-22.)

"At various times in the past and in various different ways, God spoke to our ancestors through the prophets; but in our time, the last days, He has spoken to us through His Son" (Heb 1:1-2). To "make disciples of all the nations . . . and to teach them to observe all the commands" (Mat 28:19-20) is the commission Christ gave to the Apostles and thereby to the Church, "a building that has the Apostles and prophets for its foundations" (Eph 2:20). All Catholics are the Church. Being the Church on Earth involves the task of manifesting and actualizing "the mystery of God's love for men" (*Pastoral Constitution*, 45). Everyone, however, remains also the object of the Church's ministry. Each Catholic is both a channel and a recipient of God's truth revealed partially by the prophets and "fully, by the Lord Jesus" (*Credo*, above). We are all required to receive and reveal by our lives, often by our words, the *truth* revealed to the Church by Christ.

Hans Urs von Balthazar wrote, "He who does not first listen to God, has nothing to say to the world" (*Who is a Christian?* p. 78). But all Christians, by baptism and confirmation, are included among those commissioned " to make disciples of all nations . . . and to teach them to observe all the commands" Christ gave us (Mat 28:19-20). Commanded to love as Christ loved (John 13:34); to conform our mind so that it is "the same as [that of] Christ Jesus" (Phil 2:5) who emptied Himself from Godhead to "a thing despised and rejected by men, a man of sorrows" (Isa 53:3); to be hated by the world (John 15:18-19); and to become worthy of the Lord by taking one's specific cross and following His footsteps (Mat 10:38)—this is the manner of teaching all nations by living and by dying daily (1 Cor 15:31).

All men are called to become children of God by becoming "sons in the Son" (*Pastoral Constitution*, 22), to be baptized into the Blessed Trinity (Mat 28:19). Thus in sharing "the divine nature" (2 Pet 1:4), we are to become Christlike in disposition of mind and will, by a life in accord with God's demands, recognized in faith, ventured into in hope, and thus in accord with charity. Such a life brings an understanding of Christ and the living presence of Him whose members we are, whose "true images" we are intended to become (Rom 8:29), into the world.

If Pope Paul reminds us that the Church "has the charge of guarding and teaching . . . the Truth . . . revealed . . . fully by the Lord Jesus" (*Credo*), he means not only the formal teaching in pulpit and classroom, but also the teaching our lives are to supply. Without our attempt to live and love as Christ lived and loved, verbal teaching loses its credibility and becomes ridiculous, if not scandalous. This we ought to remember when, at times with good reasons, we criticize the local Church for tolerating the teaching of false, misleading, even destructive distortions of the true faith, both in doctrine and in morals. St. John's reminder at the end of his First Epistle, to "guard against false gods" (1 John 5:21), still holds. Every distortion of teaching radically distorts our thinking about God. It falsifies the identity of the one, only, living, and true God, whose "word is something alive and active [and who can] judge the secret emotions and thoughts" (Heb 4:12); it changes Him from Redeemer and Judge into a convenient Idol that allows us to be comfortable in our sin, since this Idol guarantees our own selfish vested interest. To this Idol, we can pray, "I thank you, God, that I am not . . . like the rest of mankind" (Luke 18:11), but we cannot pray, *Kyrie eleison*, "Lord have mercy." If we reach this state, we have rationalized our mediocrity and perverted our dispositions: we are no longer attuned to the truth that is meant to liberate us—"If you make my word your home, you will indeed be my disciples, you will learn the truth and the truth will make you free" (John 8:31-32). The parable of the sower (Mat 13:18-23) shows how precarious the truth is among us, how endangered by the multiple ways we do violence to God's word; it shows how arrogant we can become in our selectiveness, as we receive the word of God.

As the Incarnate Word came and lived among us in weakness and gentleness, His word is equally exposed to man's violence and lies. Defenseless as the Child in Bethlehem, threatened by Herod, and again rendered helpless by our hardness of heart, and mocked while on the Cross, His truth—the truth of Him who is the Way, the Truth, the Life, and the Resurrection (John 14:6; 11:25)—is easily defaced and destroyed. The "rich soil" (Mat 13:23) of humility and an "abiding sorrow for sin" (Frederick William Faber, *Growth in Holiness*, Ch. XIX) requires fidelity in seeking, without which we are told we will not find (Mat 7:7-11).

In the continuity of the truth proclaimed by the Church with that fidelity which makes the Church Teaching reveal the Lord Teaching (who is Truth), we are witnessing a perpetual miracle. The Holy Spirit will be with the Church forever, "the Spirit of the truth whom the world can never receive since it neither sees nor knows Him"; but whom we know, because He is with us, He is in us (John 14:16-17). May God give us the courage to hold on to Him who is the Way, Truth, Life and Resurrection. "I believe, help my unbelief" (Mark 9:24).

58. Preparing to Receive the Word of God

"We believe all that is contained in the Word of God written or handed down, and that the Church proposes for belief as divinely revealed, whether by a solemn judgment or by the ordinary and universal magisterium."

He who eternally and immutably is the "Image of the invisible God" (Col 1:15), Himself equally invisible, "true God from true God" (Nicene Creed)—He, the Word who "was God [who] was with God in the beginning . . . through [whom] all things came to be" (John 1:1-2)—He "was made flesh [and] lived among us" (John 1:14). Then His glory was seen, "the glory that is His as the only Son of the Father" (John 1:14). He, the Eternal Word, became the Father's Word to men by being Man. "The only Son, who is nearest to the Father's heart," has made known to us God whom no one has ever seen (John 1:18). He, "the Word, who is life," who "has existed since the beginning," eternally—Him "we have heard . . . have seen with our own eyes . . . have watched and touched with our hands" (1 John 1:1). Thus wrote St. John of himself and the other Apostles, who, with the prophets, are the foundations of the building which is the Church (Eph 2:20). We, too, "in Him [that is, Jesus Christ] are being built into a house [the Church] where God lives, in the Spirit" (Eph 2:22). From Christ, through the Apostles, comes to us the "Word of God written or handed down" (*Credo*). It is the content of our faith.

Although the content of the faith comes to us clothed in words, what is actually brought to us is the reality of which the words, of which the language is only the sign. And this reality—God, the Father, the Son, and the Holy Spirit, the God whose names are "Being and Love" (*Credo*), Creator, and, for me, Redeemer—this divine reality actually shines through the revealing language. And this language, above all that of Holy Scripture, has the unmistakable tone of credibility, the witness of truth, in itself. It possesses a glow that does not come from the artistry of the author, but from the divine character of its content. As a human face, as human eyes may reveal the heart, the past and the present, as even a man's manner of walking may reveal humility or arrogance, Holy Scripture, liturgy, sacred art, and the very atmosphere of a truly Christian community, share in the life of the Church by "manifesting and actualizing the mystery of God's love for men" (*Pastoral Constitution*, 45). Holiness in its sacramental source and channel—Scripture, liturgy, any community of men reflecting the unity of Father and Son (John 17:21-22)—shines through. It is up to me to perceive and welcome it.

Is the Heart of Christ not revealed in the invitation, "Come to me, all you who labor and are overburdened, and I will give you rest. Shoulder my yoke and learn from me, for I am gentle and humble in heart, and you will find rest for your souls" (Mat 11:28-29)? Or in the words to the Apostles paralyzed by fear in anticipation of disaster, "Do not let your hearts be troubled. Trust in God still, and trust in me" (John 14:1)? Likewise, the following Scripture passages would seem to convey divine power and peace: Rev 21:1-4; Rom 8:35-39; Jas 2:13; John 17:26; Luke 13:34-35; Isa 55:6-13; Ps 103. And as we continue to seek God, we will, as promised (Mat 7:7-8), find Him in more and more of Scripture, in liturgy, in the lives of saints, in the Church teaching, ruling, and in her fruitfullness as she is instrumental in producing holiness.

But we will remain deaf and blind to the revelations of God unless we are ready to receive the Mind of Christ, the willingness to empty ourselves, to serve, and to bear our specific crosses (Phil 2:5-8; Mat 10:37-39). We must be convinced of the depth of God's wisdom and knowledge—and that it is "impossible to penetrate His motives or understand His methods" (Rom 11:33). Each of us "must learn to be a fool . . . because the wisdom of this world is foolishness to God" (1 Cor 3:18). "For God's foolishness is wiser than human wisdom, and God's weakness is stronger than human strength" (1 Cor 1:25). The outcome usually remains hidden, and will come to light only in the resurrection.

Without these expectations forming the content of our hope, Scripture and liturgy, and the life and teaching of the Church will remain, for us, superficial. They might perhaps be of historical interest, or even the subject of fascination, but they will be external. The light of faith will not penetrate to God, God will not shine "in our minds to radiate the light of the knowledge of God's glory, the glory on the face of Christ" (2 Cor 4:6), if our hope is not formed and transformed by the revealed expectations just mentioned. Only if we are ready to lose this life for His sake will we find true life (Mat 10:39). Nothing must usurp the place of God whom alone we must serve (Mat 4:10). Only then will we become able to "believe all that is contained in the Word of God written or handed down, and that the Church proposes for belief as divinely revealed" (*Credo*).

59. Papal Infallibility

"We believe in the infallibility enjoyed by the Successor of Peter when he teaches ex cathedra as Pastor and Teacher of all the Faithful, and which is assured also to the Episcopal Body when it exercises with him the supreme magisterium."

When we speak of the divine gift of faith, we do not only mean the ability to grasp revealed reality in a living way. The gift of faith implies, above all, the gift of the very realities that constitute the content of the faith. And this reminds us of the third aspect of the gift—that these realities are not only the eternal, immutable realities, the Living God, Father, Son, and Holy Spirit, but also the realities which are a gift of God Himself. Such is the drama of the stormy preparation in the history of Israel. But it all found its center and meaning in that supreme gift, when the Eternal Son of God, not clinging to His equality with God, "emptied Himself" to become Man, servant, and the crucified victim of man's sins (Phil 2:6-8).

To the Church are now entrusted not only certain powers over the realities that constitute the gift of God, above all, Jesus Christ in the Eucharist, but also the truth of it all, and the power and responsibility of guarding the very reality of God's graces and the knowledge of it, and to proclaim these glorious gifts and to carry the gifts and the knowledge of it to all men, to all nations (Mat 28:19).

Not even twenty-five years after the first Pentecost, St. Paul already had to warn the Galatians "that if anyone preaches a version of the Good News different from the one already preached to [them] he is to be condemned" (Gal 1:8). False prophets and falsehood, brazenly taught, have been with the Church at all times (1 John 4:1-6). In our times, the Church's moral teachings are being attacked, often in the name of compassion. The factual distortions in these attacks are so brazen that one might assume that Hitler's *Mein Kampf* had been the handbook of their authors. Hitler taught in word and action that when a lie, however outrageous, is repeated often enough, it will be believed. The Church's attackers confirm this principle, drawing, in their warfare against truth, a reckless caricature of the Church, past and present, which is too often uncritically accepted through ignorance and the sort of blindness that comes from proud resentment of the Church. And to reject the lies of many a so-called Catholic Theologian, even when these lies contradict the faith of the Church and are clearly proven to be lies by actual examination, is considered to be not nice and therefore uncharitable. And since "being nice" is often considered the essence of charity, especially by those whose morality is defined in the sphere of public relations, such lies remain unopposed, and they gradually undermine and destroy enough of the content of the faith and revelation, that the inner cohesion is destroyed and the faith becomes incoherent and hardly worth living or dying for.

Power and authority are given exclusively for service. Our Lord Himself came to serve (Mat 20:28). Bishops and the Supreme Pontiff "are commissioned to perpetuate the work of Christ, the eternal Pastor"; "in this Church of Christ the Roman Pontiff, as the successor of Peter, to whom Christ entrusted the care of His sheep and lambs [John 21:15-17], has been granted by God supreme, full, immediate, and universal power in the care of souls" (*Decree on the Pastoral Office of Bishops in the Church*, 2). History has made the need for a Supreme Shepherd quite clear. Therefore faith recognizes the work of Divine Providence—the infinite power and wisdom of God in the service of His mercy, of His redeeming and transforming love—in the gift of infallibility enjoyed by the Supreme Pontiff—that he cannot err when teaching solemnly in matters of faith and morals. Instead of timidly defending this marvelous gift of papal infallibility, we ought to glory in it as a safeguard of God's gifts. If it seems an obstacle in ecumenical conversations, like any other reality not part of another church's deposit of faith, it must be seen and presented as an additional gift of God. If discussion gets bogged down by some historical cases that present a true difficulty, Cardinal Newman's statement that a thousand difficulties do not make a doubt (*Discourses Addressed to Mixed Congregations*, "Faith and Doubt," p. 216) must be remembered. And we must also remember that "no one can be a Catholic without a simple faith, that what the Church declares in God's name, is God's word, and therefore true. A man must simply believe that the Church is the oracle of God" (*ibid.*).

In an age of scepticism, when perception of reality is confined to what can be tested experimentally, faith, the faith of the Catholic, is under siege. But the infallible voice of Scripture assures us that "where sin increased, grace abounded all the more" (Rom 5:20). "God is faithful, and He will not let you be tempted beyond your strength, but with the temptation will also provide the way of escape, that you may be able to endure it" (1 Cor 10:13).

Since papal infallibility is believed in only by Catholics, we are alone. It is the seal of all reunion. It is, as is all doctrine, a tremendous gift from God, but for the man who bears the responsibility, it is an awful burden as well. It also offers the faithful the assurance that God has spoken, and reveals the true contents of God's message. We approach God's word with the confidence that is to be ours "in approaching the throne of grace, that we shall have mercy from Him and find grace when we are in need of help" (Heb 4:16). It is God's healing words which the Pope speaks infallibly. And as members of Christ we will say to the Vicar of Christ what the first Vicar of Christ said to Him whose Vicar he was to be: "Lord, to whom shall we go? You have the words of eternal life" (John 6:68).

60. The Indefectibilty of True Faith

"We believe that the Church founded by Jesus Christ and for which He prayed is indefectibly one in faith, worship, and the bond of hierarchical communion."

Possibly the most important effect of the visit of Pope John Paul II to the United States has been the reassurance given to the faithful that their faith, the content of their faith and their Christian moral sense formed by their love and knowledge of Jesus Christ, is the ancient faith of the Catholic Church. They now know that they are right and they can and must now oppose what is wrong and thereby destructive of faith. They can now again face with confidence the chaos of opinions bombarding them from the pulpit and in print, the degradation of liturgy at times inflicted on them, false doctrine occasionally proposed in the Catholic press and in textbooks, taught in schools, colleges, and seminaries. They now know that the life style adopted by some priests, religious, and seminarians is simply out of harmony with the spirit and intention of Holy Mother Church. The gates of hell did not prevail, and their saving faith, the faith of the Catholic Church, was reaffirmed by the Holy Father's visit, words, and actions.

We were "all called into one and the same hope," when we were called (Eph 4:4). "There is one Lord, one faith, one baptism, and one God who is Father of all, over all, through all, and within all" (Eph 4:5-6). We "had gone astray like sheep" (1 Pet 2:25). But now we are restored to one faith—we have found and have been given the power to live by (and to repent in the light of) the eternal truths of God: His inner, immutable, and eternal life as Father and Son in the Holy Spirit, and His manifold attributes existing in the simplicity of His infinite Being and Love (the two names that "express ineffably the same divine reality of Him who has wished to make

Himself known"—*Credo*).

That this "one and the same hope" is held out to all men is part of the essential content of our faith. The truths revealed speak of the God who is Love, who desires the salvation of all, who not only dwelt among us as Man, but allowed our converging sins to test His love for us to the mysterious limit of evil unleashed against Him, torturing and crucifying Him who is our hope. Our hope is the love in His Sacred Heart upheld during the ordeal, victorious to the very end (John 13:1). This hope is the hope of the Church, indefectible, never hesitating even in the darkest hours, for "nothing . . . can come between us and the love of Christ, even if we are . . . being persecuted. . . . These are the trials through which we triumph, by the power of Him who loved us . . . the love of God made visible in Christ Jesus our Lord" (Rom 8:35, 37, 39). The prayers of the Church reach out to all mankind. The utmost is done to bring the sacraments to all the faithful, even at the risk of death.

Not only is the worship of the Church indefectibly in harmony with truth, but also by the grace of God, by the merits of Christ—the power acquired by His human Love when the Love for sinners was maintained while sin had its way, even to death on the Cross—by these merits the often all too human "bond of hierarchical communion" (*Credo*, above) is kept intact. Judas' continuing treason, Peter's occasional weakness will never prevail, even if they cause immense distress. For there are also many hidden souls, some of them contemplatives, called to this very task, but also a hidden multitude of others, who vicariously accept the crosses which have been rejected within the hierarchical communion. In the Providence of God the vicarious suffering of rejected crosses is the expiation which renders the redeeming universal expiation of Christ present in the world, absorbing evil and leavening the Mystical Body of Christ (Col 1:24; Rom 12:21). It is the new life that sets in as we die with Christ, and now live the new life which is "hidden with Christ in God" (Col 3:3). This vicarious expiation is the soul of every apostolate, incumbent on all Christians.

The indefectibilty of the unity and integrity of the faith of the Church and the purity of her worship, including the validity of the sacraments; and the preservation of the mystery of the divine reality of the bond of hierarchical commnion—these are gifts from God. The gift consists of the continuing redeeming action of grace and the living of the Law of Christ, "to bear the burden of one another's failures" (Gal 6:2). The healing power of God's redeeming love, allotted by the human Heart of Jesus to each one of us (Eph 4:7), not only repairs in a hidden way what our sins have damaged, but also through each one of us, this redeeming grace becomes visible and effective in the integrity and depth of our faith, in the purity of our prayer life, and in our harmony and holy obedience to the hierarchical life of the Church, of the diocese, and of the parish. For this, Christ prayed (Luke 22:31-32; John 17:11, 21-23, 26; Heb 5:7), suffered and died. For this the Risen Lord continues to plead, "since He is living ever to intercede for all who come to God through Him" (Heb 7:25). And thus "we believe that the Chruch founded by Jesus Christ and for which He prayed is indefectibly one in faith, worship, and the bond of hierarchical communion" (*Credo*).

61. The Rich Variety of Unity

"In the bosom of this Church, the rich variety of liturgical rites and the legitimate diversity of theological and spiritual heritages and special disciplines, far from injuring her unity, make it more manifest."

It is one of the glories of Catholicism that it creates a bond between people of the most diverse cultures and across the ages. A true priest will immediately feel at home with another true priest, even though they may differ in culture and in interests apart from their faith and priesthood. This writer has lived in community with African priests and priests from various European countries, both old and young, only to discover this brotherhood rooted in a common recognition of the "glory that is [Christ's] as the only Son of the Father" (John 1:14). This same bond is found uniting one to the poorly and the very highly educated. It is the "Catholic Thing" (G.K. Chesterton) found in the writings of the Fathers, in the ancient churches of Europe, in the moving monuments to their faith built by the poor immigrants in the ghettos of America, in the music of Mozart, the plays of Claudel, or the wit of Chesterton. It is the wisdom and the redeeming creative love of God, having entered the world in Christ, that continues to shine through men and their activities, "manifesting and actualizing the mystery of God's love for men" (*Pastoral Constitution*, 45). It is simply Christ being with the Church (Mat 28:20). It is Christ, it is the Church in the hearts of men. The greater the variety through which the face of Christ shines, the more manifest becomes the essential unity of the Church. "That they may be one . . . with Me in them and You in Me" (John 17:23)—it is the "one God who is Father of all, over all, through all, and within all'' (Eph 4:6). The one only God—in the eternal interrelation of the eternally begetting Father, the eternally begotten Son, and their eternal mutual Love, the Holy Spirit—expresses Himself through the enormous variety and plenitude of His creation, but above all, through men in the growing variety of character, vocation, and culture. It is the ''one God who is Father . . . *through* all'' (Eph 4:6; emphasis added).

The prayers and readings clothing sacramental action have developed through the centuries, giving expression to the spirituality of many varied people. The same is true of the music which gives solemnity to the words of the liturgy, and of the architecture, painting, and sculpture which lends beauty to worship and leads us to a foretaste of the glory of Heaven. For ''in the earthly liturgy we take part in a foretaste of that heavenly liturgy which is celebrated in the Holy City of Jerusalem . . . where Christ is sitting at the right hand of God'' (*Constitution on the Sacred Liturgy*, 8). The same faith finds expression in psalmtones and prefaces, in Masses of Palestrina, Mozart, and Beethoven's works of inexhaustible depth and beauty. The poetry of the *Dies Irae*, expressing the theology of human existence, its transition, fears, and expectations, given to us by divine revelation, is clothed by the somber Gregorian chant of the Middle Ages, by the music of Mozart's last work, by Verdi's highly dramatic music. Does the variety of expression not remind us that all unity derives from the one only God, who alone creates and sustains in being? Is not all true genius and its exercise a manifestation of God's creative power, which enables man to be creative in the freedom which God-given talent and discipline yield? Is not here, where nature and grace meet, the verification of St. Paul's words (although he was referring above all to the life of grace) that God, ''for his own loving purpose . . . puts both the will and the action into us'' (Phil 2:13)? It was in the presence of the Apostles that our Lord prayed that they would be one as He and the Father are one, with Jesus in them and the Father in Him (John 17:21-23). And how different were Peter and James and John and the others from each other! It is in variety that the true oneness derived from the one divine source is revealed. Variety points to the infinite riches of the Creator.

In a culture that emphasizes appearances and adamantly denies, on philosophical grounds, meaning and dependence, it is difficult to find common ground with others, even with those of one's own household. Here, too, the true faith must serve as a healing, redeeming sign of contradiction to the growing *Abolition of Man* (C.S. Lewis). The ''Dogma of Progress'' renders knowledge of the past as irrelevant as alchemy. The unity of the Church in the content of her faith, in the essence of her worship, in the validity of the sacraments, and in her common heritage and destiny, all rooted in Jesus Christ, who is "the same today as He was yesterday and as He will be forever" (Heb 13:8), is radically contradicted by the temper of our Western mentality today. That from this there will grow deep divisions and even a struggle unto death, that is, into possible martyrdom for Catholics, seems increasingly likely. As Romano Guardini wrote more than thirty years ago, "Loneliness in faith will be terrible. Love will disappear from the face of the public world [Mat 24:12], but the more precious will that love be which flows from one lonely person to another, involving a courage of the heart born from the immediacy of the love of God as it was made known in Christ." Therefore, he continues, we must live "by the key words of the providential message of Jesus: that things are transformed for the man who makes God's will for His Kingdom his first concern [Mat 6:33]" (*The End of the Modern World*, p. 132). That is God's answer to our coming struggle.

62. Divine Gifts Outside the Church

We recognize "also the existence, outside the organism of the Church of Christ, of numerous elements of truth and sanctification which belong to her as her own and tend to Catholic unity. . . ."

These words of Pope Paul's *Credo* may sound arrogant and condescending if the Church is seen as an organization of human origin. They become tolerable only if we retain a realistic view of the Catholic Church as "clasping sinners to her bosom, at once holy and always in need of purification" (*Dogmatic Constitution*, 8). If we include ourselves among those who follow the injunction of the Council to follow "constantly the path of penance and renewal" (*ibid.*), we may attain to a degree of intellectual humility that would show the statement we are considering to be one of glorious and consoling truth, a revelation of God's redeeming love. Our desire for humility can find support in the study of Church history with its monotonous litany of betrayals on the part of men and women of the Church and the usual resistance to reform coming from within. Romano Guardini wrote, "Christ lives on in the Church, but Christ crucified. One might also venture to suggest that the defects of the Church are His Cross" (*The Church and the*

Catholic, p. 55). The Church of martyrs is often also the Church of executioners. "Alas for the world that there should be such obstacles! Obstacles indeed there must be, but alas for the man who provides them" (Mat 18:7). "A prophet is only despised in his own country" (Mat 13:57).

We may have outgrown the narrowness of the ghetto, with its attitude of nervous defensiveness, and its bitter historical memories of the times "when Christians made martyrs of each other" (Hans Urs van Balthasar) (as they still do today in Northern Ireland). But this change is rarely accomplished by "penance and renewal." Shallowness and indifference, an icy pragmatism and a Christianity strictly decorative is at times all that is left. And if this condition forms the image people acquire of the Catholic Church, the statement under consideration sounds like mockery, if not blasphemy. However, the statement becomes credible if the Church is seen to be "like a stranger in a foreign land [pressing] forward amid the persecutions of the world and the consolations of God, announcing the Cross and the Death of the Lord until He comes" (*Dogmatic Constitution*, 8).

Our eyes will become perceptive if we really understand the words of St. Paul: "What do you have that was not given to you? And if it was given, how can you boast as though it were not?" (1 Cor 4:7). Then we will recognize divine gifts among non-Catholic Christians, among non-Christians, even among atheists. We will be less swayed by prejudice and resentment, and will be reminded of God's goodness as we perceive the working of grace among others.

Having heard Bach's sacred music, one could hardly deny to Lutherans the possibility of a profound spirituality rooted in revealed truth. The Credo of his B-minor Mass will remain a powerful non-verbal commentary on the faith of the Church, and the setting of the words "et unam, sanctam, catholicam, et apostolicam ecclesiam" is a firm affirmation of what it prays. Rembrandt's sacred paintings and drawings speak for themselves. The influence of Dostoevsky on Catholic thought is incalculable. The importance of Karl Barth may increase as time goes on and as Catholics seek a way out of their present confusion. This only points to some non-Catholic Christians.

But it is above all in the hidden workings of grace, in the holiness and almost instinctive understanding of the Cross among the many who do not know Christ, that we discover the universality of God's desire for the salvation of all at work in the hearts of men. Here are two prayers from pagan Africa. The first, from the Basuto:

We have remained outside,
We have remained behind outside,

We have remained behind to shed tears.
Oh, if there was only a place for me in heaven!
Why do I not have wings to fly there?
If a strong rope would hang down from heaven,
I would grasp it and would climb up,
I would mount upwards and dwell there in heaven.

The other prayer comes from the Pygmies:

To you, Creator, to you, the Powerful One,
I offer this new plant,
New fruit of an ancient tree.
You are the Master, we are your children.
To you, Creator, to you, the Powerful One.
Consider the blood that flows, the child that cries.
To you, this new plant,
New fruit of an ancient tree.

(*The Love of God in Non-Christian Religions*, trans. Thomas Ohm, O.S.B.)

Here is true hope yearning to be enlightened. The heart of man is naturally Christian, as St. Augustine tells us. The Christian shadows found outside the orbit of Christianity remind us of the awful responsibility we have to help those in darkness to find the light for which they yearn. For now we are to be "the light of the Lord . . . like children of light, for the effects of light are seen in complete goodness and right living and truth . . . but anything exposed by the light will be illuminated and anything illuminated turns into light" (Eph 5:9, 14). We are called to be "the light of the world" (Mat 5:14). If we become this light, we point to the ultimate source of the light. Therefore our "light must shine in the sight of men, so that, seeing [our] good works, they may give the praise to our Father in Heaven" (Mat 5:16).

63. Christian Unity

We believe "in the action of the Holy Spirit who stirs up in the heart of the disciples of Christ love of this unity, we entertain the hope that Christians who are not yet in the full communion of the one only Church will one day be reunited with one only Shepherd. "

The astonishing fact is not that Christendom suffered the great Schism and the break-up through the Reformation. The miracle is that the Catholic Church survived it and, pushed by historical disasters such as two world wars and the incredible horrors of totalitarianism, has become the central ecumenical force among Christians. That the road to unity can only be a way of the Cross is to be expected. The crosses may, and will, come from without through political and economic disasters, and they may, and should come from within as "the Church . . . follows constantly the path of penance and renewal" (*Dogmatic Constitution* 8). Unity can be achieved only through a continuing search (Mat 7:7), the necessary condition of finding or meeting with God's grace working mysteriously in the depth of men's hearts, because it is from the heart that the right spirit and right intentions arise (just as evil intentions do— Mat 15:19). And even these right intentions would remain sterile if there was not a growing readiness for the crosses that are always met with on the road to sanctity or union with God. But the restoring and deepening of our union with one another derives fundamentally from our union with God—"May they *all* be one in us . . . as we are one. With me in them and you in me" (John 17:21-23; emphasis added).

Christians must now live in the increasingly brutal world of the ice-cold new paganism that preaches hedonism and produces suicidal despair. They must come to perceive clearly that compromise is no longer possible, that vanity, flattery, and self-indulgence (Gal 5:19-21) are destructive of Christian life. "You cannot belong to Christ Jesus unless you crucify all self-indulgent passions and desires" (Gal 5:24)—nothing less than to crucify *all*! —and this is hardly the case in most lives. If sin, as a lived lie, did not induce blindness and self-delusion in us, we could hardly live with ourselves. The enormity of our self-deception—we call it *rationalizing*, a mockery of the gift of reason—is such that if we saw ourselves as we are, we would actually have to make a radical choice between conversion and despair. So we settle for that mediocrity, that lukewarmness, which the Lord revealed to St. John that He would spit out of His mouth (Rev 3:16).

Christians must learn to love God with their whole mind (Mark 12:30), placing their intelligence, enlightened by the light of faith, in the service of God. Security is no longer found among friends and in the family, at times not even in the parish, since all too many parishes vegetate in lifeless irrelevancies. Our Lord told us that "Heaven and earth will pass away, but [His] words will never pass away" (Mat 24:35). Many a word of His, ignored because apparently not relevant at the moment, now becomes frighteningly urgent. "Many false prophets will arise; they will deceive many, and with the increase of lawlessness, love in most men will grow cold" (Mat 24:11-12). "Brother will betray brother to death, and the father his child; children will rise against their parents and have them put to death. You will be hated by all men on account of my name" (Mat 10:21-22). And how can we fail to recognize a new actuality and an urgency in these words in the growing deception of presenting abortion, euthanasia, and selective genocide under the guise of compassion? In this new world of brutal hedonism, which sees pleasure and fun as the only meaning in life, the greatest love is no longer seen as laying down one's life for others—the Cross (Mat 10:37-39; John 15:13). Now others are to be made to lay down their lives, because they interfere with our pursuit of pleasure. And this new form of human sacrifice is done in the name of deep compassion for the victims of abortion, euthanasia, and genocide—new words for murder.

But what has all that to do with the ecumenical longings caused by the "Holy Spirit who stirs up in the heart of the disciples love for this unity"(*Credo*, above)? Is it in hope, in sharing the desire of God who "wants everyone to be saved" (1 Tim 2:4), that this longing for unity will come? Is it a growing realization of the destructive, yet almost irresistible power of the new paganism of ruthless hedonism that will unite Christ's true disciples? Is it ultimately the growing conviction that salvation is only found in Christ Jesus, who continues to draw all men to Himself (John 12:32) as He did on the Cross? And will this not open the way to making all Christians recognize that the unbroken integrity of revealed truths and the fullness of sacramental life is found where the successor of Peter, the Bishop of Rome, is acknowledgd as the Vicar of Christ? Isn't there hope that the bitter memories of past and present strife, when "Christians made martyrs of each other" (Hans Urs von Balthasar), will be taken as the most striking proof for the desperate need of salvation, of the disastrous consequences of the Fall as the Fall continues through history, among Christians and everyone else? The salvation of all mankind will be achieved when "finally the intention of the Creator in creating man in His own image and likeness will be truly realized, when all who possess human nature, and have been regenerated in Christ through the Holy Spirit, gazing together on the glory of God, will be able to say 'Our Father' "(*Decree on the Church's Missionary Activity*,7; see also the last sentence of the *Dogmatic Constitution*, 69; Rom 11:32; 1 Cor 15:28).

64. Salvation Through Christ

"We believe that the Church is necessary for salvation, because Christ, who is the sole Mediator and Way of salvation, renders Himself present for us in His Body which is the Church."

(Read *Dogmatic Constitution*, 14-16.)

"All children of the Church should . . . remember that their exalted condition results, not from their own merits, but from the grace of Christ" (*Dogmatic Constitution*, 14). The thinking of Western man seems to exist under a compulsion to reduce everything to quantitive, measurable, and mathematically predictable relations. Even personal relations are thought of in terms of a tug-of-war of opposing forces. And this reduction of our power of thinking affects even our thinking about God's dealing with men. It destroys our capacity to grasp the meaning of grace. Grace is gratuitous—a free gift from God. And instead of deep gratitude when seeing the workings of grace elsewhere, we tend to accuse God of favoritism and injustice as if we were observing business relations.

Are not envy and pride with regard to divine vocations, gifts, and favors, exactly what our Lord so violently rebuked in the Pharisees? Did He not say to them, "Serpents, brood of vipers, how can you escape being condemned to hell" (Mat 23:33)? Is not taking pride in success when working for God, and as members of the Church, in deadly contradiction to the Crucifixion? Does the Psalmist not pray, "Not to us, Lord, not to us, but to thy name give glory" (Ps 115:1)? Has not success become the sign of God's approval, with wealth and power the admired goal? But where is the cross to be taken up daily by the true follower of Chirst? Where is the eighth Beatitude? No wonder the voice of God sounding in the Church is either not heard at all or is conveniently twisted into a self-serving litany of mutual approval. Only if we are ready to accept God's wisdom—which is foolishness to men—and are willing to become fools for Christ's sake, are our hearts ready for God's truth and call (1 Cor 1:25; 4:10).

Christ, "the sole Mediator and Way of salvation," will become "present for us in His Body which is the Church" if His Voice is heard as it is truly spoken in the Church. His Word is incarnate in the life of the Church. And the sacraments, the visible sources of eternal life, are clothed in words and gestures truly expressing something not of this world. When God's word and will are heard and are humbly received by the faithful, the statement of the *Credo* under consideration becomes credible. And if we are among those "to whom the Son [has chosen] to reveal" the Father (Mat 11:27), this is not an option but a call from God, the call to be a Christian, a member of Christ, the call to acquire the Mind of Christ, to accept the conditions of true discipleship—in short, the Cross, and for us, the daily Cross (Mat 10:37-38; John 12:24; 15:2).

We are to become the means for others to see Christ crucified and risen, who lives in us—if we "have been crucified with Christ" (Gal 2:19)—the condition St. Paul lays down for no longer living with our "own life but with the life of Christ who lives in [us]" (Gal 2:20). But it is to be a life in faith—the faith that the Son of God "loved me [and] sacrificed Himself for my sake" (Gal 2:20). It is the knowledge in faith that my sins already have reached, tortured, and helped to murder Him in His historical Passion and Crucifixion, and that in spite of what I have done to Him and am liable to continue to do to Him, I was then among those—together with all of mankind—whom He drew to Himself once He was lifted up from the earth to the Cross (John 12:32). And I am now among those He continues to draw to Himself, after the second lifting-up, the Ascension. "Constituted Lord by His Resurrection and given all authority in Heaven and on earth, Christ is now at work in the hearts of men by the power of His Spirit" (*Pastoral Constitution*, 38).

This drawing of all men to Himself, when accepted, fits the individual, whether or not he knows it explicitly in faith, into the pattern of the Cross and makes him an instrument of expiation—a victim of sin, accepting and suffering without bitterness, in patience and humility. Because even those "who, without any fault of theirs, have not yet arrived at an explicit knowledge of God, and who, not without grace, strive to lead a good life" (*Dogmatic Constitution*, 16)—even they could not lead a good life without constantly resisting "evil and [conquering] it with good" (Rom 12:21). They will be among those who, at the last Judgment, will receive "the Kingdom prepared . . . . since the foundation of the world" (Mat 25:34). They too will ask of the Judge, "Lord, when did we see you . . . naked . . . sick . . . in prison?" (Mat 25:37-39). And they will hear the blessed words reserved from those who had not known the Church of Christ, and did not know Christ in His Church: "In so far as you did this to one of the least of these brothers of mine, you did it to Me" (Mat 25:40). Christ, unknown to them, had rendered Himself present to them "in His Body which is the Church" (*Credo*), equally unknown to them. And thus Christ reaches out to all, and wherever He touches anyone, there is the Church—touching, drawing toward Christ, and leading men into a hidden but real relation to herself and thus to the Lord Jesus Christ.

65. Salvation Extends to All

"But the divine design of salvation embraces all men. . . ."

One of the most difficult mysteries of God's Providence and permissiveness is the frequent violence and brutality exercised throughout the ages by some men over other men. The countless wars and untold suffering of millions from persecution, imprisonment and torture—often in the name of religion—argues for Mephistopholes' observation that man acts "more brutal than any beast" (Goethe, *Faust*, Prologue on Heaven). We may be tempted to consider our land and our age more enlightened in this regard than those of the past until we consider some of the criminal actions advocated today in the name of Christ and morality and even of compassion, although not by the Catholic Church—euthanasia, selective genocide, abortion ordered by a court, or permitted and protected as a free option on the level of removing a wart.

But human existence does not derive its meaning from what happens or is hoped for in this life. It lies exclusively in the eventual and eternal sharing of God's joy (John 15:11; 17:13) when we will see Him "face to face" (1 Cor 13:12; see also 1 John 3:2; Rev 22:3-4) in the beatific vision. And it is our task during life on earth, to reclaim all men for God and help all to seek and find God and His Will (Mat 7:7-8) so that each person can attain a greater capacity for God. This capacity is rooted and manifested in a life of faith, charity, and flowing from it, a life of apostolic hope, of active hope for the other, for others, for all others.

It has not always been easy to admit what Scripture so clearly expresses, that God "wants everyone to be saved and reach full knowledge of the truth" (1 Tim 2:4) and that "God has imprisoned all men in their own disobedience only to show mercy to all mankind" (Rom 11:32). "The Lord is not being slow to carry out His promises, as anybody else might be called slow; but He is being patient with you all, wanting nobody to be lost and everybody to be brought to change his ways" (2 Pet 3:9). Again we cannot ask why God, who protects and guides the Church even to the extent of infallibility in matters of faith and morals, did not extend this guidance in a more forceful manner to matters of relation with non-Catholics and those thought to be going astray within the Church. No glib answer should be given. It is perhaps the most difficult aspect of faith in Divine Providence. Perhaps those who have suffered here, men such as Cardinal Newman or Henri de Lubac, to name two, could have spoken about it. The fact remains that fidelity to the Church is at times severely tested from within the Church.

Jesus Himself declared that "there is no respect for a prophet in his own country" (John 4:43). Perhaps this is the most powerful way of expiation, because it lies within the very heart of the Church, a Church "clasping sinners to her bosom, at once holy and always in need of purification" (*Dogmatic Constitution*, 8).

The corruption in the human family stands out particularly painfuly at the very source of truth and life, in the continuing instrument of Him who is "the Way, the Truth, and the Life" (John 14:6): the Church. And the temptation to exclude others, to see oneself in a better light, to justify the ways of power and greed, is so much part of the continuing primeval temptation of usurping the function of God, that the very freedom of man seems to leave no way but that of a painful permissiveness. The agonizing question of so many Jews, where God was during the Holocaust, is perhaps the continuation of the cry of Him, who is the glory of His people Israel (Luke 2:32), while being murdered by our sins: "My God, my God, why have you deserted me?" (Mat 27:46). And so the Church, when she has failed in her spirit and vocation, at times shifted, by the sin of her members, the expiating crosses that should have been hers onto others who were crucified because they were outside, uncomfortable strangers. And many a Christian may have to hear the words: "I was a stranger and you never made me welcome" (Mat 25:43).

In solemn reiteration of the Dominican prayer that "all may be one" (John 17:21), the glorious teachings of Vatican II express the universal hope of salvation—the Church as "sign and instrument . . . of communion with God and of unity among all men" (*Dogmatic Constitution*, 1). It is all beautifully summarized in the very last words of the *Dogmatic Constitution* (section 69): "The entire body of the faithful pours forth urgent supplications to the Mother of God and of men that she, who aided the beginnings of the Church by her prayers, may now, exalted as she is above all the angels and saints, intercede before her Son in the fellowship of all the saints, until all families of people, whether they are honored with the title of Christian or whether they still do not know the Savior, may happily be gathered together in peace and harmony into one People of God, for the glory of the Most Holy and Undivided Trinity." In a spirit of expiation and universal hope we must fully share this prayerful hope of the Church. Refusing to do so is to repudiate Him who died for all men; it is to deny God who "wants everyone to be saved" (1 Tim 2:4). "The divine design of salvation embraces all men" (*Credo*).

66. Salvation of the Unbaptized

> *". . . those who without fault on their part do not know the Gospel of Christ and His Church, but seek God sincerely, and under the influence of grace endeavor to do His will as recognized through the promptings of their conscience, they, in a number known only go God, can obtain salvation.*

Hitler was a baptized Catholic; a vast number of his followers, torturers and executioners, were baptized Catholics. The virulent, murderous anti-Semitism of Hitler and of the many others who prepared the way for him by their nationalistic and racial arrogance and pride was largely aroused by their contact with Jews from Eastern Europe, victims of centuries of exclusion into ghettos, victims of hatred, murder, rape, and robbery at the hands of people who were baptized Christians. What aroused an almost instinctive aversion toward Eastern Europe Jews was the image of the Suffering Servant (Is 53)—and thereby of Christ crucified—which the victims of persecution showed to the world. "Without beauty, without majesty . . . no looks to attract our eyes; a thing despised and rejected by men, a man of sorrows and familiar with suffering . . . he was despised and we took no account of him" (Is 53:2-3). It was hatred of Christ Crucified in the people that gave the Savior to men, who now were crucified by the "followers" of the Crucified. The Holocaust was the final revelation of this inversion of roles—when the followers of the Crucified, who were to take up their crosses daily (Mat 10:37-39), instead crucified those from whose "flesh and blood came Christ who is above all, God forever blessed! Amen" (Rom 9:5). For centuries, Christians held the Jews in contempt and crucified Christ in His crucified kinsmen who "are still loved by God, loved for the sake of their ancestors" (Rom 11:28). Could opposition to God Incarnate go further?

In light of this aspect of the history of Christendom, one can hardly assume that salvation is reserved to baptized Christians and that a large number, if not all of those not baptized Christians and that a large number, if not all of those not baptized sacramentally are excluded from union with God now and eternally. History would make a mockery of such a view. Increasing contact with the vast majority of mankind who have not had (credible) contact with Christianity also has revealed to us that the non-Christian world shared in the virtues and goodness demanded by Christianity: that heroic goodness, the working of grace, appears quite frequently among all people of this world. It is one of the consoling experiences in meeting with people of other cultures to discover that holiness is not alien to them.

It may also be well to remember when we consider religious or philosphical systems not rooted in the concrete revelation accepted by Jews and Christians, that men are shy in giving expression to their deepest hopes and aspirations. A fear of *hubris*, a deep humility, the possibility of desecration, the desire not to expose what is sacred to the insolent curiosity of others—these may bring about a deliberate obscurity in presenting one's religion or philosophy. Only as an adherent of a public revelation, commissioned to proclaim it, can man fearlessly and without arrogance or self-seeking speak or write of his deepest convictions without embarrassment. Therefore we ought to respect the reserve of others and not interpret their hesitant stammering too quickly in terms of the concreteness of our own beliefs.

What answers would the Harris Poll have received from St. Francis to questions such as: Are you a saint? Do you love God? Do you commit sin? Do you love your father? But then, we have abdicated vast areas of intelligence, and reduced personal relations to totally predictable pool table mechanics. And great cultivated stupidity reigns in much that goes by the name of social sciences and comparative religion, infecting even theology.

Considering the history of the Western world and the extension of the West's influence into the New Worlds, the record of Christendom—cultures profoundly affected by Christianity—is a mixture of the best and the worst. Holiness has been, and still is, widespread, while unspeakable brutality, often in the name of religion, has been prominent and historically more weighty. Holiness hides itself. If we recall that love of God and love of neighbor are commanded (Deut 6:4-5; Lev 19:18; John 13:34; Mark 12:29-31) and are therefore an obedience, all self-righteous demonstration of love, all narcissism would render religous talk and practice suspect. And in spite of its many imbalances and unsatisfactory articulation, there is an immensely widespread seeking and doing of God's will.

People without in the least suspecting it—and saints usually have no idea of their own sanctity—are faithful in doing their duty, their daily chores, and assuming responsibility for their families. This is found in industrial and in tribal society, among Christians and non-Christians, and among people who regretfully see no alternative to atheism or agnosticism. And it is this hidden, unassuming, inarticulate fidelity to duty that may well be the saving sanctity for much of mankind and also a silent expiation of the appalling amount of sin continuing to poison the world.

As for Catholics, who have received the gifts of explicit faith and baptism, and who have access to the sacraments and are under the pastoral care of the Church, we must remember that "when a man has had a great deal given him, a great deal will be demanded of him" (Luke 12:48). We are the Church, the "Universal sacrament of salvation" (*Dogmatic Constitution*, 48). And in spite of so much that disfigures the Church of Christ, it is the hidden sanctity and prayer that radiate, often invisibly, to the whole world, maintaining some hope of salvation for all men. Christ remains the "only . . . mediator between God and mankind" (1 Tim 2:5). And it is His Body, the Church, that continues to be "a sign and instrument . . . of communion with God and of unity among all men" (*Dogmatic Constitution*, 1).

67. The Priest: Christ's Representative

"We believe that the Mass [is] celebrated by the priest represen-ting the Person of Christ by virtue of the power received through the sacrament of orders, and offered by him in the name of Christ and the members of His Mystical Body. . . ."

The Eternal Son of the Eternal Father, "true God from true God, one in substance with the Father" (Nicene Creed) emptied Himself by becoming Man, servant, and ultimately the brutalized victim of mankind's sins (Phil 2:6-8). He, through whom "all things came to be" (John 1:3), was rendered helpless by a few nails. Out of love, He did all this in obedience—drawing the total weight of Original Sin, and of all sins that were to flow from it until the end of human history, upon Himself as sin's target and now as its victim. God, through a vulnerable human nature, involved Himself totally in the drama of man's Fall in order to stop mankind in its journey of rebellion, a journey into nothingness, emptiness, despair, total selfishiness, and isolation—a journey into hell. While the sins of men, the Sin of the World, seemed to reach their goal, namely the degradation and destruction of the Son of Man, His human Heart went out to them, to us. And when He was lifted up from the earth to the Cross, His human love enveloped all men, his torturers and executioners, and by His divine power (2 Pet 1:3) He drew all men to Himself (John 12:32). This is how we were redeemed on that first Good Friday.

Jesus Christ, now the Risen Lord, to whom "all authority in Heaven and on earth has been given" (Mat 28:18), continues to draw all men to

Himself. He draws us by His Truth, which He Himself is (John 14:6), and by giving us whatever will bring us into active union, through Him, with the Father. Since this drawing requires on our part a response of mind and will, it has to be known in a visible manner. And the instrument through which this "manifesting and actualizing of the mystery of God's love for men" (*Pastoral Constitution*, 45) takes place is the Church. The revelation and power entrusted to the Church is for the sake of us who constitute the Church, and so that God's redeeming call might radiate through us to the whole world.

The statement of the *Credo* under consideration speaks of the priest having received power through the sacrmaent of orders to represent Christ. This power not only brings Christ to the altar, but also through Christ's presence, it makes the very Sacrifice of Calvary present. His past sufferings and death as the target and victim of sin are now eternally present in His Risen humanity, though he suffers no more (Rom 6:8-9). Whatever Christ did and suffered while on earth left an indelible mark in Him. Experiences and the heroic exercise of love transformed Him, made Him increase "in wisdom, in stature, and in favor with God and men" (Luke 2:52). The wounds in His hands and feet remained (John 20:27) to add to the eternal glory of the Risen Lord as the eternalized glory of an ordeal undergone out of love for the Father in obedience, and out of love of men in the exercise of this obedience. It was an unconditional obedience, a disposition that exends His eternal total surrender to the Father into His humanity and this by the exercise of this obedience in Incarnation (Heb 10:7) and by the folly (1 Cor 1:25) of entrusting Himself to mankind only to be murdered, so He could blot out the guilt of His murderers by His redeeming love.

We must realize that we are dealing with God the Creator and Redeemer restoring the meaning of Creation—of "the universe itself, which is so closely related to man and which attains its destiny through him" (*Dogmatic Constitution*, 48)—by enabling man to again attain grace and union with Him. Once we realize what was intended and actually done by God in Jesus Christ, we will discover a perfect continuity in the nature of the Church and the power given to some men, in and as the Church, to render the Mystery of Redemption present on earth in the Eucharist. This is reality, the Real Presence of Jesus Christ, Priest and Victim. By His divine power, the power that is His as God, He can render Himself really present through the localized presence under the appearance of bread and wine. But to bring this about, Christ speaks the transforming words of consecration through the priest who speaks in the first person—"This is my body . . . This is the cup of my blood." Are we to believe this?

The marvelous interior continuity of God's personal revelation, first "through the prophets," now "through His Son" (Heb 1:1-2); His unique presence through a human birth; and His continued effective presence is now enhanced by a sacramental presence, one equally real, brought about by His speaking in and through the priest. The divine power that is His as Son was, and continues to be, at the disposal of His human Will, and of His human Heart. This availability of divine power now extends to the ordained priest who visibly and audibly renders present on the altar Him who in Heaven is still "a Lamb that seemed to have been sacrificed" (Rev 5:6). He is now eternally "the Lamb that was sacrificed," to whom belongs "power, riches, wisdom, strength, honor, glory, and blessing" (Rev 5:12). This power to continue to draw all men to Himself (John 12:32) is now present, accessible, and salvific, in the Eucharist.

68. The Mass: A Reenacted Sacrifice

"We believe that the Mass . . . is the Sacrifice of Calvary rendered sacramentally present on our altars."

Redemption came to man when the Eternal Son, in obedience to the Father, emptied Himself by becoming Man, emptied Himself to the utmost limit (John 13:1) by allowing the Sin of the World to destroy Him—to destroy not only His dignity and freedom, but also His life, making Him, in the degradation of His last days, "more worm than man, scorn of mankind, jest of the people" (Ps 22:6). Redemption came to man when the consummation of the Fall, the converging of all the sins of mankind upon Jesus, found in His Sacred Heart a response of redeeming love, a love for mankind and for each individual human being, a love maintained, in a bitter interior struggle throughout every moment of the ordeal, from Gethsemane to the moment He expired, when all was accomplished (John 19:30). The historical, visible victory of Sin was overcome and conquered by the equally historical, simultaneous but invisible, victory of love. For during the ordeal and while being "lifted up from the earth," Christ drew all men to Himself, as He had foretold (Jn 12:32). His love reached out to all, to those already dead, and waiting liberation, to His contemporaries, to those still to be born. This is the meaning of "all men" (Consecration in the Mass), of "all mankind"

(Rom 11:32).

Through the words of consecration, the Body and Blood of Christ become present under the appearance of bread and wine. This symbolizes the cause of Christ's sacrificial death—He died by bleeding to death. In sheer obedience—"Let it be as You, not I, would have it" (Mat 26:39)—He let Himself be crushed by the Sin of the World so that He could take away the sin, the defiance of God. We must never allow ourselves to think that the brutal sufferings inflicted on Jesus, by themselves, brought our salvation. We are redeemed *in spite of* having murdered the Savior. We are redeemed by the victory of His love, a victory to be extended into history by us, as we "resist evil and conquer it with good" (Rom 12:21), as we love each other as He loved us (John 13:34). "Those who prove victorious I will allow to share my throne, just as I was victorious myself and took my place with my Father on His throne" (Rev 3:21).

Sin left its marks on Him. It no longer causes suffering, since the evil of sin has been absorbed and blotted out by a love ultimately greater than sin, and victorious. The victorious love and the marks of sin live on in the Risen humanity of Christ. In this sense, the struggle of Calvary—Life having overcome Death, and Love having embraced all sinners—will always remain present. But the mere presence of Jesus' Body and Blood do not yet constitute the presence of the Sacrifice of Calvary. This unique sacramental presence demands the mystical presence of the cause of Christ's death—the separation of His Body from His Blood, as He bled to death. It had been creatively determined by Christ at the Last Supper that the proclamation of His death by the separate consecrations would render present the pouring out of His precious Blood, "poured out for many for the forgiveness of sins" (Mat 26:28). The power of the word of Jesus Christ spoken through the celebrating priest constitutes the memorial of His death in the deepest, most real sense of the word *memorial*. He becomes present by the creative symbolism of the pouring forth of His Blood. Again, this is not only symbol but stark realization and rendering present of the past, even of Crucifixion. And the self-giving of Jesus to us, for us, can now become a sacramental, mysterious but quite real, Communion. His "flesh is now real food," and His "blood is real drink" (John 6:55). The mutual indwelling of Christ and man is reenforced. "He who eats my flesh and drinks my blood lives in me, and I live in him" (John 6:56).

Truly, "this is intolerable language. How could anyone accept it? . . . 'The words I have spoken to you are spirit and they are life' " (John 6:60, 63). Here we are deep in the mysterious, supernatural, divine reality. It is the Mystery of Faith, the mystery, symbol, and reality of Calvary through the Risen Christ present on the altar as victim and victor, as "the Lamb that was sacrificed" (Rev 5:12) and as the One whose love and fidelity were stronger than the converging rebellion of mankind.

Our Lord transformed the consummation of the rebellion of man on Calvary into a redeeming victory of love, when, on the Cross, He drew all men to Himself by the redeeming love of His Sacred Heart. The rendering present of the Sacrifice of Calvary as a real, though not new, sacrifice is the continuing redeeming reality which Christ gives us through His Church so that the Church—we, the People of God—may be renewed by our Lord, who on the Cross drew all men to Himself, and continues to do so, not only in Heaven, but above all in the Sacrifice of the Mass, when He, the Victim of Sin, comes to us and we come to Him as penitents seeking Him who is the Resurreciton and the Life (John 11:25).

O memoriale mortis Domini,
Panis vivus vitam prasestans homini.

Oh, memorial of the death of the Lord,
the Living Bread offering life to man.

(St. Thomas Aquinas)

69. The Eucharist

"We believe that . . . the bread and wine consecrated by the Lord at the Last Supper were changed into His Body and His Blood which were to be offered for us on the Cross."

"You who wanted no sacrifice or oblation, prepared a body for me. . . . then I said . . . 'God, Here I am! I am coming to obey your will.' " (Heb 10:5, 7; see also Ps 40:6-8).

The infinite power and capacity of God contains the capacity to really receive and suffer rejection by men because it is within the power of God to assume a human nature, body and soul. What no human mind could suggest as a possibility for God came to pass when the Eternal Son of the Eternal Father, "true God from true God, begotten, not made, one in substance with the Father" (Nicene Creed), became Man and dwelt among us (John 1:14). At that time, He could be seen, watched, touched (1 John 1:1), tortured, and murdered. Sin, which cannot really diminish God, reduced and killed Him in His, God's, vulnerable human nature. "The Word, who is life . . . was made visible: we saw it and we are giving our testimony, telling you of the eternal life which was with the Father and has been made visible to us" (1 John 1:2).

This is the extraordinary thing, divine in its conception and execution—that God, the Eternal Son, emptied Himself and became man, began to exist also as a human being, in Mary's womb. "His state was divine, yet He did not cling to His equality with God but emptied Himself to assume the condition of a slave and become as men are" (Phil 2:6-7). The possible complaint that this might be a flaw in God's perfection—that He could not suffer and that He could not really be affected by the rebellion of His creatures ("Have you got human eyes, do you see as mankind sees? Is your life mortal like man's, do your years pass as men's days pass?"—Job 10:4-5)—was annulled by the Incarnation. The Incarnation made the immutable God actually capable of becoming the target and victim of Sin. God in Him, whom to see is to see the Father (John 14:9), allowed the Sin of the World to destroy Him, only to exercise His always greater love, a love that has His divine power at its disposal and would direct this creative power to the salvation of men (2 Pet 1:3; John 11:41).

The mysterious harmony of His human and divine Will, of His human and divine love, was perfect obedience on the part of Jesus the Man, flawless, and yet involving a continual struggle of which we are granted a glimpse at Gethsemane. "If this cup cannot pass by without my drinking it, your will be done!" (Mat 26:42). For the embodiment of holiness—who is "gentle and humble in heart" (Mat 11:29), whose teaching of the Beatitudes was a description of Himself—for Him to be totally at the mercy of sin, of hatred, contempt, filth, rebellion, blasphemy, of the hatred of everything that speaks of God; to be completely drowned in this Hell, and yet in obedience to continue to love His very torturers, us—this is Redemption. This love, and, by implication, that which gave this love its specific character, its triumph over the evil arraigned against Him, are present wherever Jesus is present. The visible outcome of this struggle, the bleeding to death freely accepted, as Priest offering Himself, and as Victim of Sin and Sacrifice—this becomes additionally present by the separate consecration of His Body and Blood.

The Sacrifice of Christ is, in His human nature and in history, the willing acceptance of the impact of sin finding its target in Jesus, making Him the victim of sin. It is the consummation of the Sin of the World. The same Sacrifice is the victory of Jesus' love for us, His murderers, as during the ordeal He drew us all to Himself in redeeming love. His having been the victim of sin, and His maintaining His love which was tested by sin but reigned victorious, are both eternally present in Jesus, the Risen Lord. If He becomes present on the altar as He died, having bled to death, Body and Blood separated by separate consecrations, the Sacrifice of Calvary is rendered present.

But our Lord anticipated His bloody sacrifice by a sacramental separation of His Body and Blood at the Last Supper. He was unconditionally ready to accept the imminent ordeal in obedience to the Father, in the twofold love for the Father by this obedience, and the obedience of maintaining His sin-annihilating love for man. Thus interiorly, the fundamental dispositions of sacrifice were present; externally, the sacramental, anticipated separation of Body and Blood was effected. From the bloody sacrifice upon which He was about to enter, the anticipated sacrifice at the last Supper derived its fully sacrificial character. It became the Institution of the Eucharist—"do this as a memorial of me" (1 Cor 11:25). It sealed the disposition of Christ that enabled Him to be the perfect Priest: the willingness to offer up the unconditional gift of self to be annihilated by the Sin of the World; and the disposition that enabled Him to be a perfect Victim—His ability to uphold, in an inconceivable inner struggle, His love for us, His destroyers, His murderers—while being annihilated in His humanity. Priest, Victim, and Victor—almighty God, Creator of the world, eternal, infinite, incomprehensible, "whose home is inaccessible light, whom no man has seen and no man is able to see" (1 Tim 6:16), in the Son's humanity rendered helpless by nails, to expire in agony—surely, "God's foolishness is wiser than human wisdom, and God's weakness is stronger than human strength" (1 Cor 1:25). And now, in Heaven, adoration of the Lamb will continue , for "the Lamb that was sacrificed is worthy to be given power, riches, wisdom, strength, honor, glory, and blessing" (Rev 5:12). In the Eucharist, this adoration becomes accessible to men.

70. The Power of the Mass

". . . Likewise the bread and wine consecrated by the priest are changed into the Body and Blood of Christ enthroned gloriously in Heaven, and we believe that the mysterious presence of the Lord, under what continues to appear to our sense as before, is a true, real, and substantial presence."

Jesus Christ, "by His divine power . . . has given us all the things that we need for life" (2 Pet 1:3). The Eternal Son, a Divine Person, who immutably remains forever, also began to exist as Man in historical times, when Herod ruled in Judea and Tiberias was the Roman Emperor; a time from which many monuments are preserved. And once He began His public ministry, it was seen that, in His own name, by His own power, He could do things beyond the power of man. He changed water into wine, He healed large numbers of the sick, on occasion He restored the dead to life. He forgave sins. Jesus Christ, true God and true Man, used the divine power that is His as the Eternal Son, His as God from God, to establish the Kingdom of God. His creative power transforms man through grace and manifests His power and intention by miraculous events. "Here we are preaching a crucified Christ . . . to those who have been called . . . a Christ who is the power and the wisdom of God" (1 Cor 1:23,25).

Jesus as Man lived in flawless, though by no means easy, obedience to the Father. "My food is to do the will of the One who sent me" (John 4:34). And to do the Father's will, His own divine power was at His disposal. This chain of powers, from the Father to the Son in His human Will, and from there to the Church in His members, even reaches down to those not yet baptized. In order that the Church might continue her existence even under extreme conditions of emergency, the power to baptize belongs to all people, as long as they intend to do what the Church desires. We must realize what baptism accomplishes: through this sacrament, man is implanted into the very life of the Blessed Trinity, becomes a partaker of the divine nature (2 Pet 1:4), becomes a child of God, "is born through water and the Spirit" (John 3:5). It is the most enormous, astonishing transformation that we know of, and we learn its true nature only by revelation. In comparison with the effect of the sacrament of baptism, the other sacraments, apart from the Eucharist, actually accomplish less spectacular effects. Yet, the power to baptize, under certain conditions, belongs to all people. By means of this power the Church can come into being even without a Christian being present.

Our Lord, by His unity of humanity and divinity in One Person has, as Man, by His human Will, as it were, power over His divine creative power. The third Preface for Sundays expresses this: "You came to rescue us by your power as God, but you wanted us to be saved by one like us." And the Preface for the fifth Sunday of Lent declares, "as a man like us, Jesus wept for Lazarus, His friend. As the Eternal God, He raised him from the dead." Divine power was our Lord's by nature. In certain limited ways, certain divine powers needed for her sacramental and prayer life are entrusted to the Church. While some of these powers are confined to bishops and priests, the power to implant others into the life of the Trinity, to baptize into Christ (Gal 3:27; Mat 28:19) is given to all men.

All over the world Holy Mass is celebrated, in cathedrals, humble churches, and secretly in prison camps where governments have proscribed the Church: " . . . everywhere a sacrifice of incense is offered to my name, and a pure offering too" (Mat 1:11). The Council of Trent has interpreted this passage to pertain to the Mass. And the Real Presence of Jesus Christ in the Eucharist continues in our churches. We have to make a special effort in faith and meditation to nourish the conviction that the Father's intensely personal Providence extends to all of us in the workings and the power of the Catholic Church, for this conviction can only abide in a mind illuminated by God "who has shone in our minds to radiate the light of the knowledge of God's glory" (2 Cor 4:6). We do not feel, and do not necessarily experience God's grace directly. To expect, or to try to produce such experiences by manipulation is dangerous, and may lead to misleading illusions and even a loss of the Catholic sense of a universal Church, in which we all share a desperate need for pardon and redemption.

When at Mass or in visits to the Blessed Sacrament, we renew our faith in the personal love of God the Father Almighty, Creator of all, who in His inconceivable power and wisdom attends to each one of us, while in the vast universe His creative Mind and Will attend to every detail of creation, for nothing could exist or happen without God's creative power. The birds of the air do not sow or reap and yet are provided for (Mat 6:26). Our heavenly Father knows our needs (Mat 6:32)—our ultimate needs leading to holiness, to eternal life. And so, seeing God's Divine Providence in the powers and structures of the Church, we adhere, in hope, to our Lord's loving command: "Set your hearts on His Kingdom first, and on His [holiness], and all these other things" pertaining to our last end "will be given you as well" (Mat 6:33). And in an increasingly hostile world we hold fast to the reality of the Eucharist, entrusted to the Church. We believe that "the bread and wine consecrated by the priest are changed into the body and Blood of Christ enthroned gloriously in heaven, and we believe that the mysterious presence of the Lord, under what continues to appear to our sense as before is a true, real, and substantial presence" (*Credo*).

71. The Real Presence

"Christ cannot be thus present in this Sacrament except by the change into His Body of the reality itself of the bread and the change into His Blood of the reality itself of the wine, leaving unchanged only the properties of the bread and wine which our senses perceive."

"In Cruce latebat sola Deitas, Ac hic latet simul et humanitas" (St. Thomas Aquinas, from the *Adoro Te*). "On the Cross, only the Godhead was hidden, but here [in the Eucharist] His humanity is also hidden."

It was necessary for the Church, and for Pope Paul VI, to state again forcefully the faith of the Church—the realities of bread and wine are no longer, through the properties of these elements remain. Under them, there is Christ sacrificed, as He hung on the Cross, dead from having bled to death, Body and Blood separated, but in each remains the fullness of the humanity of the Eternal Son. Where the bread was, Christ is. The properties of bread indicate the Real Presence of the Body of Christ. Where the wine was, Christ is. The properties of wine indicate the Real Presence of the Precious Blood of Christ. And under these appearances that belong to bread and wine, His Body and Blood have become food for men. Christ, the victim of our sins, who conquered sin by love, can now give Himself to us visibly as spiritual food. Now even His humanity is hidden.

The infinite possibilities of almighty God include the capacity to be not only the target, but also the victim of sin; the possibility of becoming Man, of assuming a human nature. In this way, God the Immutable could become vulnerable and capable of suffering and dying: He could live a human destiny and conquer evil in real combat, by the love in His human Heart. We know what happened. The Eternal Son emptied Himself and died helplessly on the Cross. While sin destroyed Him in His existence on earth, His love went out to His murderers. Love entering a situation of sin, rebellion, hatred, contempt, murder, and blasphemy can remain love only if ready to suffer and to die—"unless a wheat grain falls on the ground and dies, it remains only a single grain; but if it dies, it yields a rich harvest" (John 12:24). Evil can be expected to be rejected freely only if it is not opposed by threat and violence, and that means that the opponent of evil must be prepared to let evil have its way, and this suffering, and possibly death. That was the way of Christ, and we are commanded to act, to love likewise, in the same spirit (John 13:34). This is the meaning of the New Commandment given after the Lord had washed the feet of the Apostles, and a few hours before He surrendered to the powers of evil, to the Sin of the World.

At His arrest, Jesus said to those who had come to arrest Him, "This is your hour; this is the reign of darkness" (Luke 22:53). To resist evil and to conquer it with good (Rom 12:21), to love one's enemy (Mat 5:44), to "follow Christ by loving as He loved" (Eph 5:2)—this is the New Commandment, by which Jesus' conquering love is concretely channeled into the world by His followers. "Just as I have loved you, you also must love one another" (John 13:34). In this way, God revealed Himself through Jesus as love (John 14:9, 1 John 4:8, 16), and He will continue to be revealed as love through us, His members and followers—"By this love you have for one another, everyone will know that you are my disciples" (John 13:35; 17:21, 23). We, the Church, by the power of Jesus, will, as a new element, a new power in history, manifest and actualize "the mystery of God's love for men" (*Pastoral Constitution*, 45). But this love, on our part, in a world deformed and permeated by sin—as even our own hearts are, though we are baptized—would be fantasy and illusion without readiness for the cross. "If anyone wants to be a follower of mine, let him renounce himself and take up his cross and follow me . . . anyone who loses his life for my sake will find it" (Mat 16:24-25).

Christ's obedience unto death on the Cross (Phil 2:8) is the injection of the eternal life of the Godhead—the total mutual surrender of the three Divine Persons that constitute the Blessed Trinity in Unity—into the hostile, rebellious world of man, God the Son emptying Himself through Incarnation even to annihilation of the Cross—"on the Cross only the Godhead was hidden" (St. Thomas Aquinas, see above). But faith, grasping the mystery of the Cross of Christ can also realize the continuation of this mystery, where "His humanity is also hidden" (St. Thomas Aquinas), when the Risen Lord, our Sacrifice, becomes present on the altar.

The tact and gentleness of Jesus Christ—coming among us again and again by the power of the priest—not compelling us to repent, to love, to remain faithful, to carry Christ into the world—this hiddenness is the mark of true Christian life. Only the desire to "have died" and to lead a life that is "hidden with Christ in God" (Col 3:2) can free us from vanity and pride, enabling us to serve—to be Church—rather than to demand to be served (Mat 4:10). Our Lord's long hidden years, His life with Mary and Joseph— they were not wasted, but were thoroughly apostolic, self-effacing, open before God. Whether we meet Christ in the Gospels, where only the Godhead is hidden, or in the Eucharist, where "His humanity is also hidden," it is the Christ who is "gentle and humble in heart" in whom we find rest for our souls (Mat 11:29). "He cured them all, but warned them not to make Him known. This was to fulfill the prophecy of Isaiah: 'Here is my servant whom I have chosen, my beloved, the favorite of my soul. I will endow him with my spirit, and he will proclaim the true faith to the nations. He will not brawl or shout, nor will anyone hear his voice in the streets. He will not break the crushed reed, not put out the smoldering wick till he has led the truth to victory: in His name the nations will put their hope'" (Mat 12:15-21).

72. Truths Anchored in the Eucharist

"This mysterious change is very appropriately called transubstantiation. *Every theological explanation which seeks some understanding of this mystery must, in order to be in accord with Catholic faith, maintain that in the reality itself, independently of our mind, the bread and wine have ceased to exist after the consecration, so that it is the adorable Body and Blood of the Lord Jesus that from then on are really before us under the sacramental species of bread and wine, as the Lord willed it. . . ."*

Pope Paul gives considerable space to the belief of the Catholic Church with regard to the Eucharist. The reasons would seem to be ecumenical, that no watering down of Catholic doctrine would enter ecumenical discussions. But more important, there has been a great deal of false teaching about the Eucharist in Catholic circles. Much of it appears to be derived from errors in philosophy and from a weakened sense of Divine Providence. But the Eucharist is so central to the life of the Church, that error here could easily have become destructive of the entire faith. Like the theology of Mary, the theology of the Eucharist anchors certain basic truths, or better, realities conceived by the creative mind of God, and discovered in revelation and its theological penetration.

The Pope, in the statement under consideration, reminds the faithful that transubstantiation and the consequent changing of the substance of bread and wine are independent of our mind. What exists in reality is independent of our mind. Our mind can learn or discover what exists in reality; but what exists, as well as what happens, has its ultimate source in the creative mind of God. Human intelligence may conform, with varying limitations, to realities, which cause us to have objective knowledge. God gives existence to His thought, and maintains it in being by His continuing creative thought.

This is the root of philosophical sanity, maintained in the theological explanation of the Eucharist by the Church.

The presence, through consecration, of Jesus' Body and Blood, and by concomitance, of His divinity—these facts form part of the faith of the Church, of the faith of every Catholic. They also safeguard our knowledge of the Incarnation, the continuing reality that began when Mary gave her consent—when the Eternal Son emptied Himself, and began to exist also as a human being, now both "true God and true Man." While on earth, His divinity was hidden. In the Eucharist, His humanity is hidden. But it is always the same Jesus Christ, target and victim of men's sins, now Risen, with "all authority in Heaven and on earth" (Mat 28:18) having been given to Him. "Jesus Christ is the same today as He was yesterday and as He will be forever" (Heb 13:8).

The theology of the Eucharist is the fulfillment of Christ's promise which was the last word He spoke while on earth—"And know that I am with you always; yes, to the end of time" (Mat 28:20). The power of the Church, through her priests, to render present the Sacrifice of Calvary, the victory of Christ's redeeming love over evil—not only evil manifest then, but in our world today, in my heart right now—this is brought home in the common, shared awareness in faith and hope of the reality of the presence of His once crucified humanity and of His redeeming, liberating power now as the Risen Lord. "Sitting at the right hand of the Father, He is constantly active in the world in order to lead men to the Church and, through it, join them more closely to Himself; and by nourishing them with His own Body and Blood, make them partakers of His glorious life" (*Dogmatic Constitution*, 48).

The Sacrifice of the Mass, which is "the Sacrifice of Calvary rendered sacramentally present" (*Credo*), is the living monument of the reality that God in His Son did more than just empty Himself by becoming as one of us: He became the revelation of the very heart, the very dispostions of God (John 14:9). In an all-embracing solidarity (Rom 12:15) with sinners, He also became literally the target of our sins in His own flesh, suffering all that men have suffered and will suffer, since all suffering is directly or indirectly a consequence of sin. All agonies which we are inflicting on one another in ever greater degrees through the social and natural sciences, the technologies of manipulation of nature and of man, were already suffered by our Lord. Yet, throughout all His suffering for our sins, that incomprehensible redeeming love of the Father channeled into and through the Heart of Jesus was always present.

In the Eucharist are anchored the marvels of God that were heard on the first Pentecost by all the assembled tribes in their own tongues (Acts 2:11)—the marvels of Incarnation, the teachings of the Lord, His miraculous signs confirming Him and His teaching, finally His placing Himself into the way of Sin in order to absorb it all by love, "to be the sacrifice that takes our sins away" (1 John 4:10). For "a man can have no greater love than to lay down his life for his friends" (John 15:13).

And the Eucharist, God's gift entrusted to the Church on her pilgrimage, in turn helps extend the Church and increases the intensity of her activity. For "as often as the commemoration of the host is celebrated, the work of Redemption is in operation" (Former Mass, Secret, Ninth Sunday after Pentecost). And this is, after all, the reason for Christ, who "for us men and for our salvation came down from Heaven" (Creed of the Mass). It is the reason for the Chruch, whose "unique mission is that of making Christ present to men" (Henri de Lubac, *Splendor of the Church*, p. 161)—to make men ready for the Eucharist. "As I, who am sent by the living Father, myself draw life from the Father, so whoever eats me will draw life from me . . . anyone who eats this bread will live forever" (John 6:57-58). Jesus is our Resurrection and our Life (John 11:25).

73. Co-Workers of God

"It is the adorable Body and Blood of the Lord Jesus that . . . are really before us under the sacramental species of bread and wine, as the Lord willed it in order to give Himself to us as food and to associate us with the unity of His Mystical Body."

"The Church has but one sole purpose—that the Kingdom of God may come and the salvation of the human race may be accomplished" (*Pastoral Constitution*, 45). The major task of the Church, the instrument and revelation of Christ, is to give, and thereby, to be, Christ to the world. In teaching, She calls mankind and disposes those who hear—forming in them the mind of Christ (Phil 2:5). In ruling, She shows the way, or rather, Him who is the Way, so that in faith and hope we will trust the Church to lead us through our obedience from sin to unity with the Father, to become children of God (John 3:5; Rom 8:14-16; John 1:12; 1 John 3:2). "May they all be one . . . in us . . . with me in them and you in me" (John 17:21-23).

Restoration of that original union or sanctity—when man was established "in holiness and justice, and in which man knew neither evil nor death" (*Credo*)—and growth in holiness, growth into God, of these things the Church is the instrument and the fruit. This is the sanctifying task of Christ and function of the Church. The Church is both the instrument and the fruit of that creative, redeeming love in the Heart of Christ by which, from the Cross, He drew all men to Himself, and continues to do so now, seated at the Father's right hand. This human-divine power was merited when sin found in Him God-made-vulnerable and found Him capable of receving the blows and insults sin is eager to inflict on the Holy One (Wisd 2). In a superhuman effort, He responded with love—His human Will bent on pleading for His torturers and murderers while suffering, while being murdered. This love, by the power of the Spirit, will be able to bring about repentance, conversion, readiness for the Cross, and the gifts of faith, charity, and hope. By the will of Jesus and the power of God we are drawn again into Christ, to "share the divine nature" (2 Pet 1:4) and to "grow into one holy temple in the Lord," and we, too, "in him are being built into a house where God lives in the Spirit" (Eph 2:21-22).

God is Creator of all. Without His creative power nothing could ever happen, nothing could grow. Our growth into Christ, the growth of our capacity to believe, to love, to hope—are all God's gifts. Even our desire for these gifts is His gift—"our desire to thank you is itself your gift" (Preface IV, Weekdays). Here we touch the mystery of human freedom, which is not a power apart from God intruding on God's omnipotence. Freedom for us is fundamentally our God-given readiness to learn God's will, both from moment to moment and also in the general scheme of our lives, so that eventually we will be led to our vocation. Freedom is furthermore the God-given, enabling powers of faith, charity, and hope, and the other virtues which these divine powers transform. "It is God, for His own loving purpose, who puts both the will and the action into you" (Phil 2:13). "We are God's work of art, created in Christ Jesus to live the good life as from the beginning He had meant us to live it" (Eph 2:10). "Glory be to Him whose power, working in us, can do infinitely more than we can ask or imagine" (Eph 3:20). "Whoever remains in me, with me in him, bears fruit in plenty; for cut off from me you can do nothing" (John 15:5). Both God's creative enabling power and our power which God made possible must never be seen as forces in mechanics which simply augment or diminish each other. This idea is an error that has come into Western thought through a fascination with physics and its phenomenal application in technology, as well as through a weakening of religious wonder. The decay of religious life and turning of religious practices into a sort of pragmatic business dealing with the All-Holy God added to this mechanization of religion.

The following might serve as a crude example illustrating the mechanistic thinking in interpersonal relations, above all in our relation to almighty God, a turn of mind in which divine grace and human freedom become two vector forces. Suppose that a man is tempted to seduce a girl; grace meanwhile would move him to go to confession and Mass, and the result, a sort of compromise, would be that the person would visit his ailing grandmother. This is not the way things work. God's infinite power and freedom—in response to the love of the Sacred Heart of Jesus, wounded by our sins—by His mysterious creative power, transforms and enables our inmost being to freely learn and do His will. That is human freedom.

To strengthen our capacities, to eradicate sin from our hearts, and thereby to become ever more single-minded members of the Mystical Body of Christ—this is the way to become co-workers of God (2 Cor 6:1) and to ready us to love as Christ loved (John 13:34). In this way, we can extend the redeeming love of Christ into a world where evil is powerful and destructive; we are enabled to "resist evil and conquer it with good" (Rom 12:21), we bear the very "cross of our Lord Jesus Christ, through whom the world is crucified to me, and I to the world" (Gal 6:14). It is then that I can begin to say with St. Paul: " I have been crucified with Christ, and I now not live with my own life but with the life of Christ who lives in me" (Gal 2:19-20).

74. Seeking a Living Faith

"The unique and indivisible existence of the Lord glorious in Heaven is not multiplied, but is rendered present by the Sacrament in the many places on earth where Mass is celebrated."

Under no circumstances must we ever apply examples from technology to help us illuminate the profound mystery of the sacramental presence of the Risen Humanity of Christ in the Eucharist. It would lead immediately to devastating illusions. The "Unique and indivisible existence of the Lord glorious in Heaven" is beyond comprehension, just as is the nature of our resurrected and glorified bodies, as St. Paul makes overwhelmingly clear in chapter 15 of First Corinthians: "Someone may ask, 'How are dead people raised, and what sort of body do they have when they come back?' They are stupid questions. Whatever you sow in the ground has to die before it is given new life and the thing that you sow is not what is going to come; you sow a bare grain, say of wheat or something like that, and then God gives it the sort of body that He has chosen" (1 Cor 15:35-37). Like all mysteries, that is, like realities beyond our comprehension while "we are seeing a dim reflection in a mirror" (1 Cor 13:12), these realities pertaining to the supernatural must be approached in meditative prayer.

This msyterious presence enters into us at Holy Communion to become "real food" and "real drink" (John 6:55). At Communion we live in Him, and He in us (John 6:56). We draw life from Him, as He Himself draws life from the Father (John 6:57)—draws it so absolutely, that He, eternally, immutably, as Son or Word, is the Life (John 11:25; 14:6). "Anyone who eats this bread will live forever" (John 6:58). For most, this was intolerable language, because their minds were no longer attuned to the supernatural. Our Lord's quotation from Isaiah (Mat 13:14-15) was verified in them. Their hearts had grown coarse, though once they had the faith of little children, ready to enter the Kingdom of Heaven (Mat 18:1-4); their ears were now dull of hearing. Only the apostles remained faithful. For them—and may it be for us, for you and me—Peter spoke those mangificent words no one could have invented: "Lord, to whom shall we go? You have the words of eternal life" (John 6:68). For Jesus' words "are spirit and they are life" (John 6:63).

It is our task to seek an ever more living faith in the presence of the Risen Lord in the Sacrament of the Eucharist, the "manner in which Christ is present in His Church, a manner which surpasses all the others" (*Mystery of Faith*, Pope Paul VI). It is a Presence to be adored, a Presence that heals, a Presence through which our feeble, uncommitted prayers, desires, and resolutions acquire strength and efficacy. Here we touch and are touched by the Source of Grace (Mat 9:20-22), the Fountain of Redemption, and of life, for He is the Resurrection and the Life (John 11:25). No wonder that Monsignor Ronald Knox could speak of the "Real Absence" he sensed when visiting a Calvinist church in Geneva.

Holiness, union with God, having the Mind of Christ—these are all aspects of the "one thing necessary" (Luke 10:42). Our part is to seek, trusting Christ's promise that we shall find (Mat 7:7), in God's own time and (often hidden) way. "I did the planting, Apollos did the watering, but God makes things grow . . . we are fellow workers with God; you are God's farm; God's building" (1 Cor 3:6-9). "It is God, for His own loving purpose, who puts both the will and the action into you" (Phil 2:13). It is for us to listen, to hear, to trust, to accept, and to live in accord with what we have heard in prayer—so we can begin to say, "Your will be done." To love God (Mark 12:29-30) and our neighbor as Christ loved (and continues to love) us (John 13:34)—even, and especially, if our neighbor is seen as hostile and destructive—these loves are commanded, and at the same time, this love is strictly a gift from God, grace. We will it, desire it, pray for it, that we may learn what love demands and have the strength to do it; but God gives "the will and the action." And if our faith, trust, and hope draw us to the Sacrifice of the Mass and to the continuing presence of Christ in the tabernacle, our faith in the reality of Christ's sacrifice and presence allows us to touch Him and power goes out from Him (Luke 8:43-48); then He will continue to draw us to Himself (John 12:32), and we too will hear His word, "your faith has restored you to health; go in peace" (Luke 8:48).

"Glory be to Him whose power, working in us, can do infinitely more than we can ask or imagine" (Eph 3:20).

75. The Living Heart of Our Churches

"And this existence remains present, after the Sacrifice, in the Blessed Sacrament which is, in the tabernacle, the living heart of each of our churches."

The frequent downgrading of the continuing presence of our Risen Lord in the Blessed Sacrament in our churches and chapels is perhaps the most saddening result of the betrayals in the Catholic Church in our time in the affluent countries of the once Christian "Free World." Should we not meditate on the two heart-rending lamentations of our Blessed Lord? "Jerusalem . . . how often have I longed to gather your children, as a hen gathers her brood under her wings, and you refused! So be it! Your house will be left to you. Yes, I promise you, you shall not see me till the time comes when you say: Blessings on him who comes in the name of the Lord!" (Luke 13:34-35); and these words spoken as He shed tears over Jerusalem: "If you in your turn had only understood on this day the message of peace!" (Luke 19:42). But we no longer come in the name of the Lord— our churches, and chapels on campuses and in religious houses are often deserted when there is no Mass, and we no longer understand the message of peace, because it is not communicated to us. The silence of too many shepherds is deafening. It comes from bored rejection and studied ignorance, at times accompanied by a ridicule that makes "the living heart of each of our churches" a place where Christ is repudiated.

One begins to realize that there may be a close relation between frequent abortion among Catholics (one of two pregnancies in once Catholic Austria is terminated by abortion) and the secularized hedonism of people no longer intent on seeking God, of people who refuse to knock and to ask. For without the longing to express and the will to accept what is found, we remain deaf and blind before revealed reality. This results in the paralysis, if not the death, of our faith. The "living heart . . . of our churches" is the living Heart of the Church. To ignore one is to ignore the other.

To seek the presence of Christ in the Blessed Sacrament, to dwell in that presence is much more than a gesture of prayer: it is to enter the supernatural radiance of the healing love of God that fills the human Heart of Christ. "In His body lives the fullness of divinity . . . in the one who is the head of every sovereignty and power" (Col 2:9). If all of us who labor and are overburdened follow His invitation to come to Him, He will give us rest. I must take the cross He has willed for me, His yoke, and learn from Him, for He is gentle and humble in heart (Mat 11:28-29). He is the Lord, because in Him "lives the fullness of divinity,"and to His humanity, to His victorious love, has been entrusted the power and authority to bring all men to salvation and growth in holiness. His human Heart, by His divine power, can now bring about the purifications of the heart, and fill the heart with faith, charity, and that hope which is the very form of charity while we are on earth, the wish that God, who wants "everyone to be saved" (2 Tim 2:4), will prevail in all hearts.

We are "to become true images of His Son" (Rom 8:29), "reflecting like mirrors the brightness of the Lord, [growing] brighter and brighter as we are turned into the image that we reflect" (2 Cor 3:18). We have entered His presence, finding Him whom to seek is already to have found. We seek to become Christlike, to love as He loved (John 13:34; Eph 5:2), with a love characterized by that inner God-given freedom which is poverty of spirit, without which we cannot even begin to say "Thy will be done." Nor could we be gentle without the detachment that comes from the sense of poverty of spirit which enables us to accept "the loss of everything and look on everything as so much rubbish if only we can have Christ and be given a place in Him" (Phil 3:8). The other Beatitudes presuppose this inner poverty, as in turn they clothe that poverty which is the following of Him who "emptied Himself . . . even to accepting death" (Phil 2:6-8). Then we become capable of carrying the actual Cross of Christ, capable as His members and likenesses of extending the Cross into our own historical situation. The Beatitudes are a description of what it is to be Christlike. They are descriptions of our Lord (and His Mother), who, in the tabernacle, is "the living heart of . . . our churches."

"The Word was made flesh, He lived among us" (John 1:14). He still lives among us in the tabernacles of our churches. When we enter His presence, we should keep in mind that He is the Child of Bethlehem, the carpenter of Nazareth, the One who "taught . . . with authority" (Mat 7:29), the tortured and crucified Victim, and the Risen Lord. "Jesus Christ is the same today as He was yesterday and as He will be forever" (Heb 13:8). He is now and forever the Lamb to whom "be all praise, honor, glory, and power, for ever and ever" (Rev 5:13).

"Come, Lord Jesus" (Rev 22:20).

76. The Presence of the Risen Lord

"And it is our very sweet duty to honor and adore in the Blessed Host which our eyes see, the Incarnate Word whom they cannot see, and who, without leaving Heaven, is made present before us."

"Let us be confident, then, in approaching the throne of grace, that we shall have mercy from Him and find grace when we are in need of help" (Heb 4:16). There we find mercy that has at its disposal the infinite power, knowledge, and wisdom of the Divine Son. We are in the presence of a Heart that transforms God's infinite love into human mercy, into human tears: "As He drew near and came in sight of the city, He shed tears over it and said, 'If you in turn had only understood on this day the message of peace. But, alas, it is hidden from your eyes' " (Luke 19:41-42). And every word He ever spoke while among us continues to be spoken to all of us, if only we would listen, as we are urged by the voice of the Eternal Father on the Mountain of the Transfiguration: "This is my Son, the Beloved . . . Listen to Him" (Mat 17:5). This was not meant only for the three Apostles present, but for the Church, of which the Apostles are the foundations, and Peter the Rock. The words of Jesus are revelations of God, of God's disposition and will. "Heaven and earth will pass away, but my words will not pass away" (Mark 13:31). The words are still spoken through the

Church, and lived by saintly people, of whom there are many, though they are hidden from view.

Before the tabernacle we are in the presence of Him who "will wipe away all tears" from the eyes of those (Rev 21:4) who, on earth, have wept; they will now be comforted eternally (Mat 5:5). Any word of Christ found in Scripture is here and now spoken to us with the nearness and intensity of those words when they were spoken historically in Palestine.

We are now in the presence of the Risen Lord as we shall be in Heaven. Faith is the God-given ability that enables us to "prove the existence of the realities that at present remain unseen" (Heb 11:1). The gift of faith makes real the content of the faith which we share with the Catholic Church, which inspired St. Thomas Aquinas to write the great Eucharistic hymns, and Mozart to write music to the "Ave Verum." It is the faith of saints, sinners, scholars, and children, the faith that assures us of the Real Presence of the Risen Lord in our churches. The presence is the same, whether we see God face to face or know ourselves in His presence by faith. "In the earthly liturgy we take part in a foretaste of the heavenly liturgy which is celebrated in the Holy City of Jerusalem toward which we journey as pilgrims, where Christ is sitting at the right hand of God" (*Constitution on the Sacred Liturgy*, 8).

But this tremendous Presence, renewed at every Mass, and continued in the tabernacle, is accessible to us all. That we no longer seek the Lord Jesus where He is waiting is a frightening symptom of the massive betrayal on the part of some theologians who have abandoned orthodoxy and have largely monopolized the attention of the media. The passivity of so many bishops remains a mystery, and not exactly a mystery of God's power. We simply see again what Isaiah already described, "Our watchmen are all blind, they notice nothing. Dumb watchdogs all, unable to bark, they dream, lie down, and love to sleep" (Is 56:10).

Decline and betrayal in the Church are the occasion for hearing a new call of God to realize that we are members of One who was destined to be "a sign that is rejected" (Luke 2:34), that with Him we are to be ready to be hated—because His choice withdrew us from the world (John 15:19). Through the life of the Beatitudes we must prepare for the eighth Beatitude: "Blessed those who are persecuted in the cause of right: theirs is the Kingdom of Heaven" (Mat 5:10). The signs of the times are also given by deficiencies in the Church. Rot in the Church not only provoked the Reformation of the sixteenth century, but also brought forth the great reformers within the Catholic Church, and the Council of Trent.

In "approaching the throne of grace" we carry our sadness to the Lord.

At Mass, the sadness is offered to Him in the tabernacle in the Sacrifice of Expiation as we remember that "during His life on earth, He offered up prayer and entreaty, aloud and in silent tears" (Heb 5:7). What Christ began on earth, the Church continues. The Eternal High Priest, Jesus our brother, "because He remains *forever*, can never lose His priesthood. It follows, then, that His power to save is utterly certain, since He is living forever to intercede for all who come to God through Him" (Heb 7:24-25). To come to the Father through Him; for the Father to come and speak to us through Him; to remain quietly in the Divine Presence—that "is our very sweet duty to honor and adore . . . the Incarnate Word . . . who, without leaving Heaven, is made present before us" (*Credo*).

Adoro te devote, latens Deitas,
Quae sub his figuris vere latitas;
Tibi se cor meum totum subiicit,
Quia te contemplans, totum deficit.

Devoutly I adore you, hidden Godhead,
Truly hidden under these signs.
My heart is given totally to you,
My heart knows nothing else, when contemplating you.

(St. Thomas Aquinas)

77. The Kingdom of God

"We confess that the Kingdom of God begun here below in the Church of Christ is not of this world whose form is passing. . . ."

(Read *Pastoral Constitution*, section 39.)

"Mine is not a kingdom of this world; if my kingdom were of this world, my men would have fought to prevent my being surrendered to the Jews" (John 18:36). The Kingdom of God begins to take root in the heart when man first enters into communion with the Triune God, that is, when He is baptized into the name and into the life of the Divine Persons, and begins to partake of the divine nature (2 Pet 1:4). At this time something comes to man which will last forever and which will not be lost by death: it is the divine life which at death becomes an irrevocable, eternal possession.

Eternal life, which alone gives meaning to human existence, has been restored. It is that which allows all men to share a dignity and destiny which creates an equality that transcends all human achievements, all qualities, and all talents. All historical distinctions are then transcended. "All baptized [into] Christ, you have all clothed yourselves in Christ, and there are no more distinctions between Jew and Greek, slave and free, male and female, but all of you are one in Christ Jesus" (Gal 3:27-28). Here lies the root of true equality, true dignity, of human duties, of human rights. And these rights begin when the human person comes into being, when God creates "in each man his spiritual and immortal soul" (*Credo*) at conception.

As the new life of grace grows and draws into its service more and more human talents and achievements, creation is thereby drawn into eternity—through men, the use of created things and the splendor of nature, as discovered by man, enter eternity. "In the glory of Heaven when will come the time of the renewal of all things (Acts 3:21) [then] together with the human race, the universe itself, which is so closely related to man and which attains its destiny through him, will be perfectly reestablished in Christ (Cf. Ep 1:10; Col 1:20; 2 Pet 3:10-13)" (*Dogmatic Constitution*, 48).

The form of the world, of the universe "which attains its destiny through man, " will pass. But when we come to see in the splendor of nature a reflection of the Creator, we discover something of the greatness of God, and of our own capacity for God. "The heavens declare the glory of God, the vault of heaven declares His handiwork" (Ps 19:1). The majesty and beauty of nature—of mountains, waters, and prairies—speaks of God's power, the detail of growing and living things, and above all, man himself, in their coordination and purpose speak of God's wisdom. It is the Creator who enables man to achieve, to organize his life, to use nature in technology, to bring incredible beauty into his own world, and to use the beauty he makes in the service of God.

The Kingdom of God, of Christ, is not of this world. But this world—creation, nature, and man in his wholeness—are to become again restored to God's purpose and thus to His Kingdom. Man was originally created, and all men were meant, to live "In holiness and justice, [knowing] neither evil nor death" (*Credo*). The growing knowledge of nature and the right use of its in God's service would bring, through us, the universe and the earth as the habitat of men, ever more into the service of God, to His eternal glory. "Fill the earth and conquer it" (Gen 1:28) were God's instructions to our first parents. Man's fulfillment of this command takes many forms. And although often marred by vanity and pride, human activities that are constructive and that are performed with a generous spirit enter into eternity with the souls who shared in their existence. Great music, for example, through the composer and through all those who share in its joy by performing and hearing it, lives on in those who find in it a source of purification and strength. When they enter eternal life, the very music enters in and with them into the Kingdom of God. It can be said of every unselfish thought or action, that somehow, by raising us, and through us, others, to a higher and purer existence, they will enter eternity through men. Nothing truly good and unselfish is ever lost; it always, however hidden, raises the spiritual level of mankind.

"It was not for any fault on the part of creation that it was made unable to attain its purpose. . . . Till now the entire creation . . . has been groaning in one great act of giving birth" (Rom 8:20,22). Creation fell with man and it is to be restored through man; it will become eternal glory through man and in man; and in man it will be brought into the Kingdom, to be, again in man, an integral part of the Kingdom. Christ came and placed Himself into the path of sin, of which He is always the target (Mat 25:45), and sin sought to destroy, to crucify Him. But His love for us sinners prevailed. Thus, "He would bring everything together under Christ, as head, everything in the heavens and everything on earth" (Eph 1:10). When the Kingdom of God is established, the love of Christ will have reached all who are saved, and in and through them all creation and all true achievements of men will become part of the Kingdom of God. It will be "a Kingdom of truth and life . . . of holiness and grace . . . of justice, love, and peace" (Preface, Feast of Christ the King).

78. Material Progress and the Kingdom of God

We confess that the Kingdom of God's "proper growth cannot be confounded with the progress of civilization, of science, or of human technology. . . ."

The optimism that characterized the period before World War II is no longer credible. The somewhat naively entertained hopes that the explosion of historical, scientific, and psychological knowledge would lead to ever greater happiness for increasingly large numbers of people have not been fulfilled. The enormous progress in the conquest of bodily diseases has been accompanied by a growing inability to cope with life, marriage, children, death; to cope with the addictive escape from increasing boredom into television and elsewhere. Mental breakdowns have become more common and the very fear of them torments more and more people. One would think that the myth of progress would have been discarded. However, it seems that we tie our hopes again and again to some actual or hoped-for discoveries, only to find them chimerical. It all should point to the revealed fact that unless the Kingdom of God is our first and absorbing concern, nothing else will bring lasting solutions. "No one can serve two masters . . . you cannot serve both God and mammon" (Mat 6:24). "Set your hearts on His [God's] Kingdom first, and on His righteousness, and all these other things will be given you as well" (Mat 6:33). "What, then, will a man gain if he wins the whole world and ruins his life?" (Mat 16:26).

The growth of God's Kingdom in us—the growing dominion of God in our lives; our increased willingness and ability to mean what we say when we pray, "They will be done"; our acquisition of the Mind of Christ (Phil 2:5) by becoming more generous, self-effacing, and ready for crosses; our growing into union with God, letting the divine life in us grow; our living increasingly "with the life of Christ" who comes to live in us (Gal 2:19-20), being "crucified with Christ," and living less with our own life—this is a life of growth in faith, hope, and charity, a life in which Christ becomes more and more our Way, Truth, and Life (John 14:6). This is growth in holiness (1 Thess 4:3), growth of union with God (John 17:3; 23; Eph 3:17-19); it is becoming an extension, a member of Christ, of coming to be Church, and coming to contribute to the Church's task of revealing and actualizing God's redeeming love for all men (*Pastoral Constitution*, 45). It is the apostolate into which we have been baptized and confirmed.

The fascination with technology seems to obscure the "one thing necessary" (Luke 10:41). Only by faith can we really adhere to the invisible, where reality is anchored, where God dwells "whose home is in inaccessible light, whom no man has seen and no man is able to see" (1 Tim 6:16), where the destiny toward which we journey, in which we already share by the life of grace, lies. "We have no eyes for things that are visible, but only for things that are invisible; for visible things last only for a time, and the invisible things are eternal" (2 Cor 4:18).

Man's ability to "fill the earth and conquer it" (Gen 1:28) has enormously expanded in the last five hundred years, and this expansion is constantly accelerating. It is natural to expect new knowlege and its application to resolve difficulties, to improve life, and to spread the new benefits to all men on this earth. It is natural to expect education to make men more moral, and finally bring about relative Heaven on earth. But this is not happening. This accounts for the upsetting growth of disillusionment and the fact that the new powers of man are being increasingly monopolized and used for destruction. We are now able to destroy mankind, and the statistical likelihood of major nuclear war is growing. How can we balance progress of science and technology, so necessary for survival and for providing decent conditions for all of mankind, with that wisdom without which all good turns into means of oppression, exploitation, and destruction? The ancient problem, now becoming critically decisive, is the question of power and responsibility. But responsibility is the will to respond to the fullness of reality, above all to essential revealed reality, without which we cannot know the meaning of human existence and our true priorities, and without which we would not know that we could gain the whole world and yet lose God (Mat 16:26): that it is not technology but eternal life for which we exist and which will be our eternity. Death, though it appears to be extinction, is actually transition, and the assurance of resurrection of the body and of ultimate integrity and joy will allow us to live in hope, holding on to the revealed fact "that what we suffer in this life can never be compared to the glory, as yet unrevealed, which is waiting for us" (Rom 8:18).

God will continue to show up "the foolishness of human wisdom" (1 Cor 1:20). And the invitation of Jesus who "suffered outside the gate to sanctify the people with His own blood" (Heb 13:12) continues, and "God's foolishness" continues to prove "wiser than human wisdom, and God's weakness [to be] stronger than human strength" (1 Cor 1:25). It is Christ Crucified and Risen to whom we turn and whom we follow.

79. Growth in Holiness

The Kingdom of God "consists in an ever more profound knowledge of the unfathomable riches of Christ."

The concept of infinity will always remain an inexhaustible mystery to men, even when we see God "face to face" (1 Cor 13:12). But we can always deepen our knowledge of God, a knowledge which leads to the hope of union with God, and in turn, elicits from us, by the grace of God, a response of love, as God becomes known as Love.

Knowledge of God is rooted in our love for Him, our union with Him. And His Love for us—"He loved us first" (1 John 4:19)—is the creative source of our capacity to love Him and to love our neighbor as we are commanded (John 13:34). And His creative Love is the cause both of the capacity to love and of every exercise of love, for God "puts both the will and the action" into us (Phil 2:13). "We are God's work of art, created in Christ Jesus to live the good life as from the beginning He had meant us to live it" (Eph 2:10).

What God and His grace enable us to be and to do is far beyond our natural capacity. His "power, working in us, can do infinitely more than we can ask or imagine" (Eph 3:20). Grace is a sharing in the very mystery which God is, yet its workings remain largely hidden (Eph 3:16) as we are purified and transformed by it and as it allows us "to share the divine nature" (2 Pet 1:4). Now I begin to "live . . . not with my own life but with the life of Christ who lives in me" (Gal 2:20; see also Eph 3:17). As a branch of the vine, remaining in Him and He living in men, I will, hidden even from myself, bear "fruit in plenty"; but cut off from our Lord, I can do nothing (John 15:5). Our true life, the life of grace, is hidden, because God is a hidden God (Is 45:15), "whose home is in inaccessible light" (1 Tim 6:16).

What we have considered in the words of our Lord, of St. Peter, St. John, and St. Paul, is the Kingdom of God, enveloping us, drawing us, and incorporating us, as we become stronger members of Christ's Mystical Body, of the Church, as we are "being built into a house where God lives, in the Spirit" (Eph 2:22). The "profound knowledge of the unfathomable riches of Christ" (*Credo*) is already eternal life (John 17:3), which began with our baptism "into Christ" (Gal 3:27; see also Mat 28:19). As this life grows, purifies, permeates, and transforms our whole being, it strengthens our capacity to believe, to hope, to love. As we learn to die to ourselves—"you cannot belong to Christ Jesus unless you crucify all self-indulgent pasions and desires" (Gal 5:24)—we acquire, we are given the Mind of Christ, who, as God, "emptied Himself" by becoming Man, became in His humanity a servant, and in the obedience of love, humbled Himself "even to accepting death, death on a cross" (Phil 2:5-8). We know of the horrors these last words evoke.

The Kingdom of God—where God prevails, rules, and dwells—is meant to embrace all men. All men are called into this Kingdom, and by becoming part of it, are called to extend the Kingdom of God. And this call from Christ should go forth through us. "It is as though God were appealing through us" (2 Cor 5:20). For all men are called to salvation and to growth in holiness. Holiness is eternal life begun and growing now in this life, which will become our irrevocable possession at the moment of death, and will open up either then or after purification unto the beatific vision, when we will see God face to face (1 Cor 13:12; Rev 22:4) and reign with Him "forever and ever" (Rev 22:5). Our quest, our essential life now, is to set our "hearts on His Kingdom first," and on His (God's) holiness (Mat 6:33). We are to come to "an ever more profound knowledge" (*Credo*) of God's holiness in Christ in whose "body lives the fullness of divinity" (Col 2:9), and, in setting our hearts on God's holiness, to seek to share it by becoming holy. "Yahweh spoke to Moses; He said: 'Speak to the whole community of the sons of Israel and say to them: "Be holy, for I, Yahweh your God, am holy" ' "(Lev 19:1-2). "What God wants is for you all to be holy" (1 Thess 4:3). Growth in holiness, growth in the capacity for eternal life, growth in actual union with God, with the Father in Christ and Christ in us (John 17:23), that is the essential task and vocation of man, and all else must be in its service. "And eternal life is this: to know you, the only true God, and Jesus Christ whom you have sent" (John 17:3).

And so we pray: "thy Kingdom come," "come, Lord Jesus" (Rev 22:20).

80. The Virtue of Hope

The Kingdom of God "consists in . . . an ever stronger hope in eternal blessings, an ever more ardent response to the Love of God. . . ."

The more we become victims of the illusionary hopes and escapes of modern life, whether chemically or psychologically induced, the more unreal, even unthinkable becomes the promise, the hope, and the reality of eternal life. Eternal life is then relegated to the realm of fantasy. On the other hand, disillusionment and boredom bordering on despair can create a deep thirst for something real, for real peace, for true meaning of life extending beyond death into an eternity of true joy, of true love. But unless the realities, "the glory, as yet unrevealed which is waiting for us" (Rom 8:18), are credibly proclaimed and grasped in faith, where can man turn to? Man's thirst for something that would draw him out of his despondency, boredom, and despair is certainly exploited by many religious enterprises, often calculating, at times simply naive, always embarrasssing.

For Christians, the Kingdom of God into which we have been called is not simply our own personal hope. It is something we must spread to others. As we enter more deeply into this Kingdom and the Kingdom into us, we become signs and instruments of this Kingdom, for the Lord and King (Rev 19:16) Jesus Christ comes to rule in us and to avail Himself of us as He shines through us, because He now lives in us. "I have been crucified with Christ" (Gal 2:19)—to be crucified is the means of purification and growth, the act of emptying oneself unto death (Phil 2:7-8)—so that "I live . . . not with my own life but with the life of Christ who lives in me" (Gal 2:20).

This transformation into the life of Christ must go on because we are "intended to become true images of His Son" (Rom 8:29), "reflecting like mirrors the brightness of the Lord, all grow brighter . . . as we are turned into the image that we reflect" (2 Cor 3:18). We become "light in the Lord" (Eph 5:9), because "anything illuminated turns into light" (Eph 5:14). We will become the "light of the world" (Mat 5:14), because by following Him, who is in Himself "the light of the world," we "will have the light of life" (John 8:12). And through us, Jesus Christ, who is the light, will "give light to those who live in darkness and the shadow of death" (Luke 1:79). And through us as humble revelations and signs of Christ, He will restore hope to men who are "immersed in this world, without hope and without God" (Eph 2:12). As Vatican II teaches, "in the lives of those . . . more perfectly transformed into the image of Christ . . . God shows to men . . . His presence and His face" (*Dogmatic Constitution*, 50). This is the soul of the apostolate of all who are the Church, who are members of Christ. "It is as though God were appealing through us" (2 Cor 5:20).

My "hope in eternal blessings" (*Credo*) is never an isolated hope only for myself. God loves me with a love that fills the human Heart of Jesus and was extended to me from the Cross, since I was known to Him though I was not yet born (John 12:32). He continues now from Heaven to draw me to Himself—"constituted Lord by His Resurrection and given all authority in Heaven and on earth [Mat 28:18], Christ is now at work in the hearts of men. . . ." (*Pastoral Constitution*, 38). He is at work in my heart, even if I resist Him, rebel against Him, or hide from Him as our First Parents did (Gen 3:8) and as men continue to do when they become guilty of sin. Jesus Christ still is the Good Shepherd (John 10:14; Mat 18:12-14) who will forgive seven times seventy times as we as His members are told to do (Mat 18:22), that is, again and again, if we only seek Him (Mat 7:7).

But as Christ's love embraces and seeks to lead all men, our love must also embrace all men in hope for their salvation. If hope is a "response to the Love of God'' (*Credo*) for others, even for all men, then our hope must enter into the same range and cannot remain confined to ourselves. We must desire and learn to hope for the salvation and growth in holiness of others, and with and as the Church, even for *all* others. Hope, a supernatural virtue, a gift from God, is given to us by God ''for his own loving purpose'' (Phil 2:13), which is the salvation of others (1 Tim 2:4), the salvation of all. As Christ's members we cannot withdraw from our share in the work of Redemption. ''It was God who reconciled us to Himself through Christ, and gave us the work of handing on this reconciliation'' (2 Cor 5:18). For this we must hope, and our hope must be an active hope through prayer and expiation.

This active desire is the essential core of love of neighbor, which, as God's redeeming Love for all men, has its origin in the Father, fills the Heart of Jesus, and from there seeks entrance into our hearts, to make us true members and instruments of our Lord and Redeemer. This is our apostolate, which belongs to the very nature of the Christian vocation. ''The Lord's greatest commandment,'' charity, ''urges all Christians to work for . . . the communication of eternal life to all men'' (*Decree on the Apostolate of Lay People*, 2 and 3). And the form of this charity is hope—in love—that His Kingdom may come to all.

81. Solidarity in Grace

The Kingdom of God consists in ''an ever more generous bestowal of grace and holiness among men.''

Sanctifying grace makes us capable of being ''partakers of the Divine Nature'' (2 Pet 1:4), of becoming one with God, of Christ dwelling in our hearts (Eph 3:17), with the Father in Him (John 17:23). The condition—loving the speaker of these words, Jesus Christ—is fulfilled by keeping His word. It is an obedience, because, as our Lord had just said, to love Him is to receive and keep His commandments—if we do so, then we are among those who love Him (John 17:21). Verses 21 and 23 of St. John's Gospel are to be meditated on in all simplicity; they are meant for us all.

Recognizing the necessity of obedience, we then must inquire what His commandments really are. We are dealing not with suggestions, but with commandments that give divine life, with decisions determining our eternity—whether this will be eternal joy, seeing God "face to face" (1 Cor 13:12) in the beatific vision (Heaven) or whether in lukewarmness and indifference, or in rebellion and diabolical pride, we keep away from us the Creator of Heaven and earth, repudiating His saving Love that comes to us in Jesus, helpless in the manger, and in Jesus, helpless on the Cross. Eternal loss is the persistent repudiation until the moment of death of God, who comes to us with "tender mercy" to give light to us "who live in darkness and the shadow of death" (Luke 2:78-79). It is man's malice in the rejection of "the kindness and love of God our Savior" (Titus 3:4), who "will disown us" "if we disown Him," but who "is always faithful" even while we are unfaithful (2 Tim 2:12-13).

We are created to be saints, to be restored to the life of grace and union with God begun in baptism, to grow in holiness. Holiness is to be united to God, it is to have our "hidden self . . . grow strong, so that Christ may live in our hearts through faith" (Eph 3:17). It is to be "planted in love . . . [to be] filled with the utter fullness of God" (Eph 3:17, 19).

But we live in a certain solidarity of sin with the rest of mankind. We have inherited the deprivations due to Original Sin and continue to live in an atmosphere, a situation of sin, where success comes more easily through sin, and where seeking and serving God often leads to crosses. "If anyone wants to be a follower of mine, let him renounce himself and take up his cross every day and follow me" (Luke 9:23). But there is a solidarity in grace, implied when we speak in the plural in prayer. These two solidarities transcend all distances and physical communication. The spiritual level of our milieu or community is affected by our prayers. But since prayer can embrace all people, including people we do not know, failure to pray well—to become slack in prayer because of our mediocrity, or not to pray at all, while our evil intentions, even if never translated into actions, grow—all this depresses the spirit of the individual person and even spreads its ill effects to the whole world.

The prayers of the Church and the existence of contemplative orders bear witness to the solidarity in grace, rooted in the common destiny of all men, who are all enveloped by the one God's love. We were all drawn by Christ to Himself while He was apparently defeated by the Sin of the World during the Crucifixion (John 12:32). The now Risen Lord continues to draw all men to Himself, now through the Church "a sign and instrument . . . of communion with God and of unity among all men" (*Dogmatic Constitution*, 1). This involves all the baptized in the responsibility for the salvation of the whole world, and obliges all of us to the essential apostolate of prayer and expiation.

We ask Mary to "pray for us sinners." It is a universal prayer, an entering into God's desire that all men find salvation, especially those who are on a disaster course, hiding from God, defying Him, seducing others to do so (Rom 1:32). And as members of Jesus Christ, Redeemer of the whole world, we are commanded to love as He loves (John 13:34). With Him and for Him—to render His love a historical revelation in this world (Col 1:24)—we are to love our enemies (Mat 5:44) who by wrongdoing are defying God. We are to pray for our persecutors. In this way we become sons of our Father in heaven (verse 45). And by thus extending God's love to our opponents, we come to share this very perfection of God, we are "perfect as our Heavenly Father is perfect" (verse 48)—we reveal and actualize His redeeming love.

When we pray "thy Kingdom come," trying to realize and mean what we say, we are praying as children of God and members of Christ who "came into the world to save sinners" (1 Tim 1:15). Although we thus pray, more truly than St. Paul we must say that we are among the greatest of sinners (1 Tim 1:15).

Following the words of Christ, in seeking single-minded service of God (Mat 6:24), we again and again tear ourselves away from worrying about our life, what we are to eat and how to clothe our bodies (Mat 6:25). We "set [our] hearts on His Kingdom first, and on His holiness" (Mat 6:33), to become vessels and channels of God's redeeming love. Then we, and others aided by us, will enter more deeply "the Kingdom of God" which "consists in . . . an ever more generous bestowal of grace and holiness among men" (*Credo*).

82. Christian Renewal of Society

"But it is [the ardent response to the love of God] which induces the Church to concern Herself constantly about the true temporal welfare of men."

It is God's redeeming love that moves people to be concerned about human dignity and friendship, and inspires man to live on earth in justice and holiness, fighting evil and alleviating suffering, "to live religious and reverent lives in peace and quiet" (1 Tim 2:2). Evangelical inspiration is the leaven of justice on all levels of human relations, both in the family, and in the varied communities we find ourselves in, communities that are becoming increasingly diverse and more representative of all mankind. What Christ gave us in the Parable of the Good Samaritan (Luke 10:29-37), in the admonition on the danger of riches (Mat 19:23-26)—His proclamation that we cannot serve both God and money, and must not allow temporal cares, however justified, to crowd out the thought of God and of trust in Him (Mat 6:24, 33)—is the kind of divine, corrective leavening that He continues to proclaim through His Church. Vatican II in the *Pastoral Constitution* (sections 38-45) deals at great length with the relation of temporal responsibilities to our journey toward death and resurrection, toward eternal life. We find in the life and teachings of Christ the incentive and motivation for assuming responsibility in caring for our neighbor, for doing our part for the good of society—to work for improvements, and to labor for justice and the alleviation of suffering. We show love of our neighbor—always an act of obedience to God's commandment (John 13:34)—in part by our service to society; but service to society must be put in its right place in a hierarchy of values, an order of priorities totally directed to the goal of our common pilgrimage toward eternal life, union with God, the beatific vision—to the eternal joy that God in His love wishes to share with us (John 17:13). We must learn to thirst for these things. "God, you are my God, I am seeking you, my soul is thirsting for you" (Ps 63:1). And if we find in our hearts no response, if longing for God is difficult for us or impossible, then we must, in faith, long for the ability to thirst for God, and pray Psalms such as 42 or 63 as an expression of what we would like to share in, but are not yet capable of sharing—"My soul thrists for God, the God of life; when shall I go to see the face of God?" (Ps 42:2).

"Grace and holiness among men" (*Credo*) are alone the inspiration, motive, and foundation of a true self-effacing concern for temporal welfare. Enlightened self-interest is a mockery of Christ. If we will not learn to desire the Mind of Chirst, and like Him empty ourselves, and "assume the condition of a servant" (Ph 2:5-8), and prefer even death to committing injustice (John 15:13; 1 John 3:16; cp. Socrates), our contribution to social, economic, and political justice will be nil. We will join the chorus of self-righteous, smug, blind pretenders to Christianity, who happily lay down their conditions for accepting Christ, and who pray, "I thank you, God, that I am not grasping, unjust, adulterous like the rest of mankind. . . . I pay tithes on all I get" (Luke 18:11-12). Respectability is not holiness; public relations devices and illusions do not deceive Almighty God. To the affluent hypocrite, who denies the Cross by thinking that success is a sign of God's approval, and the popularity is a foretaste of Heaven, these words continue to be spoken: "You say to yourself, 'I am rich, I have made a fortune, and have everything I want,' never realizing that you are wretchedly and pitiably poor and blind and naked too" (Rev 3:17).

At all times, and today more than ever, Christian existence demands of those who have received the gifts of faith and baptism a readiness for heavy crosses—an inescapable element of putting on the Mind of Christ who, in obedience to the Father, emptied Himself even unto death, death on a cross (Phil 2:8). That is why Maritain wrote: "Christian heroism has not the same sources as heroism of other kinds. It has its source in the Heart of God scourged and turned to scorn and crucified outside the city gate" (Heb 13:12—*Freedom in the Modern World*, p. 145). And, to "work for a renewal of the temporal order on Christian principles yet not to work in a truly Christian spirit would be to spoil the thing in an effort to bring it into being: which is the most subtle form of treason" (op. cit. p. 141). To seek Christian renewal of society is to let the leaven of sanctity permeate society (Mat 13:33), quite invisibly, hidden from the world, known only to God and the blessed in Heaven. Christianity of appearance not only does not exist, it is hypocrisy. As St. Paul wrote, many in the last days "will keep up the outward appearance of religion, but will have rejected the inner power of it" (2 Tim 3:5). This is treason.

"Grace and holiness bestowed on man" (*Credo*), through the hearts of men "induces the Church to concern Herself . . . about the true temporal welfare of men" (*Credo*). Thus the love, originating in the Father, the Origin without origins, descends through men into the world to return to God in the sanctified hearts of men. "This may be a wicked age, but your lives would redeem it" (Eph 5:16). "Brotherly love brings to earth, through the heart of man, the fire of eternal life; which is the true peacemaker" (Jacques Maritain, *The Range of Reason*, "Christian Humanism," p. 196). Thus we become ambassadors of Christ (2 Cor 5:20), "fellow workers with God" (1 Cor 3:9).

83. A Christian Attitude Toward Suffering

"Without ceasing to recall to Her children that they have not here a lasting dwelling, [the Church] also urges them to contribute, each according to his vocation and his means, to the welfare of their

earthly city. . . . "

Law is an educator. Obedience to law is meant to form our minds, our judgments, the direction of our lives in the spirit of the law. We are commanded to love God and our neighbor (Mark 12:29-30), the latter seeking its pattern in Christ's love for us (John 13:34). We serve the law by seeking, finding, and fulfilling the demands of love. Love of God is formed by obedience to the Church, love of neighbor by the teaching and life of the Church as a commentary on the life and teaching of Christ. The liturgy is central to the life of the Church, especially the liturgy of the Eucharist, where adoration and gratitude have their center and source, and where the true interests of men are brought before God.

As our love of God grows, our capacity for God and union with Him becomes deeper, and our transformation into a likeness of Christ becomes more pervasive. The life of faith, charity, and hope begins to replace a life of self-indulgence (Gal 5:19-21) and the believer comes to see the world, and especially other people, with the Mind of Christ (Phil 2:5-8). In union with the Redeemer he will increasingly share the desire of the Father for the salvation of all men, that all might "reach full knowledge of the truth" (1 Tim 2:4). And, imperceptibly at first, there will grow that divine pity that is especially drawn by temporal and spiritual deprivation and sufferings. The believer's share in Christ's compassion, the God-given ability to share vicariously in the sufferings of others, will grow.

Sadness shared with those who are sad (Rom 12:14) will grow into a burning desire to assist—and assistance is always possible through prayer, and by Christlike acceptance of the suffering shared by compassion (which means a "suffering-with").

There now seems to be a new form of suffering in the world, one not even perceived by the sufferer. It is the suffering that results when emptiness and boredom are assumed to be the normal condition of life, a condition experienced by increasing numbers of people, especially those who are relatively affluent. Their home-life is largely empty of warm human relations, education is for them unmitigated boredom, and the inanities and vicarious thrills of television and commercialized entertainment drain any vestige of longing for human warmth. Sex as the only thing remaining to break the hellish monotony of life becomes the source of an even deeper feeling of futility and emptiness. Life is seen as absurd, escapes soon fail, and what is left is that stark paganism described by St. Paul as being "immersed in this world, without hope and without God" (Eph 2:12). It is a real foretaste of hell, where total selfishness bears the eternal fruit of total isolation—a self-inflicted destiny for those who have continued to defy the Lord and giver of life, even at the moment of death. they have made themselves incapable of love, and thus of God, whose name is Love.

Every situation of suffering cries for Redemption. There can never be for us a question of assigning guilt and of deciding that some suffering people are not deserving of Redemption. There can be nothing more radically opposed to the Mind of Christ than to hold that certain people have their suffering "coming to them." For such people, the inspired words of St. James hold: "There will be judgment without mercy for those who have not been merciful themselves; but the merciful need have no fear of judgment" (James 2:13).

Relieving the despair of people is not merely one aspect of the welfare of the earthy city; contributing to the good of the earthly city is clearly a major responsibility, so that people can find the peace and justice that will enable them to "live religious and reverent lives in peace and quiet" (1 Tim 2:2). Doing this would enable people to receive a glimpse of true joy on their journey to eternal life as they find liberation from the deadly lifestyles our civilization imposes on us by the power of commercial persuasion, peer pressure, and the constant din of clichés presented as if they were expressions of divine truths. Our civilization offers other things too. But to discover and cultivate the nobler things offered we have be become truly free—it is the Truth that shall make us free (John 8:32), He who is the Way, the Truth, the Life, and our Resurrection (John 14:6; 11:25). It is He, our Lord Jesus Christ, who continues through the Church to bring us the innumerable manifestations and actualizations of the mystery of God's redeeming, liberating, transforming, creative love (*Pastoral Constitution*, 45)—in word and sacraments. He teaches us, in the Beatitudes (Mat 5:3-12) and in the New Commandment (John 13:34) of that love which was maintained by Him for His murderers—"all men"—while their, our, murderous pursuits found in Him their, our, goal, target, and victim.

There is no solution to the many historical dilemmas infecting our times—South Africa, the Middle East, Northern Ireland, rebellions within the Catholic Church, nations strangled by atheistic regimes, widespread destitution paralyzing and killing millions, nuclear armament—apart from the wisdom of God that is foolishness to men (1 Cor 1:27). There is no salvation from the gross injustices on earth without the Cross. We need no more proof that "the wisdom of this world is foolishness to God" (1 Cor 3:19); we see the bankruptcy of the world's wisdom everywhere. "The human race has nothing to boast about to God." But "God has made [us] members of Christ Jesus and by God's doing He has become our wisdom, and our virtue, and our holiness, and our freedom'' (1 Cor 1:30). Our Lord Jesus Christ is not only the Way: He is the only Way.

84. Being Fools for Christ

The Church urges her children "to promote justice, peace, and brotherhood among men, to give their aid freely to their brothers, especially to the poorest and most unfortunate."

We are told, we are commanded by our Lord to become and to be "the light of the world" and "the salt of the earth" (Mat 5:14, 13). To become light we must let Him, who is in Himself "the light of the world" (John 8:12), shine through us. We are to carry His light, His "tender mercy" among the spiritualy and temporally deprived, "to give light to those who live in darkness and the shadow of death," and to let Christ, through us, guide them "into the way of peace " (Luke 1:78-79). This is the apostolic task into which we are baptized and confirmed—to become, by our very being, by living with the Mind of Christ (Phil 2:5), effective revelations and instruments of Christ.

We are to promote justice in a world filled with gross injustice, to promote peace where there is contempt and hate, to promote brotherhood where the only true source of it—God's redemptive love and our common pilgrimage toward eternal life—is largely unknown or discredited by lies and cheap rhetoric. The attempt to bring about justice, peace, and brotherhood as a utopia, as an inevitable goal of progress in history, leads to ideological rigidities rooted in fantasy, to manipulation of people, and growth of an immovable, inefficient bureaucracy, as seen in so many countries living by some form of atheistic Marxist socialism. The sacrifices of human life, dignity, and freedom; the absence of justice and peace; and the caricature of brotherhood among men who are seen as nothing but the chance product of determinist evolution, is appalling. Such a system now enslaves more than a billion people and keeps their countries impoverished by mismanagement and the building of armaments capable of annihilating mankind. But what can we, what can I, do to hold back this flood of suicidal and murderous madness, especially when one considers that the statistical likelihood of nuclear holocaust grows as more powers come to possess nuclear weapons? Meanwhile, as the powers of oppression expand and grow, through the media and education, in psychological, and also in chemical efficiency, the powers of spiritual and temporal Redemption are becoming more hidden, moving toward a more precarious confrontation with the brute power of the state, while the minds of men are being conditioned and thereby paralyzed by the dominating powers.

As believers, we know that evil and suffering have their root in sin, the sin of Adam and its fruits, the sins of men ever since. To counteract the destructive power of sin and to alleviate suffering, ultimately caused by sin, is the task of seeking (Mat 7:7), hearing (Mat 13:23), and responding (Luke 6:47-49) to God in meditative prayer, and in bearing the crosses rejected in sin (Col 1:24) as part of sharing in the Crucifixion of Christ (Rom 6:5). In doing this, we introduce the sin-destroying power of love into the life of men on earth as an active element of history: we "resist evil and conquer it with good" (Rom 12:21).

This is the way Christ walked: confronting the powers of evil and destruction with weakness, "God's weakness" being "stronger than human strength" (1 Cor 1:25). "It was to shame the wise that God chose what is weak by human reckoning . . . those who are nothing at all to show up those who are everything" (1 Cor 1:27-28). Here lies the root of the utter folly of Mother Teresa of Calcutta in being willing to accept every unwanted child rather than letting the child become a victim of abortion. Here lies the source of the folly of the innumerable "fools for the sake of Christ" (1 Cor 4:10), most of them hidden, who by their hidden crosses, by their fidelity of hope "against hope" (Rom 4:18) and the fidelity of their burning charity are battling the powers of evil. Only a few of these have been canonized by the Church—St. Peter Claver and St. Vincent de Paul, for example. Millions remain hidden, yet they have prevented the world from being completely drowned in immovable stagnation in evil, in the immobility of hell.

Without God's aid, the helplessness of goodness before organized evil, which has the power of the state as its employer, would be complete, and the only thing left would be to abandon the world to evil. But "God loved the world so much," and continues to do so, "that He gave His only Son" (John 3:16) to redeem us while rendered helpless by the Cross. Sin rendered Him helpless, while love achieved its hidden victory.

We, His members, must learn that our strength lies in our weakness, "so that the power of Christ may stay over me . . . for it is when I am weak that I am strong" (2 Cor 12:10). In the conviction that nothing "can ever come between us and the love of God made visible in Christ Jesus our Lord" (Rom 8:39), we must become His crucified members, so that "the power of His resurrection" (Phil 3:10) may counteract the evil that seeks to remove the Love—the Name of God—from the world. Christians, in promoting justice, peace, and brotherhood in whatever situation they find themselves, in the achievement of these ends and in the patient acceptance of the ill-treatment they are made to suffer, try to be without hatred and without pride; they exert a stern measure of self-control so as not to be wanting in justice, and they do not allow falsehood or anything else that degrades man to dishonor their actions. They truly love those against whom they are fighting as they truly love those for whom they are fighting; all the evil that is done to them is engulfed in their charity. Before they bear witness aginst evil, love has consumed the evil in their heart.

85. Solicitude for Others

"The deep solicitude of the Church, the Spouse of Christ, for the needs of men, for their joys and hopes, their griefs and efforts, is therfore nothing other than her great desire to be present to them, in order to illuminate them with the light of Christ and to gather them all in Him their only Savior."

These words of the *Credo* expand on the words of Vatican II, that "the Church has but one sole purpose—that the Kingdom of God may come and the salvation of the human race may be accomplished" (*Pastoral Constitution*, 45). The Church finds herself in growing contradiction to the promises of the world, the world for which our Lord did not wish to pray (John 17:9), the world that "did not know Him" (John 1:10), "a world that is sunk in vice" (2 Pet 1:4), a world in which, without grace, we would inevitably be "immersed . . . without hope and without God" (Eph 2:12).

The task of bringing hope and Redemption to all men is not rooted in Christ's command to "make disciples of all nations" (Mat 28:19). Rather, Christ's command is rooted in the very purpose of the creation of men, the attainment of the blessedness of Heaven, eternal life. To leave people without this knowledge of God's love and design would be utterly inhuman. It would be refusing to share the Gospel, the Good News of salvation, without which man's life on earth can only be a life of despair, or of fleeting escapes, or for a few affluent people, consolation through the kind of precarious happiness that is accessible through money. To carry the Good News, the hope and the gift of salvation to all men is the task of the Church. And every Catholic *is* that Church. This responsibility which constitutes the reason for the Church's existence is called the apostolate, the "being sent" which is an integral part of the Christian vocation (*Decree on the Apostolate of the Lay People*, 2).

For every Catholic there is that task of really sharing "the solicitude of the Church . . . for the needs of men." But how do I acquire this solicitude? How do I enter into the mind and desires of the Church, that is, of Christ? What if I feel indifferent, even callous, and do not even want to know of men's needs, joys, hopes, griefs, and efforts? For such concern cannot be turned on and off at will like a physical action. How do I live honestly by St. Paul's injunction, to "rejoice with those who rejoice and be sad with those in sorrow" (Rom 12:14)? This dilemma is often felt, and tempts us to distrust the sincerity of many who show deep concern for the victims of injustice, a distrust nourished by our desire to see ourselves correct before God—an attitude that elicited from our Lord the following deprecations— "hypocrites . . . blind guides . . . whitewashed tombs . . . full of dead men's bones . . . serpents, brood of vipers" (Mat 23:13-33), deprecations that should truly arouse our consciences and make us approach the Lord "in fear and trembling" (Phil 2:12).

Here may well lie the strange hardening of hearts in some people who consider themselves right-minded, orthodox, "conservative," on the side of the angels—though embarrassed by papal teachings on social justice. Could it be that the words of Isaiah, quoted by our Lord, are spoken to me, to them: "The heart of this nation has grown coarse, their ears are dull of hearing and they have shut their eyes, for fear they should see with their eyes . . . understand with their hearts, and be converted and be healed by me" (Mat 13:15)? Can we really assume, without presumption (a sin against hope), that our hearts are that "rich soil" which alone enables us to hear the word of God and understand it (Mat 13:18-23)? Is not the deafness of Christians often in high places of Church and society, *the* scandal, creating that vacuum which Marxism seems rapidly to be filling? Is our hardness not the beginning of hell? Are not self-righteousness, spiritual snobbery, and smugness the attitudes wich rendered even the Son of God helpless? Guardini wrote:

> God grant us the fear without which we shall never enjoy salvation! . . . Lord, let me be among your chosen. . . . Do not add: 'for I have done no real wrong.' If you are tempted to, fear for your chances. Before this tremendous mystery [of God's] divine will which chooses as it pleases, giving those it has selected to the Son it matters little

whether or not you have done your duty. . . . You must know only this, but as profoundly as possible: that you are a sinner and lost. In this knowledge fling yourself on God's heart and say: Lord, will that I be chosen, that I am among those given to your Son never to be lost— my loved ones and I and all mankind '' (*The Lord*, p. 378).

This is the way, the only way to appeal to the mercy of God filling the human Heart of Jesus who pleads for me. ''His power to save is utterly certain, since He is living forever to intercede for all who come to God through Him'' (Heb 7:25).

He alone is the Way—''no one can come to the Father except through Me'' (John 14:6). But His is the Way of the Cross. And ''anyone who does not take his cross and follow in [His] footsteps is not worthy of [Him]'' (Mat 10:38). ''The deep solicitude of the Church, the Spouse of Christ'' (*Credo*) is ours only if we are willing to suffer persecution, in our own person, and through compassion with a world in agony. Then ours will be the Kingdom of Heaven (Mat 5:10). If we harden our hearts, there will be no Kingdom of Heaven, only hell, eternal isolation, eternal despair. ''If only you would listen to him today, 'Do not harden you hearts.' '' (Ps 95:7).

86. The Hidden Battle in Our Hearts

''This solicitude can never mean that the Church conform herself to the things of this world. . . .''

''The things of this world'' are what we are to give up. ''You must give up your old way of life; you must put aside your old self, which gets corrupted by following illusory desires. Your mind must be renewed by a spiritual revolution'' (Eph 4:22-23). ''Do not model yourselves on the behavior of the world around you'' (Rom 12:2). The *Credo* speaks of the continuous temptation the Church and her members face at all times to yield to the ways and promises of the world. But the betrayals due to our weakness of faith and hope are neutralized in their destructive and corruptive effects by the silent, largely hidden life of prayer and expiation of millions of saintly people, many of whom are quite unaware of their cooperation in the work of Redemption.

Our solidarity in sin is confronted by our solidarity in grace, in prayer and suffering. St. Paul advises Timothy that prayers are to be offered for all, especially for kings and others in authority, and that this will please God our Savior, because He wants everyone to be saved (1 Tim 2:1-4). Our prayers and sufferings may be totally hidden. But "God does not see as man sees; man looks at appearance but Yahweh looks at the heart" (1 Sam 16:7). We must all adhere to the words of St. Paul, "It makes me happy to suffer for you, as I am suffering now, and in my own body to do what I can to make up all that has still to be undergone by Christ for the sake of His Body, the Church" (Col 1:24). Thus Christ's redeeming love in and through us, becomes the revelation and concrete historical application of the "healing power of God's love" (Prayer after communion, 21st Sunday). It is a mystery in its power and effects taking place in the depths of men's hearts. It is a hidden apostolate, open to all, as hidden as the victory of Christ's redeeming, crucified love on Calvary, when He drew all men, all mankind, to Himself.

He continues to draw all men, now from Heaven, allotting to "each one of us . . . his own share of grace" (Eph 4:7), to be given to us "by His Power" (2 Pet 1:3). But men are needed to reveal Christ to other men, for He "gave us the work of handing on this reconciliation" (2 Cor 5:18). "He has entrusted to us the news that they are reconciled. So we are ambassadors for Christ; it is as though God were appealing through us" (2 Cor 5:19-20).

And so the spiritual combat of and on behalf of the Church continues, largely hidden in the hearts of men. It is a battle each one must fight in his own heart. But alone, or in union with others, we pray that the Church, in her solicitude for men's needs, joys, hopes, griefs, and efforts, will be present to give Christ, who alone is the Way, the Truth, and Life, and the Resurrection, to all men, in open proclamation, and will also embrace all men in the secrets of their hearts. Because Christ "the Word was the true light that enlightens all men" (John 1:9), all men are being reached.

For the Church "to conform herself to the things of this world" (*Credo*) is treason, though it does happen. The Church is the sacrament of Him who is "destined to be a sign that is rejected" (Luke 2:34), also that in His Heart love may annihilate evil, by being target and victim of sin. "He was bearing our faults in His own body on the Cross . . . through His wounds you have been healed" (1 P 2:24). Now Christ continues to be "at work in the hearts of men by the power of His Spirit" (*Pastoral Constitution*, 38). But it is through the Church, through you and me, that the mystery of God's love for men is at once manifested and actualized (*Pastoral Constitution*, 45).

The solicitude of the Church, its longing to overcome evil and bring truth and life to men, demands poverty of spirit; the Church must be gentle and willing to suffer sadness, especially over sins in and of the human

Church; She must thirst for holiness and justice, must be merciful and pure in heart; she must reconcile men with God as the foundation of all reconciliation on earth, and must be ready to be persecuted in the cause of right (Mat 5:3-13).

"This may be a wicked age, but your lives should redeem it" (Eph 5:16).

87. Longing for Christ

"This solicitude can never mean that [the Church] lessen the ardor of her expectation of her Lord and of the eternal Kingdom."

(Read Mat 25:31-46; Rev 19:11-16; 21:1-8)

"He will come again in glory to judge the living and the dead, and His Kingdom will have no end" (Creed of the Mass). History, our pilgrimage, will come to an end, though we do not know the "day or hour" (Mark 13:32). After the Second Coming and the Last Judgment, when men will be given again their completeness through the resurrection of the body, everything will be "subjected to Him," Jesus Christ. "Then the Son Himself will be subject in His turn to the One who subjected all things to Him so that God may be all in all" (1 Cor 15:28).

St. Paul spoke of the prize of victory (eternal life) being awarded to "all who have loved [the Lord's] appearing" (2 Tim 4:8). It is incumbent upon us to look toward the end of our pilgrimage, the end of history, to look toward the end which is truly a transition to eternal life—this is of the very essence of Christian existence. If love does not hope for perpetual unity of life and love, it simply is not that holy, pure, expectant love that has its root in the divine reality of total mutual self-giving in triune life. Cardinal Daniélou considered this love, this longing for Christ, one of the most beautiful definitions of a Christian *(Salvation of the Nations,* p. 85). How impoverished is a life in which the final goal, the ultimate purpose of our pilgrimage has no share! Rather it is the expectation of a glorious consummation of the human journey from Paradise through Fall, Redemption, Death, and Resurrection to eternal life, where "God lives among men, [where] He will make His home among [us], [where we] shall be His people . . . [where] He will wipe away all tears from [our] eyes" (Rev 21:3-4), where we shall see Him "face to face" (1 Cor 13:12)—it is this promise and expectation, that vivifies our faith in the God-Creator whose name is Love (1 John 4:8, 16).

The true living God, "the Father almighty," is the God whom we see when we see Jesus (John 14:9), "who is nearest to the Father's heart, who has made Him known" (John 1:18). Jesus is both the eternal and the created human "Image of the unseen God" (Col 1:15). God is truly seen in the Child in Bethlehem, in the carpenter of Nazareth, in Jesus' weeping, healing, teaching, and pleading for us. The eternal Image of the Father, the Word, became incarnate in Jesus Christ. The Son's infinite power, knowledge, and wisdom are now in the service of His redeeming love and mercy, at the disposal of the human Heart of Jesus (2 Pet 1:3), to whom "all authority in Heaven and on earth has been given" (Mat 28:18). Jesus the Man now possesses the authority to allot to us whatever graces we need (Eph 4:7). Certainly, God "loved us first" and therefore we are to love Him (1 John 4:19).

But how can we love when we feel dry, when we are drowned in anxieties, when the reality of God seems so remote, when we do not even know whether we possess the faith that we profess—whether we really "believe in one only God, Father, Son and Holy Spirit [whose] two names Being and Love, express ineffably the same divine reality of Him who has wished to make Himself known to us" (*Credo*)?

In this dilemma—a dilemma possibly more often felt than admitted, even to oneself—it should come as a great relief to learn that loving God and neighbor are commandments, and love therefore is an obedience that can be given independently of feeling. "Anyone who receives my commandments and keeps them will be the one who loves me." "This is what loving God is—keeping His commandments" (1 John 5:3). "His commandments are these: that we believe in the name of His Son Jesus Christ and that we love one another as He told us to" (1 John 3:23; see also John 13:34). To love our neighbor, even our enemy (Mat 5:43-48), is simply to realize God's will toward those He loves, and this includes all men, since Christ's redeeming love drew *all* men to Himself (John 12:32) and continues to now from Heaven. This is the meaning of His being "the King of kings and the Lord of lords" (Rev 19:16). The prayer "Thy will be done" is an act of love.

While on earth, we are on a common journey to eternal life, to Heaven. As Christians we are the Church, which is "a sign and instrument . . . of communion with God and of unity among all men" (*Dogmatic Constitution*, 1). As Church we are called to manifest and actualize "the mystery of God's love for men" (*Pastoral Constitution*, 45)h. In our solicitude for all men and our expectation of the eternal Kingdom we pray, "Come, Lord Jesus" (Rev 22:20).

88. The Way to Eternal Life

"We believe in the life eternal."

How can we speak of the ineffable—"the things that no eye has seen and no ear has heard, things beyond the mind of man, all that God has prepared for those who love Him" (1 Cor 2:9)? Our Lord prayed thus to the Father: "Eternal life is this: to know you, the only true God, and Jesus Christ whom you have sent" (John 17:3). It is seeing the Triune God "face to face" (1 Cor 13:12). It is sharing the very joy of God (John 15:11; 17:13).

If all genuine, unselfish love is a gift from God, a reflection of God; if all true friendship, all real community has its exemplar in God—"that they may be one *as* we are one" (John 17:22; emphasis added); if this unity has its source in God—"with me in them and you in me" (John 17:23)—is a gift of God, then a true reflection of divine joy can be found here on earth. The Kingdom of God has already begun on earth in the hearts of those of generous dispositions—it is promised to those who are poor in spirit, who are willing to suffer persecution "in the cause of right" (Mat 5:10; see also 5:3).

To long for God Himself, not only for deliverance from the burden of living, is a grace. "I want to be gone and be with Christ" (Phil 1:23). "Like the deer that yearns for running streams, so my soul is yearning for you, my God. My soul is thirsting for God, the God of my life; when can I enter and see?" (Ps 42;1-2).

Human love and community also give us an inkling of eternity—"How good, how delightful it is for all to live together like brothers" (Ps 133:1)—for there God can enter and transform human relations into a school for and a foretaste of Heaven. Nature, its grandeur and beauty, its order and wisdom as increasingly laid open by the sciences—"the heavens declare the glory of God" (Ps 19:1)—if adoringly perceived by man will enter in him into eternity. But above all, it is God—Creator, and Savior, whose "two names, Being and Love, express ineffably the same divine reality" (*Credo*, "who has called us by His own glory and goodness" (2 Pet 1:3), "who has shone in our minds to radiate the light of the knowledge of God's glory, the glory on the face of Christ" (2 Cor 4:6)—it is He whom we seek.

Our longing for God is grace; it is the God-given power of hope springing from charity, the hope that I may be a fellow worker of God now (1 Cor 3:9), because apostolic hope is the sharing of God's desire for "everyone to be saved" (1 Tim 2:4). My desire for Heaven must be joined to a desire for the salvation of others, of all others, a desire rooted in faith; that is, in all reality revealed and grasped by the light, the power of faith. We are to "love one another" as Jesus loved, and loves us (John 13:34; 15:12). And we enter Heaven through and with Him who is the Way; there is no other way to the Father (John 14:6).

"I saw the holy city, and the New Jerusalem, coming down from God out of Heaven, as beautiful as a bride all dressed for her husband. Then I heard a loud voice call from the throne, 'You see this city? Here God lives among men. He will make His home among them; they shall be His people, and He will be their God; His name is God-with-them. He will wipe away all tears from their eyes; there will be no more death and no more mourning and sadness' " (Rev 21:2-4).

89. The Mission of the People of God

"We believe that the souls of all those who die in the grace of Christ, whether they must still be purified in Purgatory, or whether from the moment they leave their bodies Jesus takes them to Paradise as He did for the Good Thief, are the People of God in the eternity beyond death. . . ."

To become "the People of God in the eternity beyond death" is our common goal. How do we, how does each one of us, grow into eternal life, into the beatific vision?

"If we live by the truth and in love, we shall grow in all ways into Christ" (Eph 4:15). We "live by the truth" if we "listen to Him," the "Son, the Beloved," who enjoys the Father's favor (Mat 17:5), who is "the Truth" (John 14:6). We "live . . . in love" if we keep His word (John 14:23), because only he who receives His commandments and keeps them loves Him (John 14:20). To obey from love and in love is to follow Him who "became obedient unto death, even death on a cross" (Phil 2:8). This is the New Commandment, to love one another just as He loved us (John 13:34), to "follow Christ by loving as He loved" (Eph 5:2). This is commanded.

We are "baptized into Christ" (Gal 3:29), we are to "grow in all ways in Christ" (Eph 4:15). Thus we become His members, His Church, to whom "He has entrusted . . . the news . . . that [we] are reconciled" (2 Cor 5:19). But this news is not only given to us for our own consolation, but that we may become "ambassadors for Christ," that by becoming Christlike and obedient, we may, *as* Church, be able to become living signs of Christ and His mission—"as though God were appealing through us" (2 Cor 5:20). God's gifts are never to rest in the one to whom they are given. They are to benefit others, and the entire Church on Pilgrimage as well. When we grow "into Christ, who is the head," it is He, our Lord Jesus Christ, who is fitting and joining the whole body together, "every joint adding its own strength, for each separate part to work according to its function. So the body grows until it has built itself up, in love" (Eph 4:15-16).

God "wants everyone to be saved" (1 Tim 2:4); He "has imprisoned all men in their own disobedience only to show mercy to all mankind" (Rom 11:32). It is true, Christians are to be revelations and instruments of Christ and are thereby to become lights of the world (Mat 5:14), lights that "must shine in the sight of men, so that, seeing their good works, they may give the praise to your Father in Heaven" (Mat 5:16). But what of those, the majority of mankind, whom the light of Christ does not reach? How does Jesus Christ, the Word, who is the true light, enlighten "all men" (John 1:9)? Vatican II assures us that Divine Providence does not "deny the assistance necessary for salvation to those who, without any fault of theirs," have not come to know the living God, but to whom grace is given to "strive to lead a good life" (*Dogmatic Constitution*, 16). Must not Christians, although not in personal contact with those who have not come to know the living God, participate in this distant apostolate? It can hardly involve any external activity.

Christ's central act of Redemption was hidden. When, lifted up from the earth to the Cross, He drew *all* men to Himself, this remained invisible. Invisible to the world, the final victory was accomplished in the Heart of Christ, the Heart that was faithful to us, His murderers, and loved us "to the end" (John 13:1). The victory of Christ was the victory of His love for those desiring to destory Him—the One whom we see and hear when we see and hear Jesus (John 14:9). Through this victory Christ merited His Lordship. Now He can continue to intercede for us (Heb 7:25), and to allot to each "his own share of grace" (Eph 4:7).

If we begin to love as He loved and still loves (John 13:34; Eph 5:2), that is, to love our enemies (Mat 5:43-48) as He did, and thereby share His supreme quality of love which is from the Father, we too will become perfect *as* the Heavenly Father is perfect (Mat 5:48), we too will "prove victorious" and be allowed to share His throne (Rev 3:21).

Every cross has its origin in sin, Original Sin, and the sins permeating the world which are all the result of Original Sin. To accept sin's consequences (crosses), however remote in time and space the sin may be from us now, crucifies us with Christ. If we respond as He did, we share in His expiation, through us, an active element of history, blotting out evil with good (Rom 12:21). Without it, our prayers for others would remain somewhat empty, and could hardly be serious. The Law of Christ is to bear one another's troubles, one another's "failings" (Gal 6:2 Knox translation). Thus, every cross can become expiation and contribute to the extension of Christ's victory to all men. This is the apostolate open to all men and incumbent on all Christians. In its hiddenness, it is probably much more common than we are inclined to think. It is "the cross of our Lord Jesus Christ, through whom the world" was crucified to St. Paul, and he to the world (Gal 6:14). These crosses are the birthpangs of the People of God enabling all others to become the People of God until Christ is formed in all (Gal 4:19).

90. Victory over Sin and Death

"We believe that the souls of all those who die in the grace of Christ . . . are the People of God in the eternity beyond death which will be finally conquered on the day of the Resurrection when these souls will be reunited with their bodies."

Death, the wages of sin (Rom 6:23) will be conquered "when everything is subjected to" Jesus, when God will "be all in all" (1 Cor 15:28). The day of "the resurrection of the dead" (Nicene Creed), of Christ's return the Day of Judgment (*Dies Irae*), is the end of the drama of mankind which, but for the Cross of Christ and His victory of redeeming love and fidelity, would have been tragedy. Or does it even rise to the level of tragedy, for apart from the redeeming Cross, man's existence, his living "in wickedness and ill will, hating each other and hateful ourselves" (Tit 3:3), without promise and without hope, would not even have been a tragedy, but total, brutal absurdity. Creation of the universe without man to give meaning to it (*Dogmatic Constitution*, 48), and without the possibility, through man's own resurrection, of bringing the world into the eternity of Heaven, would only have added to the absurdity of existence.

But God "let us know the mystery of His purpose, the hidden plan He so kindly made in Christ from the beginning to act upon when the times had run their course to the end: that He would bring everything together under Christ, as Head, everything in the heavens and everything on earth" (Eph 1:9-10).

Sin implanted absurdity and division into the world, and an impelling force in the hearts of men to destory any trace of God. The original temptation, to usurp God's place, to decide autonomously what is good and evil, right and wrong (Gen 3:5), continues as a temptation in us all. When accepted, it becomes Sin, destructive of the sinner himself and of the world around him. Through a sinner, sin seduces and lies, multiplying evil in the world and discouraging the seeking of God. And all sin is a lived lie. Lies and their destructive potential grow with the powers man acquires as civilization advances. Material and psychological technologies vastly enlarge man's power to achieve in common endeavor, liberation from much toil, much pain, and many hazards. But it also enlarges the power to dominate, manipulate, enslave, exploit, and ultimately extend the seeds of destruction into fruits of destruction. And since total self-destruction is now possible to man, we must reckon with the possibility that the end of history will come about by man's own power over nature. What St. Peter describes (2 Pet 3:10) man can now unleash.

The inner consistency of all we believe, of the content of the faith, cannot be broken without eventually dissolving the faith. One truth, not easily integrated into the mind of Western man, but the ignoring of which would make all else meaningless, is that human nature was originally "established . . . in holiness and justice . . . in which man knew neither evil nor death" (*Credo*). But mankind chose evil by the Sin of Adam, and continues to choose it in the sinfulness of individuals. In consequence, death, the violent tearing apart of body and soul, came into the world. What are we to make of it?

In repudiating Him whose names are Being and Love, man rejects the source of his life, and the meaning of his life, which is to share God's love, life, and joy. He repudiates the one only God without whose creative thought man could not function, could not even exist. The Creator sustains "the universe by his powerful command" (Heb 1:3). But mankind's course was reversed by Adam's rebellion against the Author of truth and life. Now man finds himself naked and helpless, and he hides from his God and Father (Gen 3:7-8). Mankind is set on a course of practical atheism, living as if there were no God. Man is on a course of destruction. Death is inevitable if man is left to nature without the gifts of God that established him "in holiness and justice" untouched by evil. Death became the necessary consequence of mankind's choice made by Adam, a choice repeated again and again throughout history by his descendants. When God is rejected, and His special graces are lost, death follows as a natural consequence.

The incredible fidelity of God's love promised from the very beginning the eventual conquest of sin and death (Gen 3:15), in anticipation of God the Son emptying Himself, through love, into mankind, into service, and into an obedience even including the horrors of His Crucifixion. There, from the Cross, Christ's tortured and rejected love embraced all men (John 12:32), going back to Adam, Eve, and all who had died. It embraced His own contemporaries and all those still to come whom He foresaw in their stumbling, sin-ridden journey to a goal still hidden from most of them. Thus, "death is swallowed up in victory" (1 Cor 15:54). The victory of love sustained for mankind, for every individual human being, was achieved during the agony of His Passion and Crucifixion in inconceivable inner, hidden struggle. "Death and life have contended in that combat" (Sequence, Mass of Easter Sunday).

Full restoration of what was lost by sin will take place on the "Day of Resurrection when these souls will be reunited with their bodies" (*Credo*). Then the dreadful deprivation of man, the death inevitably willed by his rebellion, the separation of body and soul, the punishment for defying God, will ultimately be conquered.

"So let us thank God for giving us the victory through our Lord Jesus Christ. Never give in then, my dear brother, never admit defeat; keep on working at the Lord's work always, knowing that, in the Lord, you cannot be laboring in vain" (1 Cor 15:57-58).

91. Eternal Beatitude

"We believe that the multitude of those gathered around Jesus and Mary in Paradise forms the Church of Heaven, where in eternal beatitude thay see God as He is. . . ."

To "see God as He is," to see "face to face" (Rev 22:4, 1 Cor 13:12) Him "whose home is in inaccessible light, whom no man has seen and no man is able to see" (1 Tim 6:16), this is the heart of man's purpose, the reason for the creation of man and of man's habitat, the universe. Paradise is where all men who have found God's favor, who have not persisted in their rebellion, are gathered in the full unconditional response to God's love, drawn irresistibly into God's life by God's "glory and goodness" (2 Pet 1:3). But what can be said in human language, what can be conceived in terms of human experience and concepts, of "eternal beatitude"? It is revealed that no man is able to see God (1 Tim 6:16). St. Paul, by his inspired word, speaks of "what Scripture calls: the things that no eye has seen and no ear has heard, things beyond the mind of man, all that God has prepared for those who love Him" (1 Cor 2:9).

Heaven is not a fantasy, projected by man to make life tolerable, by setting before us a hope that has no support in reality. It is that to which we are traveling—eternal life. It is "the Holy City of Jerusalem toward which we journey as pilgrims, where Christ is sitting at the right hand of God" (*The Constitution on the Liturgy*, 8). It is the supreme liturgy, where the *Credo* has become immediate beatific vision, the *Gloria* eternal adoration springing irresistibly from the very vision of the Glory that is God, the *Kyrie* and *Agnus Dei* turned into the glory of consummated repentance and conversion. The *Sanctus* is the very vision granted to Isaiah—"I saw the Lord Yahweh seated on a high throne, [and seraphs] cried out one to another in this way, Holy, holy, holy is Yahweh Sabaoth" (Is 6:1-3)—the vision toward which we are journeying, as "in the earthly liturgy we take part in a foretaste of that heavenly liturgy which is celebrated in the Holy City of Jerusalem" (*The Constitution on the Liturgy*, 8).

Without necessarily seeking reasons or attributing guilt, we may well quietly allow great sorrow to seize us when we witness so many of our drab liturgies, performed as an expression of boredom, at times cluttered up with cheap tricks to attract people, aggravated by a mindless recitation of the prayers clothing the sacred action of Holy Mass. There may be hardly an attempt made to attend to what the words, spoken or sung, express. If we cannot avoid such situations, we must, peacefully, try to be among those called "blessed," because they mourn: "they shall be comforted" (Mat 5:5). If we are resentful and indignant, we are only escaping from the cross of liturgical deterioration by carrying anger into the very heart of the sacred liturgy. We should rather stay with our Blessed Lord who wept when He looked upon Jerusalem, because the city, then, like us today, did not understand "the message of peace" hidden from their eyes. Jerusalem was destroyed and has since remained a monument to division and hatred, hardness and irreconcilable factions, who seemingly invoke the same One Only God. And today more than ever. "All because you did not recognize your opportunity when God offered it!" (Luke 19:41-44).

As sin and blindness infiltrated Israel and the Holy City, they continue to infiltrate the Church on Pilgrimage, the Church "clasping sinners to her bosom, at once holy and always in need of purification, following constantly the path of penance and renewal" (*Dogmatic Constitution*, 8). Yet it is the same Church that gives us the Holy Eucharist, and is built up by the continuing presence of the redeeming love of our Blessed Lord, when again and again we "eat this bread and drink this cup . . . proclaiming His death" (1 Cor 11:26). But then, as now—such is our condition after the Fall—"a person who eats and drinks without recognizing the Body, is eating and drinking his own condemnation" (1 Cor 11:29).

"The Church of Heaven"—are there things in creation, are there reflections in human life, that allow us to have some foretaste of Heaven? The longing for Heaven must be more than mere release from loneliness, torture, nausea, despair. It is "the glory, as yet unrevealed, which is waiting for us" (Rom 8:18). Where do we find today "the love of God made visible in Christ Jesus our Lord" (Rom 8:39)? Where do we find traces of the "God that said, 'Let there be light shining out of darkness, [God the Creator], who has shone in our minds to radiate the light of the knowledge of God's glory, the glory on the face of Christ' " (2 Cor 4:6)? Where is the face of Christ?

It is we who are to have the mind of Christ in our humility (Phil 2:5-8), who are to "shine in the world like bright stars," "innocent and genuine, perfect children of God among a deceitful and underhand brood" (Phil 2:16, 15). Holiness comes from the Son of God extending Himself through us, into the world, to become a sign of redeeming contradiction (Luke 2:34), to confront the world that is "sunk in vice" (2 Pet 1:4). Sanctity among men is the revelation and instrument of God, of Jesus Christ, the "Image of the invisible God" (Col 1:15). In Him was seen "the glory that is His as the only Son of the Father, full of grace and truth" (John 1:14). If we truly seek, we will surely find God in Christ; we will be "exposed by the light" and "will be illuminated, and anything illuminated turns into light" (Eph 5:13-14). Thus, by reflecting Him who dwells in us (John 14:23) we will become the "light of the world" (Mat 5:14), "more perfectly transformed into the image of Christ" (cf. 2 Cor 3:18). It is in such lives that "God shows to men, in a vivid way, His presence and His face" (*Dogmatic Constitution*, 50). In the sanctity of the myriads of saints here on earth, Heaven descends among men and hope is aroused and maintained among the vast multitudes still "immersed in this world, without hope and without God" (Eph 2:12). It is through us, drawn into divine life by faith and baptism that the love of God, invisibly drawing all men to Himself through the Heart of Jesus, becomes visible and extends hope and the call of God. As we fail, we understand the words of Leon Bloy, "there is only one unhappiness, and that is—NOT TO BE ONE OF THE SAINTS" ("The Woman who Was Poor," *Pilgrim of the Absolute*, p. 268).

92. The Role of the Saints in Heaven

In the Church of Heaven, the blessed souls "also, in different degrees, are associated with the holy angels in the divine rule exercised by Christ in glory, interceding for us and helping our weakness by their brotherly care."

We are commanded to love one another as Jesus Christ has loved us (John 13:34; Eph 5:1-2). And "what proves that God loves us is that Christ died for us while we were still sinners" (Rom 5:8). This love continues to envelop us still, as Christ's love descends upon us from Heaven. It is the love of the Good Shepherd, who laid down His life for His sheep (John 10:14, 15). This is how we, too, should love one another. This is commanded. It is the Law of Christ, to "carry each other's troubles" (Gal 6:2), to support one another on our journey to Heaven.

Vocations—the manner and scope of being "fellow workers with God" (1 Cor 3:9)—differ. The care or apostolate of Mary, of Joseph, of John the Baptist, of the Apostles is universal. They helped establish the "building that has the Apostles and prophets for its foundations, and Christ Jesus Himself for its main cornerstone" (Eph 2:20).

Some were called to initiate Christ's Kingdom among a particular people, as St. Patrick did in Ireland, St. Boniface in Germany, and St. Cyril and Methodius among the Slavs. Individual missionaries, having begun missions in a tribe or geographic section, are considered spiritual fathers by their people, and are venerated after they have died. I knew an old missionary (Father Andreas Krieger) who laid the first foundation of the church among the Kondoa tribe in Tanzania, prior to World War I. He lived long enough to see many men of the tribe ordained priests, and one ordained as their bishop. Father Krieger is venerated as the founder of that church, now a diocese, and his prayers are sought by the people.

It would be strange if entrance into eternal life cut off the blessed from actively caring for those whom they served and aided on their journey to Heaven. It would be quite incongruous if Mary, who stood under the Cross, praying and pleading together with her Divine Son for His murderers, for mankind, would, after the Assumption, be deprived of the very glory that was hers on earth—to share intimately in the work of her Son, the Redeemer. When she allowed herself to suffer the impact of Sin, she responded with the mercy and pity of God that flooded her Immaculate Heart. Her love for those who are struggling, alternately stumbling and rising on their pilgrimage toward seeing the face of God, could not be set aside when she had reached Heaven. Now the beatific vision draws her irresistibly into the infinite current of God, whose name, whose very Being is Love.

If eternal life is sharing the very nature of God (2 Pet 1:4), it is thereby also a sharing if God's desire that "everyone be saved" (1 Tim 2:4). The apostolate on earth, in another form, continues in Heaven. Otherwise, eternal life could hardly be seen as completion and perfection of the life on earth. Until God becomes "all in all" (1 Cor 15:28), the blessed in Heaven will continue their apostolate in an expanded and new manner, responsive to the prayers on earth which ask for their intercession and help. Their crosses, their vicarious expiation suffered on earth are now applicable to those still on pilgrimage.

Mary, Mother of the Redeemer, became by her vicarious compassion under the Cross the Mother of all men, since her crucified love went out to us all in union with the love of her crucified Son. St. Joseph, Protector of the Child and Boy Jesus, has been declared by the Church, Protector of the Church, as he continues his function toward those still on earth.

And so, the Church, by the unerring instinct of the faithful, has always believed that the founders of churches among various people continue to be involved "in the divine rule exercised by Christ in glory" (*Credo*). "If we have died with Him, then we shall live with Him. If we hold firm, then we shall reign with Him" (2 Tim 2:11-12). "To reign with Him," to have a share in the task of gathering all unto God—this simply means that the blessed, in a mysterious and exalted manner, continue actively as "fellow workers with God" (1 Cor 3:9), by interceding, with Mary, for us sinners, "now and at the hour of our death."

And if we are disturbed by the thought that our eternity should, in its intensity of bliss, depend on the hope, care, and intercession of others, let us condsider the alternative—that the blessed in Heaven could no longer desire, care, and intercede for those whose burden they once shared. If we are disturbed by what we perceive seeming unfair in God's dealings, we ought to remember the parable of the laborers in the vineyeard, and the word of our Lord, "Why be envious because I am generous?" (Mat 20:1-16). Why have resentment against God's generosity, if others gain by it? In strict commutative justice we are all lost. God's wisdom may be foolishness to our unredeemed minds (1 Cor 1:27), because we demand mercy but are slow to grant it. But then, we really must try to hear the hard but consoling word of St. James, inspired by God, "There will be a judgment without mercy for those who have not been merciful themselves; but the merciful need have no fear of judgment" (James 2:13).

93. The Communion of Saints

"We believe in the communion of all the faithful of Christ, those who are pilgrims on earth, the dead who are attaining their purification, and the blessed in Heaven, all together forming one Church. . . ."

"All baptized in Christ, you have all clothed yourselves in Christ, and there are no more distinctions between Jew and Greek, slave and free, male and female, but all of you are one in Christ Jesus" (Gal 3:27-28). All men are called to redeemed unity. Therefore our Lord prayed before going to His death, "May they all be one. Father . . . in us, as You are in Me and I am in You . . . with Me in them and You in me" (John 17:21-22). When God the Eternal Son became Man, He came and dwelled among us to bring mankind home to unity with the Father, to enable us to become the Father's children again, "sons in the Son" (*Pastoral Constitution*, 22), by being reborn into new life (John 3:5), and "to become true images of His Son" (Rom 8:29). Here lies the root of that new communion of faith, the Church, the Mystical Body of Christ, the People of God. "Called into one and the same hope" (Eph 4:4), it is our common journey in this hope, being drawn by Christ (John 12:32), until we reach that city, where "God lives among men" (Rev 21:3), "the New Jerusalem" (Rev 21:2).

"There is one Lord, one faith, one baptism, and one God who is Father of all, over all, through all, and within all" (Eph 4:6). God wills to restore all mankind to redeemed unity. This unity is to have its exemplar and source in the uncreated unity of Father, Son, and Holy Spirit, through the mediation of the unity between God and mankind, which was created in historical times, less than two-thousand years ago and will last forever. This mediation was achieved through Jesus Christ, in whose "Body lives the fullness of divinity" (Col 2:9). He is true Man, "equal . . . to the Father according to His humanity, and Himself one . . . by the unity of His person" (*Credo*).

As "pilgrims on earth," we are involved in a twofold struggle. First, by ongoing conversion (Mark 1:15) we must struggle to continually prepare ourselves to be given "the power through His Spirit for our hidden self to grow strong, so that Christ may live in your hearts through faith, and then, planted in love and built on love . . . you are filled with the utter fullness of God" (Eph 3:16-19). Second, we, as members of Christ, are involved in our apostolate, which is an essential part of the Christian vocation (*Decree on the Apostolate of Lay People*, 2) and we must struggle with the difficulties this entails. "It was God who reconciled us to Himself through Christ and gave us the work of handing on this reconciliation. . . . So, we are ambassadors for Christ; it is as though God were appealing through us" (2 Cor 5:18-20). We are recipients and channels of God's redeeming action. The Risen Lord possesses the authority to allot to all men their "own share of grace" (Eph 4:7), in continuing to extend His human-divine love, that we repudiated by crucifying Him, but which we have not succeeded in extinguishing. And so, at the bidding of His human Heart, "by His divine power He has given us all the things that we need for life" (2 Pet 1:3).

And so we continue together on our pilgrimage, aided by the prayers of those who have died into God and are now seeing the Risen Lord in His glory, face to face, along with God the Creator and Redeemer, the Father, and the Holy Spirit. Here on earth we aid and harrass each other on this journey, often acting as the blind misleading the blind (Matt 15:14), and sometimes crucifying each other. The many hidden saints among us pick up the crosses we have refused by our rebellion, resentments, contempt, hatred, and other forms of murder (1 John 3:15). And the sins not turned into someone's crosses are still to be expiated in Purgatory.

Pilgrims, those being purified, and the blessed, all constitute the one Church, "a house where God lives in the Spirit" (Eph 2:22). But the day will come when, "finally, the intention of the Creator in creating man in His own image and likeness will be truly realized, when all who possess human nature, and have been regenerated in Christ through the Holy Spirit, gazing together on the glory of God, will be able to say 'Our Father' " (*Decree on the Church's Missionary Activity*, 7).

94. The Power of Prayer

"And we believe that in this communion the merciful love of God and His saints is ever listening to our prayers, as Jesus told us: Ask and you will receive."

In the first Preface for the Mass of Christian Death, the Church prays, "for your faithful people life is changed, not ended." Human nature risen is the same as it is in this life, though transfigured and perfected. Man is essentially a social being. Failure to relate to anyone destroys one's capacity for God. For those who persist in total selfishness at death, eternity will be one of total isolation, and this is hell. "The sorrow, the unutterable loss of those charred stones which once were men, is that they have nothing more to be shared" (George Bernanos, *Diary of a Country Priest*). They are eternally petrified in their own self-centeredness. The blessed, on the other hand, are those who spend themselves for souls in Christ (cf. 2 Cor. 12:15).

In Heaven, man irrevocably shares in the divine nature (2 Pet 1:4), seeing God "face to face" (Rev 22:4). He is totally drawn into the life of the Eternal Son. In Him, through Him, the blessed receive their glorified life from the Father. Through the Son they are now sons in the Son, "crying out in the Spirit: Abba, Father" (*Pastoral Constitution*, 22). There is nothing held back, all is surrendered in total generosity, with and in the Son, to the Father. Their mutual Love, the Holy Spirit, finds no resistance as He envelops the blessed with His Love, drawing them into the uncreated unity of the Blessed Trinity. Our Lord's prayer—"Father, may they be one in us, as You are in Me and I am in You . . . that they may be one as We are one. With Me in them and You in me" (John 17:21, 22)—has found answer in the blessed. The continuing prayer of the Church, the Great Doxology at the end of the Canon of the Mass, is answered in the blessed, for "through [Jesus Christ], with Him, in Him, in the unity of the Holy Spirit, all glory and honor is yours, almighty Father, for ever and ever."

The perfection of the blessed is the transfiguration of what is redeemed while on earth. Everyone's capacity for God will then be totally filled. Man's social nature will have reached perfection. Of man on pilgrimage the Church teaches: "Life in society is not something accessory to man himself: through his dealing with others, through mutual service, and through fraternal dialogue, man develops all his talents and becomes able to rise to his destiny" (*Pastoral Constitution*, 25). In Heaven, the blessed in their concern for their brothers who are still on the Way of the Cross to Resurrection, continue their "dealing with others, through . . . service" (see above). This service is to intercede out of their own, now glorified, love of neighbor, for those still struggling—those who were their neighbors on earth, and are still the object of their helping love. But the blessed will also intercede in response to prayers coming to them from earth.

When a paralytic was brought to our Lord, "seeing *their* faith, Jesus said . . . .'courage, my child, your sins are forgiven' " (Mat 9:2, emphasis added). He saw *their* faith, *their* hope, for the man paralyzed in his heart and in his body, hope flowing from *their* love of the paralyzed man and *their* trust in the divine power of Jesus.

And yet we cannot help being uneasy, perhaps embarrassed, by the statement of the *Credo* we are considering. That God's mercy should be influenced by man's prayer on earth and by the continuation of it, the intercession of the saints, seems to lack equity and fairness. Perhaps a hindrance to our understanding the fairness or justice of the spiritual interdependence of all people is that its closest analogy—interdependence in the political and economic spheres—is largely a means of oppression and exertion of power, a way for the powerful to take advantage of the weak. And so we find it difficult to understand that God, listening to men's deep desires expressed in prayer is moved to greater mercy. The following two considerations may help turn an embarrassing part of our faith into a deeply consoling mystery of God's justice, of His holiness most profoundly revealed in His mercy, which makes the Crucifixion a bitter and glorious reality.

First, "how impossible to penetrate His motives or understand His methods": "how deep His wisdom and knowledge" (Rom 11:33). If God would remain deaf to men praying on behalf of each other, the God of whom Jesus is the visible Image would have deceived us in Christ. As we can and must help each other on the road to Heaven, the faith, hope and charity involved are God's gifts. To express in prayer our desire for the salvation of others is simply to share God's universal salvific will. The impossibility of being heard by God would change the image of God into that of an icy, totally rigid monster. There is no trace of this in revelation. Abraham pleaded for his people (Gen 18:22-23). Today's contemplative orders witness to the continuation of this practice, rooted in God's being *Our Father*.

Second, whenever we pray for others, we must also have a willingness to apply the Law of Christ, to carry each others' burdens and failures (Gal 6:2). There must be a willingness to do on a small scale what our Lord did on a cosmic scale, for all men, of all times—to allow oneself to be victim of others' sins, and in redemptive love to accept it in expiation.

The Passion and Death of Christ are the price paid for our salvation. The icy horror which we feel if we consider the contrary to be true—namely that God and the saints never listen to us—should make us see our hesitancy and incomprehension, if not resentment, to be a temptation. And if we still find the transition from what we consider "justice" into the true, living, divine, and merciful justice of God difficult, we must accept and live the truth under consideration in the obedience of faith. And we will recall the words of St. James that "the merciful need have no fear of judgment" (James 2:13). We will learn to "live by the truth and in love [and] we shall grow in all ways into Christ, who is the head" (Eph 4:15).

95. The Power of the Resurrection

"Thus it is with faith and in hope that we look forward to the resurrection of the dead, and the life of the world to come."

"We look for the resurrection of the dead and the life of the world to come" (Creed of the Mass). It is this promise and this hope that alone prevent human existence and human history from being the brutal absurdity they would otherwise be. Revelation of the helplessness that is ours as creatures, further debilitated by original and personal sin, and the promises of God, generate the content of our hope, which the virtue or power of hope now allows us to live by. Only then can we know that, left to ourselves, we would inevitably drown in evil. But now we also know in hope that salvation can be ours again (Rom 7:24-25). We now know that we are on pilgrimage toward eternal life, towards an eternity of joy, of beatific vision. "Thus it is with faith and in hope that we" are enabled by God's redeeming love, with us in Christ Jesus, in His Church, to "look forward to the resurrection of the dead, and the life of the world to come" (*Credo*).

The Resurrection of Jesus Christ is the central saving event in the drama of mankind, not primarily because "on the third day He rose again . . . ascended into Heaven," but because "He is seated at the right hand of the Father" (Creed of the Mass), so that every tongue should acclaim that Jesus Christ is Lord (see Phil 2:11 and Rom 10:9), and that "all authority in Heaven and on earth has been given" to Him (Mat 28:18). Our hope is rooted in the fact, central to the total situation in which we find ourselves, that the Risen Humanity of Jesus is now "the King of kings and the Lord of lords" (Rev 19:16), the "only . . . mediator between God and mankind, Himself a Man, Christ Jesus" (1 Tim 2:5).

Belief in the Resurrection is above all the acceptance of the victory accomplished on Good Friday by the Father, in appointing Jesus Lord. For this means that now, and till the end of history, "when He shall come again in glory to judge the living and the dead" (Creed of the Mass), His human-divine love will continue to draw all men, each man, to Himself. This is the "power of His Resurrection" (Phil 3:10). That is why, in faith and hope, we are called, in obedience to the Commandments to love God (Mark 12:30) and each other as Christ loved and loves us (John 13:34; 15:12); to return God's love who "loved us first" (1 John 4:19), by obedience to His commandments (John 14:15).

And with all this in mind, we pray, "Come, Lord Jesus" (Rev 22:20).

96. The Prayer of Adoration

"Blessed be God Thrice Holy. Amen."

Eternal life is to know the Father, "the only true God, and Jesus Christ" whom the Father, by the Eternal Son's incarnation, willed to be present and visible among us (John 17:3). Jesus as Man became the visible "Image of the unseen God" (Col 1:15). To see the Man, Jesus, at any stage of His life, was to see the Father (John 14:9). It was the way by which "the only Son, who is nearest to the Father's heart . . . made [the Father] known" (John 1:18). Then the Apostles and others were able to see "His glory, the glory that is His as the only Son of the Father, full of grace and truth" (John 1:14).

To see "the glory that is His," "the radiant light of God's glory" that belongs by His divine nature to the Eternal Son, who is "the perfect copy" of the Father's nature (Heb 1:3) (the one divine nature shared by the Father, Son, and Holy Spirit), to see the "one only God Father, Son, and Holy Spirit" (*Credo*) "face to face" (Rev 22:4)—that is our destiny. Our life on earth is redemptive preparation. What eternal life is to be in the fullness of the beatific vision, when we will be irresistibly drawn by and to God by His "glory and goodness" (2 Pet 1:3), has its roots in baptism. We are baptized into the life of the Trinity (Mat 28:19), into Christ (Gal 3:27). A life of union with God, relating man to God by the gifts of faith, hope, and charity begins with baptism. What is grasped and integrated by faith, the content of what is revealed and believed, will be completed in the beatific vision. The tension between a growing realization that without God we can do nothing (John 15:5), that we are "naked" (Gen 3:7), and the promise of God, whose mercy has His infinite power, knowledge, and wisdom at its disposal, is lived in hope. In eternity, when God will be "all in all" (1 Cor 15:28), the "peace the world cannot give" (John 14:27) will eternally be ours in the total repsonse of ours in that God-given love, the love of God that "has been poured into our hearts by the Holy Spirit which has been given to us" (Rom 5:5). Our hope here on earth, born in patience and perseverance in suffering, has not been deceptive (Rom 5:4). In Heaven all tears will be wiped away (Rev 21:4), and eternal life, eternal joy, will then be ours.

Love of God, enjoined upon us while we are on earth (Mark 12:30), consists of "keeping His commandments" (1 John 5:3), "and that we love one another as He told us to" (1 John 3:23). Our love of God is the same obedience that brough Christ to the earth (Heb 10:7) and to the total empty-ing of Himself when "He humbled Himself and became obedient unto death, even death on a cross" (Phil 2:8). That God's will be done, the living desire that His Kingdom will come, to all and in all, is man's response to God who "loved us first" (1 John 4:19). It is to "put our faith in God's love toward ourselves" (1 John 4:16). And all this is revealed in Jesus Christ whom we are to follow (Mat 10:37-39) "by loving as He loved" us, "giv-ing Himself up in our place as . . . a sacrifice to God." Thus, we "imitate God, as children of His that He loves" (Eph 5:2,1).

In Heaven, when faith will have become beatific vision and hope will have become irrevocable fulfillment of our capacity for God, love will be eternal gratitude and adoration in response to the vision of God. The Risen Lord, "the Lamb that was sacrificed" is recognized as "worthy to be given power, riches, wisdom, strength, honor, glory, and blessing" (Rev 5:12). The Latin of the *Gloria* of the Mass says, "gratias agimus tibi propter magnam tuam"—we give you thanks for your great glory. To thank someone for what He *is* rather than for what one has received—to adore uncondi-tionally the God of Glory, the glory of power, wisdom, knowledge, mercy—all in the oneness of God, whose name is Love and who is to us the revela-tion of the fullness of His triune life as Father, Son, and Holy Spirit, who are One in substance with one another—to Him we give thanks for what *He is*.

While on earth, on pilgrimage, burdened with the consequences of sin, with our minds obscured and weakened, our wills torn in different directions—in this condition adoration and gratitude rarely arise spontaneous-ly in our hearts. And yet, our eternity will be unconditional, unhampered adoration and gratitude in irresistible response to the beatific vision of God. Love, which on earth is largely obedience (1 John 5:3), in Heaven will be total ecstasy. On earth we must live with the often powerful, if not intolerable contradiction and attraction of evil, and can bring ourselves to adoration and gratitude often only in the obedience of faith. But it remains an essen-tial preparation for what we are destined to be eternally.

That incredible expression of adoration, the great hymn, the *Gloria* of the Mass, which is given such sublime settings in the music of Bach's B-Minor Mass, and Beethoven's *Missa Solemnis*, is the fruit of genius, of a great tradition, of superhuman labor and discipline, and of the desire in faith, hope, and charity to sing the glory of God. For us, without genius and with only a dwindling sense of tradition, labor and discipline in faith, hope, and charity are still needed to adore God's glory.

We will make the last and crowning words of the great *Credo of the People of God* our own and pray, "Blessed be God Thrice Holy. Amen."

Appendix:
The "Credo" of the People of God
of Pope Paul VI (June 30, 1968)

With this solumn liturgy we end the celebration of the nineteenth centenary of the martyrdom of the holy Apostles Peter and Paul, and thus close the Year of Faith. We dedicated it to the commemoration of the holy Apostles in order that we might give witness to our steadfast will to be faithful to the Deposit of faith[1] which they transmitted to us, and that we might strengthen our desire to live by it in the historical circumstances in which the Church finds herself in her pilgrimage in the midst of the world.

We feel it our duty to give public thanks to all who responded to our invitation by bestowing on the Year of Faith a splendid completeness through the deepening of their personal adhesion to the Word of God, through the renewal in various communities of the profession of faith, and through the testimony of a Christian life. To our Brothers in the Episcopate especially, and to all the faithful of the Holy Catholic Church, we express our appreciation and we grant our blessing.

Likewise we deem that we must fulfill the mandate entrusted by Christ to Peter, whose successor we are, the last in merit; namely, to confirm our brothers in the faith.[2] With the awareness, certainly, of our human weakness, yet with all the strength impressed on our spirit by such a command, we shall accordingly make a profession of faith, pronounce a creed which, without being strictly speaking a dogmatic definition, repeats in substance, with some developments called for by the spiritual condition of our time, the creed of Nicea, the creed of the immortal Tradition of the Holy Church of God.

In making this profession, we are aware of the disquiet which agitates certain modern quarters with regard to the faith. They do not escape the influence of a world being profoundly changed, in which so many certainties are being disputed or discussed. We see even Catholics allowing themselves to be seized by a kind of passion for change and novelty. The Church, most assuredly, has always the duty to carry on the effort to study more deeply and to present in a manner even better adapted to successive generations the unfathomable mysteries of God, rich for all in fruits of salvation. But at the same time the greatest care must be taken, while fulfilling the indispensable duty of research, to do no injury to the teachings of Christian doctrine. For that would be to give rise, as is unfortunately seen in these days, to disturbance and perplexity in many faithful souls.

It is important in this respect to recall that, beyond scientifically verified phenomena, the intellect which God has given us reaches *that which is*, and not merely the subjective expession of the structures and development of consciousness; and, on the other hand, that the task of interpretation—of hermeneutics—is to try to understand and extricate, while respecting the word expressed, the sense conveyed by a text, and not to recreate, in some fashion, this sense in accordance with arbitrary hypotheses.

But above all, we place our unshakeable confidence in the Holy Spirit, the soul of the Church, and in theological faith upon which rests the life of the Mystical Body. We know that souls await the word of the Vicar of Christ, and we respond to that expectation with the instructions which we regularly give. But today we are given an opportunity to make a more solemn utterance.

On this day which is chosen to close the Year of Faith, on this Feast of the Blessed Apostoles Peter and Paul, we have wished to offer to the Living God the homage of a profession of faith. And as once at Caesarea Philippi the Apostle Peter spoke on behalf of the Twelve to make a true confession, beyond human opinions, of Christ as Son of the Living God, so today his humble Successor, Pastor of the Universal Church, raises his voice to give, on behalf of all the People of God, a firm witness to the divine Truth entrusted to the Church to be announced to all nations.

We have wished our profession of faith to be to a high degree complete and explicit, in order that it may respond in a fitting way to the need of light felt by so many faithful souls, and by all those in the world, to whatever spiritual family they belong, who are in search of the Truth.

To the glory of God Most Holy and of Our Lord Jesus Christ, trusting in the aid of the Blessed Virgin Mary and of the Holy Apostles Peter and Paul, for the profit and edification of the Church, in the name of all the Pastors and all the faithful, we now pronounce this profession of faith, in full spiritual communion with you all, beloved Brothers and Sons.

PROFESSION OF FAITH

We believe in one only God, Father, Son and Holy Spirit, Creator of things visible such as this world in which our transient life passes, of things invisible such as the pure spirits which are also called angels,[3] and Creator in each man of his spiritual and immortal soul.

We believe that this only God is absolutely one in His infinitely holy essence as also in all His perfections, in His omnipotence, His infinite knowledge, His providence, His will and His love. He is *He Who Is*, as revealed to Moses;[4] and He *is love*, as the Apostle John teaches us:[5] so that these two names, Being and Love, express ineffably the same divine Reality of Him Who has wished to make Himself known to us, and Who "dwelling in light inaccessible",[6] is in Himself above every name, above every thing and above every created intellect. God alone can give us right and full knowledge of this Reality by revealing Himself as Father, Son and Holy Spirit, in Whose Eternal Life we are by grace called to share, here below in the obscurity of faith and after death in eternal light. The mutual bonds which eternally constitute the Three Persons, Who are each one and the same Divine Being, are the blessed imost life of God Thrice Holy, infinitely beyond all that we can conceive in human measure.[7] We give thanks, however, to the Divine Goodness that very many believers can testify with us before men to the Unity of God, even though they know not the Mystery of the Most Holy Trinity.

We believe then in the Father who eternally begets the Son, in the Son, the Word of God, who is eternally begotten, in the Holy Spirit, the uncreated Person who proceeds from the Father and the Son as their eternal Love. thus in the Three Divine Presons, *coaeternae sibi et coaequales*,[8] the life and beatitude of God perfectly One superabound and are consummated in the supreme excellence and glory proper to uncreated Being, and always, "there should be venerated Unity in the Trinity and Trinity in the Unity."[9]

We believe in Our Lord Jesus Christ, Who is the Son of God. He is the Eternal Word, born of the Father before time began, and one in substance with the Father, *homoousios to Patri*,[10] and through Him all things were made. He was incarnate of the Virgin Mary by the power of the Holy Spirit, and was made man: equal therefore to the Father accoridng to His divinity, and inferor to the Father according to His humanity,[11] and Himself one, not by some impossible confusion of His natures, but by the unity of His person.[12]

He dwelt among us, full of grace and truth. He proclaimed and established the Kingdom of God and made us know in Himself the Father. He gave us His new commandment to love one another as He loved us. He taught us the way of the Beatitudes of the Gospel: poverty in spirit, meekness, suffering borne with patience, thirst after justice, mercy, purity of heart, will for peace, persecution suffered for justice sake. Under Pontius Pilate He suffered, the Lamb of God bearing on Himself the sins of the world, and He died for us on the Cross, saving us by His redeeming Blood. He was buried, and of His own power, rose the third day, raising us by His Resurrection to that sharing in the divine life which is the life of grace. He ascended to heaven, and He will come again, this time in glory, to judge the living and the dead: each accoridng to his merits—those who have responded to the Love and Piety of God going to eternal life, those who have refused them to the end going to the fire that is not extinguished.

And His Kingdom will have no end.

We believe in the Holy Spirit, who is Lord, and Giver of life, Who is adored and glorified together with the Father and The Son. He spoke to us by the Prophets; He was sent by Christ after His resurrection and His Ascension to the Father; He illuminates, vivifies, protects and guides the Church; He pruifies the Church's members if they do not shun His grace. His action, which penetrates to the inmost of the soul, enables man to respond to the call of Jesus: Be perfect as your Heavenly Father is perfect (Mt. 5:48).

We believe that Mary is the Mother, who remained ever a Virgin of the Incarnate Word, our God and Saviour Jesus Christ,[13] and that by reason of this singular election, she was, in consideration of the merits of her Son, redeemed in a more eminent manner,[14] preserved from all stain of original sin[15] and filled with the gift of grace more than all other creatures.[16]

Joined by a close and indissoluble bond to the Mysteries of the Incarnation and Redemption,[17] the Blessed Virgin, the Immaculate, was at the end of her earthly life raised body and soul to heavenly glory[18] and likened to her risen Son in anticipation of the future lot of all the just; and we believe that the Blessed Mother of God, the New Eve, Mother of the Church,[19] continues, in Heaven her maternal role with regard to Christ's members, cooperating with the birth and growth of divine life in the souls of the redeemed.[20]

We believe that in Adam all have sinned, which means that the original offense committed by him caused human nature, common to all men, to fall to a state in which it bears the consequences of that offense, and which is not the state in which it was at first in our first parents, established as they were in holiness and justice, and in which man knew neither evil nor death. It is human nature so fallen, stripped of the grace that clothed it, injured in its own natural powers and subjected to the dominion of death, that is transmitted to all men, and it is in this sense that every man is born in sin. We therefore hold, with the Council of Trent, that original sin, is transmitted with human nature, "not by imitation, but by propagation" and that it is thus "proper to everyone."[21]

We believe that Our Lord Jesus Christ, by the Sacrifice of the Cross redeemed us from original sin and all the personal sins committed by each one of us, so that, in accordance with the word of the Apostle, "where sin abounded, grace did more abound."[22]

We believe in one Baptism instituted by Our Lord Jesus Christ for the remission of sins. Baptism should be administered even to little children who have not yet been able to be guilty of any personal sin, in order that, though born deprived of supernatural grace, they may be reborn "of water and the Holy Spirit" to the divine life in Christ Jesus.[23]

We believe in one, holy, catholic, and apostolic Church, built by Jesus Christ on that rock which is Peter. She is the Mystical Body of Christ; at the same time a visible society instituted with hierarchical organs, and a spiritual community; the Church on earth, the pilgrim People of God here below, and the Church filled with heavenly blessings; the germ and the first fruits of the Kingdom of God, through which the work and the sufferings of Redemption are continued throughout human history, and which looks for its perfect accomplishment beyond time in glory.[24] In the course of time, the Lord Jesus forms His Church by means of the Sacraments emanating from His Plenitude.[25] By these she makes her members participants in the Mystery of the Death and Resurrection of Christ, in the grace of the Holy Spirit who gives her life and movement.[26] She is therefore holy, though she has sinners in her bosom, because she herself has no other life but that of grace: it is by living by her life that her members are sanctified; it is by removing themselves from her life that they fall into sins and disorders that prevent the radiation of her sanctity. This is why she suffers and does penance for these offences, of which she has the power to heal her children through the Blood of Christ and the Gift of the Holy Spirit.

Heiress of the divine promises and daughter of Abraham according to the Spirit, through that Israel whose Scriptures she lovingly guards, and whose Patriarchs and Prophets she venerates; founded upon the Apostles and handing on from century to century their ever-living word and their powers as Pastors in the Successor of Peter and the Bishops in communion with him; perpetually assisted by the Holy Spirit, she has the charge of guarding, teaching, explaining and spreading the Truth which God revealed in a then veiled manner by the Prophets, and fully by the Lord Jesus. We believe all that is contained in the Word of God written or handed down, and that the Church proposes for belief as divinely revealed whether by a solemn judgment or by the ordinary and universal magisterium.[27] We believe in the infallibility enjoyed by the Successor of Peter when he teaches ex cathedra as Pastor and Teacher of all the Faithful,[28] and which is assured also to the Episcopal Body when it exercises with him the supreme magisterium.

We believe that the Church founded by Jesus Christ and for which He prayed is indefectibly one in faith, worship and the bond of hierarchical communion. In the bosom of this Church, the rich variety of liturgical rites and the legitimate diversity of theological and spiritual heritages and special disciplines, far from injuring her unity, make it more manifest.[30]

Recognizing also the existence, outside the organism of the Church of Christ, of numerous elements of truth and sanctification which belong to her as her own and tend to Catholic unity,[31] and believing in the action of the Holy Spirit who stirs up in the heart of the disciples of Christ love of this unity,[32] we entertain the hope that Christians who are not yet in the full communion of the one only Church will one day be reunited in one Flock with one only Shepherd.

We believe that the Mass, celebrated by the priest representing the person of Christ by virtue of the power received through the Sacrament of Orders, and offered by him in the name of Christ and the members of His Mystical Body, is the Sacrifice of Calvary rendered sacramentally present on our altars. We believe that as the bread and wine consecrated by the Lord at the Last Supper were changed into His Body and His Blood which were to be offered for us on the Cross, likewise the bread and wine consecrated by the priest are changed into the Body and Blood of Christ enthroned gloriously in Heaven, and we believe that the mysterious presence of the Lord, under what continues to appear to our sense as before, is a true, real and substantial presence.[35]

Christ cannot be thus present in this Sacrament except by the change into His Body of the reality itself of the bread and the change into His Blood of the reality itself of the wine, leaving unchanged only the properties of the bread and wine which our senses perceive. This mysterious change is very appropriately called by the Church *transubstantiation*. Every theological explanation which seeks some understanding of this mystery must, in order to be in accord with Catholic faith, maintain that in the reality itself, independently of our mind, the bread and wine have ceased to exist after the Consecration, so that it is the adorable Body and Blood of the Lord Jesus that from then on are really before us under the sacramental species of bread and wine,[36] as the Lord willed it, in order to give Himself to us as food and to associate us with the unity of His Mystical Body.[37]

The unique and indivisible existence of the Lord glorious in Heaven is not multiplied, but is rendered present by the Sacrament in the many places on earth where Mass is celebrated. And this existence remains present, after the Sacrifice, in the Blessed Sacrament which is, in the tabernacle, the living heart of each of our churches. And it is our very sweet duty to honor and adore in the Blessed Host which our eyes see, the Incarnate Word Whom they cannot see, and Who, without leaving Heaven, is made present before us.

We confess that the Kingdom of God begun here below in the Church of Christ is not of this world whose form is passing, and that its proper growth cannot be confounded with the progress of civilization, of science or of human technology, but that it consists in an ever more profound knowledge of the unfathomable riches of Christ, an ever stronger hope in eternal blessings, an ever more ardent response to the Love of God, and an ever more generous bestowal of grace and holiness among men. But it is this same love which induces the Church to concern herself constantly about the true temporal welfare of men. Without ceasing to recall to her children that they have not here a lasting dwelling, she also urges them to contribute, each according to his vocation and his means, to the welfare of their earthly city, to promote justice, peace and brotherhood among men, to give their aid freely to their brothers, especially to the poorest and most unfortunate. The deep solicitude of the Church, the Spouse of Christ, for the needs of men, for their joys and hopes, their griefs and efforts, is therefore nothing other than her great desire to be present to them, in order to illuminate them with the light of Christ and to gather them all in Him, their only Saviour. This solicitude can never mean that the Church conform herself to the things of this world, or that she lessen the ardour of her expectation of her Lord and of the eternal Kingdom.

We believe in the life eternal. We believe that the souls of all those who die in the grace of Christ, whether they must still be purified in Purgatory, or whether from the moment they leave their bodies Jesus takes them to Paradise as He did for the Good Thief, are the People of God in the eternity beyond death, which will be finally conquered on the day of the Resurrection when these souls will be reunited with their bodies.

We believe that the multitude of those gathered around Jesus and Mary in Paradise forms the Church of Heaven, where in eternal beatitude they see God as He is,[38] and where they also, in different degrees, are associated with the holy Angels in the divine rule exercised by Christ in glory, interceding for us and helping our weakness by their brotherly care.[39]

We believe in the communion of all the faithful of Christ, those who are pilgrims on earth, the dead who are attaining their purification, and the blessed in Heaven, all together forming one Church; and we believe that in this communion the merciful love of God and His Saints is ever listening to our prayers, as Jesus told us: Ask and you will receive.[40] Thus it is with faith and in hope that we look forward to the resurrection of the dead, and the life of the world to come.

Blessed be God Thrice Holy. Amen.

FOOTNOTES

[1] Cfr. 1 Tim. 6:20.
[2] Cfr. Lk. 22:32.
[3] Cfr. Dz.-Sch. 3002.
[4] Cfr. Ex. 3:14.
[5] Cfr. 1 Jn. 4:8.
[6] Cfr. 1 Tim. 6:16.
[7] Cfr. Dz.-Sch. 804.
[8] Cfr. Dz. Sch. 75.
[9] Cfr. Dz. Sch. 75.
[10] Cfr. Dz. Sch. 150.
[11] Cfr. Dz. Sch. 76.
[12] Cfr. *ibid.*
[13] Cfr. Dz.-Sch. 251-252.
[14] Cfr. *Lumen Gentium* 53.
[15] Cfr. Dz.-Sch. 2803.
[16] Cfr. *Lumen Gentium* 53.
[17] Cfr. *Lumen Genitum* 53, 58, 61.
[18] Cfr. Dz.-Sch. 3903.
[19] Cfr. *Lumen Gentium*, 53, 56, 61, 63; Cfr. Paul VI, Alloc. for the Closing of the Third Session of the Second Vatican Council: AAS LVI [1964] 1016; Cfr. Exhort. Apost. *Signum Magnum*, Introd.
[20] Cfr. *Lumen Gentium* 62; Cfr. Paul VI, Exhort. Apost. *Signum Magnum*, P. 1, n. 1.
[21] Cfr. Dz.-Sch. 1513.
[22] Cfr. Rom. 5:20.
[23] Cfr. Dz.-Sch. 1514.
[24] Cfr. *Lumen Gentium* 8 et 5.
[25] Cfr. *Lumen Gentium* 7, 11.
[26] Cfr. *Sacrosanctum Concilium* 5, 6; Cfr. *Lumen Gentium* 7, 12, 50.
[27] Cfr. Dz.-Sch. 3011.
[28] Cfr. Dz.-Sch. 3074.
[29] Cfr. *Lumen Gentium* 25.
[30] Cfr. *Lumen Gentium* 23; Cfr. *Orientalium Ecclesiarum* 2, 3, 5, 6.
[31] Cfr. *Lumen Gentium* 8.
[32] Cfr. *Lumen Gentium* 15.
[33] Cfr. *Lumen Gentium* 14.
[34] Cfr. *Lumen Gentium* 16.
[35] Cfr. Dz.-Sch. 1651.
[36] Cfr. Dz.-Sch. 1642, 1651-1654; Paul VI, Enc. *Mysterium Fidei.*
[37] Cfr. S. Th., III, 73, 3.
[38] 1 Jn. 3:2; Dz.-Sch. 1000.
[39] Cfr. *Lumen Gentium* 49.
[40] Cfr. Lk. 10:9-10; Jn. 16:24.

The publication of this book was made possible in part through the support of the Christendom Publishing Group. Members are listed below:

Anonymous
Anonymous
Anonymous
Mrs. Marie Barrett
Mr. Daniel Bauer
LCDR C. W. Baumann
Mr. & Mrs. John and Opal Baye
Mr. Joseph C. Berzanskis
Mr. Joe Bierek
Mr. A. J. Birdsell
Mr. & Mrs. Joseph C. Bowling
Mr. John F. Bradley
Mr. George Bridgman
Mr. & Mrs. Robert Brindle
Mrs. Martha Brown
Mr. James G. Bruen Jr.
Mrs. Robert C. Bryant
Mrs. Edith L. Buckley
Mr. Doyle G. Burke
Paul A. Busam M.D.
Mrs. Marie Butkus
Mrs. Margaret Buyaert
Mr. Thomas J. Calvo
Mr. Charles M. Campbell
Miss Priscilla Carmody
Joseph C. Cascarelli Esq.
Rev. Francis A. Cegielka SAC
Mrs. Virginia J. Chipp
Mrs. S. J. Conner
Rev. Edward J. Connolly
Mr. John W.W. Cooper
Msgr. Henry Cosgrove
CH (Maj) Alfred M. Croke
Mr. & Mrs. Chris N. Cuddeback
Reverend John J. Cusack
Mr. Robert J. Cynkar
Mrs. Ellen L. Dalby
Sister M. Damian
The Dateno Family
Mr. B. P. Davidson
Mrs. W. J. Davies
Mrs. George de Lorimier
Mr. William De Lozier
Mrs. Jack Deardurff
Reverend Herman J. Deimel
Reverend Robert J. Dempsey
Dr. Joseph L. DeStefano
Mrs. Mary L. Dix
Reverend Daniel B. Dixon
Mr. Thomas C. Domeika
Mr. & Mrs. Leon W. Doty
Mr. Thomas J. Dowdall
Mr. Edward A. Dreis
Mr. D. J. Duckworth
Mr. John H. Duffy

Reverend J. A. Duraczynski
Mrs. James Ebben
Mrs. Clarence Ebert
Mr. D. N. Ehart
Mr. Clinton M. Elges
Sister Ellen S.J.W.
Mr. William W. Elliott
Mrs. Betty Emilio
Reverend George S. Endal S.J.
Mrs. Frances A. Esfeld
Mr. Francis G. Fanning
Mr. & Mrs. Victor Fernandez
Mrs. Gilda Fidell
Mr. & Mrs. James G. Fischer
Miss Margaret C. Fitzgerald
G. F. Flagg Family
Mr. Emmet Flood
Mr. Eugene P. Foeckler Sr.
Mr. John F, Foell
Mrs. Donald B. Fox M.D.
Mr. & Mrs. J. P. Frank Jr.
Mrs. Claudette Fredricksen
Mrs. Adele Fricke
Mr. Martin Froeschl
Mr. Eduardo Garcia-Ferrer
Mr. & Mrs. John Gardner
Mr. Edward Patrick Garrigan
Mrs. Shirley Gasquet
Mr. Richard L. Gerhards
Msgt. R. P. Gideon
Mr. Carl J. Graham
Cpt & Mrs. James P. Guerrero
Mr. Patrick Guinan
Mrs. Paula Haigh
Reverend A. A. Halbach
Mr. Robert E. Hanna
Mrs. Mary J. Hart
Mrs. Mary T. Hatfield
Mr. Frank E. Hauck
Mr. David Havlicek
Reverend Brian J. Hawker
Mrs. Francis Heaverlo
Reverend Herman L. Heide
Reverend Hugh P. Henneberry S.S.J.
Reverend Albert J. Herbert S.M.
Mrs. W. Herbert
Mr. Ronald H. Herrmann
Mr. Joseph L. Holtz
Arthur Hopkins M.D.
Mr. John C. Horan
Mr. & Mrs. André Huck
Mrs. Doris L. Huff
Edgar Hull M.D.
Mrs. Carmen Iacobelli
Reverend Jeffrey A. Ingham

Mr. Herman Jadloski
Mr. J. Janeski
Mr. & Mrs. Dave Jaszkowiak
Mrs. Kathleen C. Jones
Mr. Marley Francis Jones
Mr. Daniel P. Judge
Mr. Edward E. Judge
Rev. Matthew S. Kafka
Mr. & Mrs. Albert Kais
Miss Betty Kelly
Reverend Michael J. Kelly
Mr. & Mrs. Frank Knoell
Mr. John R. Knoll
Mr. Augustine Kofler
Mr. William C. Koneazny
Dr. Edward J. Krol
James W. Lassiter M.D.
Miss Thérèse Lawrence
Mr. Edward A. Lewandowski
Reverend Harry J. Lewis
Very Rev. Victor O. Lorenz
Mrs. Jan Lundberg
Mrs. Carolyn C. MacDonald
Miss Katherine I. MacDonald
Mr. George F. Manhardt
Mr. Thomas Manning
Miss Jeanette Maschmann
N. Anthony Mastropietro M.D.
Mr. Thomas J. May
Reverend Mark G. Mazza
Mrs. Verlie McArdle
Mr. Steven McCallan
Mr. Thomas J. McCann
Mr. W. C. McCarthy
Reverend William R. McCarthy
Mr. John A. McCarty Esq.
Mr. James McConnell
Mr. Robert McConville
Mrs. Miriam McCue
Robert E. McCullough M.D.
Mr. Joseph D. McDaid
Mr. & Mrs. Dennis P. McEneany
Reverend P. J. McHugh
Mr. Thomas A. McLaughlin
Mr. J. R. McMahon
Mr. Robert Cruise McManus
Mrs. Kenneth McNichol
Reverend Edward J. Melvin C.M.
Patrick A. Metress
Mr. Larry G. Miezio
Mr. & Mrs. Larry Miggins
Mrs. Robert L. Miller
Mr. Michael P. Millner
Mr. Joseph Monahan
Reverend Hugh Monmonier
Mr. James B. Mooney
Mrs. Gertrude G. Moore
Miss A. Morelli
Col. Chester H. Morneau

Mr. Nicholas J. Mulhall
Mrs. Joseph P. Mullally Ph.D.
Mr. & Mrs. G. W. Muth
Mrs. Marie Mutz
Mr. L. J. Netzel
Mr. Frank Newlin
Mr. Joseph F. O'Brien
Reverend Philip O'Donnell
Mr. & Mrs. Tim O'Donnell
Mr. John F. O'Shaughnessy Jr.
Mr. Lawrence P. O'Shaughnessy
Mrs. Josephine K. Olmstead
Mrs. Veronica M. Oravec
Mrs. John F. Parker
Mr. Ernest Patry
Reverend Angelo Patti
Reverend Laszlo Pavel
Mr. & Mrs. Joseph and Mary Peek
Bill and Mary Peffley
Mr. Alfred H. Pekarek
Robert N. Pelaez M.D.
Mr. & Mrs. Gerald R. Pfeiffer
Mr. & Mrs. Pat Pollock
Mr. & Mrs. William H. Power Jr.
Dr. & Mrs. C. Pruzzia
Mr. E. K. Quickenton
Mr. Stuart Quinlan
Mrs. Mary F. Quinn
Mr. Thomas J. Quinn
Dr. William E. Rabil
Miss Beatrice A. Rappengluck
Mr. & Mrs. Joseph E. Rau
Reverend Robert A. Reed
Dr. & Mrs. Francis C. Regan
Mrs. John F. Reid
Mr. & Mrs. John J. Reuter
Dr. Charles E. Rice
M. V. Rock M.D.
Brother Philip Romano OFMCap
Mrs. Mary A. Rosenast
Mr. Bernard J. Ruby
Mrs. Agnes Ryan
Mr. G. Salazar
Mr. Richard W. Sassman
Mr. & Mrs. George Scanlon
Miss Marian C. Schatzman
Miss Constance M. Scheetz
Mrs. Margaret Scheetz
Mr. Peter Scheetz
Mrs. Francis R. Schirra
Mrs. Claragene Schmidt
Mrs. Job A. Schumacher
Mr. & Mrs. Ralph Schutzman
Mr. P. J. Schwirian
Mr. Frank P. Scrivener
Mr. & Mrs. Robert R. Scrivener
John B. Shea
John R. Sheehan M.D.
Miss Anne Sherman

Mr. W. R. Sherwin
Mr. & Mrs. Dale P. Siefker
Mrs. Bernice Simon
Mr. Richard M. Sinclair Jr.
Capt. Arthur Sippo
Mrs. Walter Skorupski
Mr. S. C. Sloane
Miss Mary Smerski
Mr. Vincent C. Smith
Mr. William Smith
Mrs. William Smith
Mrs. Ann Spalding
Mrs. James Spargo
Mr. & Mrs. Victor Spielman
Miss Anne M. Stinnett
Mr. Michael Sullivan
Mr. John Svarc
Mr. Edward S. Szymanski
Mr. Raymond F. Tesi
Reverend Clyde Tillman
Mr. Dominic Torlone
Rev. Chris Twohig
Mr. & Mrs. Albert Vallone

Mr. Wil Van Achthoven
Mrs. Alice Vandenberg
Reverend Frederick J. Vaughn
Mr. William C. Vinet Jr.
Mrs. Margaret Vogenbeck
Reverend George T. Voiland
Mrs. Catherine Wahlmeier
Mr. David P. Walkey
Miss Kathleen Walsh
Honorable Vernon A. Walters
Mrs. Alice V. Ward
Mr. Fulton John Waterloo
Mr. Ralph A. Wellings
Mrs. Joan Weth
Mr. J. Weusten
Mr. Alfred L. White
Miss Penny Wiest
Mr. John R. Wilhelmy
Mrs. Mary Williams
Mrs. Mary Wimmenauer
Mr. Michael C. Winn
Mrs. Marguerite A. Wright
James F. Zimmer M.D.